MW01259128

TODAY
with the King

TODAY

with the King

Daily Meditations with...

VICTOR
BOOKS a division of SP Publications, Inc.
WHEATON. ILLINOIS 60187

Offices also in
Whitby, Ontario, Canada
Amersham-on-the-Hill, Bucks, England

All Scripture quotations are from the *King James Version.*

Cover photography by Robert Cushman Hayes.
Inside photo illustrations by Tom Fawell: 10, 276, 308, 374; Ewing Galloway: 110;
  Gary Irving: 76, 208, 342; H. Armstrong Roberts: 142, 176, 242; Paul M. Schrock:
  44.
Copy for December 31 meditation adapted from *The Hiding Place,* by Corrie ten
  Boom with John and Elizabeth Sherrill, ©1971 by Corrie ten Boom and John and
  Elizabeth Sherrill.

Recommended Dewey Decimal Classification: 242.2
Suggested Subject Heading: DEVOTIONAL

Library of Congress Catalog Card Number: 85-50313
ISBN: 0-89693-364-4

Contents

To Coreen
Who made a journey of fifty years together
seem short indeed

Foreword

Nothing is so vital for the Christian's spiritual health as a daily walk with God through His Word, the Bible. Centuries before Christ, King David declared, "Thy Word is a lamp unto my feet, and a light unto my path" (Ps. 119:105). In the midst of a dark and confusing world, believers throughout the ages have discovered that only God's Word can give life and light, comfort and hope.

In this volume, my longtime friend, Dr. Robert A. Cook, has written a series of daily meditations which will help introduce many to Scripture's eternal truths. His insights are both biblical and practical, and clearly demonstrate that the Word of God still has the power to change our lives. I commend this helpful book of meditations to all who today and every day desire a closer walk with the King.

Billy Graham

Author's Preface

When my longtime friend Roy Irving approached me with the idea of producing a book of daily devotions, two thoughts crossed my mind. One was that there is a plethora of such books, from the classics to those now offered by radio and television ministries: who needs another? The other thought was based on realities. There simply was not enough time to take care of my assigned responsibilities and do a devotional book as well.

Roy assured me that he would help in preparing some of my materials already on tape or in print, if I would come up with the balance of the book. I must say that it has been a good experience for me to pray, wait on God, and then put down in some semblance of order the thoughts that have come to me.

In this volume, we hope to present a friendly, informal treatment of the great truths of God's Word; and to make practical the dynamic concepts of vital Christian living as contained in Scripture. We trust the book reveals a fresh approach, practical applications, and a loving spirit.

So, my thanks to Roy Irving and my friends at Scripture Press/Victor Books. Thanks also to my sister, Miss Mildred Cook, and my longtime assistant, Miss Louise Alfors, for their invaluable help in editing and compiling many of the source materials we have used for these devotional studies. And special thanks to my friend of forty years, Dr. Billy Graham, for his kindness in providing a foreword for this volume.

Robert A. Cook

January

I can't think of a better way to begin the New Year than at the feet of our blessed Lord, can you? This first series has to do with the life of Christ. What it does, actually, is to give us a "piece of the action," as the young folks might say. A sort of window on the earthly ministry of our Lord Jesus Christ. This month I want you to look with me through that window into some of our Lord's teachings from the Gospels. Not a formal study, you understand. Rather a touching down together, here and there, to draw spiritual refreshment for our souls—so we'll be able to walk with the King and be a blessing.

BY WAY OF THE STORM

Scripture, Mark 4:35—5:20
And there arose a great storm of wind, and the waves beat into the ship, so that it was now full.
(Mark 4:37)

Can you think of some experience in your life where God has led you straight into a storm? Oh, the turbulence, the tension, the worry, the fret, and maybe the heartache! And no one seemed to understand all you were going through, and nobody seemed to care. But then our blessed Lord delivered you. He calmed the storm and proved Himself to be the Master. What a delicious, wonderful, thrilling experience *that is!*

In Mark 5 is the account of a man whose soul was turbulent and Christ's mastery of that violent inner storm. The demon-possessed man bore the trademarks of the world's culture: restlessness, violence, and nudity. Do these strike a familiar note in your own thinking? Restlessness, violence, and nudity are all around us today. Yet when the Lord Jesus had met and mastered this poor man's need, he was seated and sane; he was calm and clothed; and he was listening to the Saviour. Can there be such a change in one's life? Yes, there can! There's another truth here. What is more important, 2,000 head of swine or one person delivered from the power of Satan? What are your priorities today?

Small thought here

Why should Jesus have sent the disciples across the Sea of Galilee when He knew the storm was coming? Why should He have gone into the ship and then fallen asleep when He knew that He was going to be needed to quell the storm? Well, simply this, my friend: *God's plans include taking you from Point A to Point B by way of the storm and, thank God, by way of the miracle!*

DIVINE HEALING

Scripture, Matthew 9:27-31
Then touched He their eyes, saying,
"According to your faith be it unto you."
And their eyes were opened.
(Matt. 9:29-30)

Today's text has to do with healing: healing of body, mind, soul, and spirit. Though there are many points of view about healing, every person who knows the Lord Jesus and believes the Word of God agrees on at least two basic truths:

• *God is God and He can heal.* He built our bodies and He can heal them. There's no question in anyone's mind who reads and believes his Bible that Almighty God, who created us and redeemed us through the Lord Jesus Christ, can heal us.

• *God does heal, at times and in situations where it pleases Him, and where people meet His conditions.* It's evident, to some of us at least, that God doesn't always choose to heal. I've conducted quite a few funerals in my time. But God *can* and *does* heal when it is in His perfect will and when persons meet His conditions.

How precisely and beautifully our Lord Jesus met the needs of people during His earthly ministry. Matthew's Gospel speaks plainly about the blind men who followed the Lord Jesus. When they cried out, "Have mercy on us, Son of David!" He asked, before restoring their sight, "Do you believe that I am able to do this?" My friend, do you believe that the Lord Jesus can do anything you need Him for today?

Small thought here

Many people lack the power of God in this area of bodily healing because they don't really believe God can heal them. Decide in your own heart today how much you believe your God can do. After you've settled *that*, you'll be able to share with others these precious Scripture passages where our Lord Jesus heals eyes and bodies, minds and hearts.

HOW MUCH DO YOU CARE?

Scripture, Matthew 9:35—11:1
But when He saw the multitudes, He was moved with compassion on them, because they fainted, and were scattered abroad, as sheep having no shepherd.
(Matt. 9:36)

Everything grows out of your heart attitude. "Out of the abundance of the heart," said our Lord, "the mouth speaketh" (Matt. 12:34). "As [a man] thinketh in his heart," the wise man said, "so is he" (Prov. 23:7). So it is not by chance that today's Scripture emphasizes the concern and compassion of our blessed Lord which led to His commissioning the disciples. When our Lord Jesus saw the multitudes, He was deeply moved because they wandered aimlessly, "as sheep having no shepherd."

Have you ever thought about how one shows concern for others? And how concern and compassion find their way into the whole fabric of living with hurting people? Dr. Clyde Narramore says if you don't get past small talk when you know that a person is really hurting, you're not showing concern. Narramore says you show concern by turning on your heel, going back, and saying, "Oh, I'm sorry. What seems to be the matter?" And Suzy can explain that her mother has fallen down the stairs and broken her hip, and she's in the hospital, and Suzy's worried sick about her. That shows real concern.

Small thought here

Did you know that one of the attitudes most easily discernible by others, yet probably the most difficult to communicate, if you don't possess it, is this matter of personal concern and compassion? How much do you really care about people?

DEAL WITH DISCOUR-AGEMENT

Scripture, Matthew 11:1-11
Now when John had heard in the prison the works of Christ, he sent two of his disciples and said unto Him, "Art Thou He that should come, or do we look for another?"
(Matt. 11:2-3)

Faithfulness to the Lord Jesus Christ doesn't always mean you're going to be a great success—as the world knows success. Jesus said there was none greater born of women than John the Baptist. He called him a burning and shining light. Yet our Lord allowed John to finish his life in a prison cell and to die by an executioner's ax. Why does God allow these things? Well, I don't know. I only know that God does right. He never makes a mistake. His purposes are perfect and His timing is exquisitely beautiful. You can count on your blessed Lord. John was great. Herod was weak. Herodius was filled with hatred. The combination cost John his life and Herod his soul (and Herodius with him).

Have you ever gotten discouraged? John did. He had preached to great crowds, then saw the crowds diminish. But that didn't shake him. He responded: "Christ must increase, but I must decrease." Now John has told the truth to Herod: "You're living in sin. You have no right to live with another man's wife." And as a result, John is in jail, thinking: *I wonder, oh, I wonder. Is Jesus really the Messiah? If He were, would He let me rot in jail?* Discouragement comes to us all. What's the answer to it? Jesus said, "Go tell John what you see and hear. Does He heal? Yes. Tell John that."

Small thought here

The answer to discouragement is found by asking: "What is God doing?" And when you see *that*—when you see what God is doing in your life—you will find discouragement vanishing and the light and joy of God's assurance coming into your heart. Hallelujah for that!

TAKE A BREAK!

Scripture, Mark 6:30-46
And He said unto them, "Come ye yourselves apart into a desert place and rest a while": for there were many coming and going, and they had no leisure so much as to eat.
(Mark 6:31)

Have you ever been so busy you just didn't think you could stand it? So busy you didn't have time to eat or sleep or pray? There is some comfort, it seems to me, in realizing that this happened to our Lord Jesus. Not in vain does the Scripture say that He was tested in all points "like as we are, yet without sin" (Heb. 4:15). Oh, He knows the press and the pressure of the many duties that are yours and mine day by day. Today's text says there were so many coming and going that Christ and His disciples had no leisure so much as to eat. And so they departed into a desert place to rest a while.

God wants you to have times when you rest with Him. Somewhere I ran across a little leaflet that said, "Plan to spend a whole day with God sometime." What a refreshing concept that is. Set aside some time to be alone with your Lord, for a whole day. Have an agenda of things to talk about with Him. Frequently, when I have a long drive, I'll make a list of things about which I wish to talk to my blessed Lord. What joy there is in talking with Him hour after hour.

Small thought here

The Lord Jesus Christ can start where you are with what you have. Will you make a list of some of your limitations? Limitations of talent, ability, time, money, physical strength, emotional strength, whatever? Jesus will start with you where you are, take what you have, and multiply it for His glory—if you will let Him have it. What a tremendous, encouraging thought!

FOCUS YOUR FAITH

Scripture, Matthew 14:22-33
And He said, "Come." And when Peter was come down out of the ship, he walked on the water, to go to Jesus.
(Matt. 14:29)

Faith has to have a focus. Faith for what? Faith for the situations of everyday life. Our Lord Jesus met His disciples in the middle of the storm. This is the second occasion in the Gospels where a storm had arisen. But despite the wind and waves, in the fourth watch of the night Jesus went to His disciples, walking on the sea. When they saw Him, they thought it was a spirit or an apparition. Though they were grown men, they were troubled and cried out for fear because they were scared to death. The Lord Jesus said, in effect, "Be of good cheer. Don't worry, fellows, it's only I. Be not afraid." Then Peter said, "Lord, if it be Thou, bid me come unto Thee on the water." Peter made two mistakes, really. First, he said "if"; and second, he looked at the wind and the waves around him, the tempest, and lost his focus of faith.

Never say "if" and never look only at the tempest. If you look at the circumstances, inevitably you'll start to sink. If you look to Jesus, you'll weather the storm. "Looking unto Jesus, the author and finisher of our faith," says the writer to the Hebrews. No wonder there is faltering faith and strong faith. No wonder there are people who are sinking and people who are swimming; people who are trusting and people who are doubting. And the difference, my dear friend, lies in focusing your faith on our blessed Lord.

Small thought here
Be Exhibit "A" in this matter of faith. Don't go to your tasks today until you determine in your heart to really believe God for at least one area of personal weakness. Focus your faith on some specific need and see God work in your life. You'll be a blessing to others too.

BREAK WITH TRADITION?

Scripture, Mark 7:1-23
And He said unto them: "Full well ye reject the commandment of God, that ye may keep your own tradition."
(Mark 7:9)

Someone said to me years ago there are two reasons for turning down anything at the local church level. The first is, "We never did it before." The second is, "We've tried it before." You could vote no on anything on the basis of those two distinct points of view.

When should you break with tradition? I think we have an answer in today's text that will help us distinguish between God's truth and man's tradition. Take the matter of unwashed hands, for example (Mark 7:1-8). We are reminded that unkept commandments (vv. 9-13) are much more important. Then we have the distinction between superficial defilement and the real source of defilement (vv. 14-23). A very illuminating passage indeed!

And what about Christ Himself? Our Lord Jesus didn't hesitate to break with tradition *when it involved real heart holiness.* He said, in effect: "Isaiah certainly told Me the truth about you people. He said, 'These people come near to Me with their mouths and honor Me with their lips, but their hearts are far from Me. They worship Me in vain: teaching for doctrines the commandments of men and laying aside the commandment of God for the traditions of men.'" Then Jesus went on to point out that an unclean heart, an immoral spirit, and a dishonest tongue—all the things that distinguish the simple human being—are the real defilements.

Small thought here

Break with tradition any time it keeps you from being real with your God. Practice that principle and you will come out on top every time.

HARDNESS OF HEART

Scripture, Mark 7:24—8:26

Jesus . . . saith unto them, "Why reason ye, because ye have no bread? Perceive ye not yet, neither understand? Have ye your heart yet hardened? Having eyes, see ye not? And having ears, hear ye not?"
(Mark 8:17-18)

In today's passage we have a number of needs outlined for us, all but one of which our Lord Jesus met: the demon in the life, the impediment of speech, the unsatisfied hunger, the hardness of heart, and the blindness of eyes. Our Lord Jesus cast out the demon; He loosed the mute tongue; He fed the multitude; and He opened the eyes of the blind man. There is just one need that wasn't met: hardness of heart. This is now the second time in a very short space of study that we've heard about hardened hearts. Indeed, the matter comes up again and again. Herod's heart was hardened; so were the disciples'. Our Lord Jesus looked round about with anger on the crowd that surrounded Him one day, being grieved, it said, for the hardness of their hearts. There is no cure for the life that keeps God out. One more thought before we leave this message: Our Lord Jesus—in dealing with this man who had been blind—touched him and made him look up. And he was restored and saw every man clearly. What a beautiful picture of what God can do in giving you the proper perspective on other people.

Small thought here

Our Lord Jesus can meet every need of the life except hardheartedness. Why? Because a hardened heart keeps God out. When God's touch is on your life, you can see people as God sees them. You can bless them as God wants to bless them. You can reach them as Christ wants to reach them.

IT'LL COST YOU SOMETHING

Scripture, Matthew 16:13-27
Then said Jesus unto His disciples, "If any man will come after Me, let him deny himself, and take up his cross, and follow Me."
(Matt. 16:24)

What a difference between the questions, "Whom do *people* say that I am?" (v. 13) and "Whom do *you* say that I am?" (v. 15) It's the difference between being a spectator and a believer. The great weakness, it seems to me, among God's workers today is that too many of them can tell you all about what others are saying about Christ but flinch and wince a little when confronted with the matter of a *personal abandonment* of themselves to the Lord Jesus.

Simon Peter, whatever else you may say of him, certainly gave a good account of himself at this point. He said to our blessed Lord, "You are the Christ, the Son of the living God" (v. 16). Where are *you* in this matter of identifying yourself with the Lord Jesus? You say, "Well look, I'm a Christian (and perhaps a Sunday School teacher), so why ask *me* that? That is precisely why I'm asking you. Because there are "Christians" and then there are Christians. There are people who know about Jesus Christ and there are people who are the very living demonstration of Christ within. And what a difference between them! Which variety are you?

Small thought here
What is the cost of really following the Lord Jesus? We speak so easily of sacrifice that it's become a tired word without much meaning. But our Lord Jesus laid it on the line for us. He said that if anyone is really serious about following Him, it involves a *cost*—and a *cross*. So make up your mind, take up your cross, and live your life for Christ *today*. What a tremendous challenge!

TOWARD HIS LIKENESS

Scripture, Luke 9:26-36
And as He prayed, the fashion of His countenance was altered, and His raiment was white and glistening.
(Luke 9:29)

Something happens when you pray. A change occurs. The same can be said about the Lord Jesus Christ at the Transfiguration. Today's text tells us that as He prayed on that mountaintop with Peter, James, and John, the appearance of His countenance was dramatically altered and His garments became as "bright as a flash of lightning." Of course, you and I will never approximate—we'll never begin to come anywhere near—the radiant glory that was shining from our Lord Jesus at that wonderful transfiguration event. But we need to be confronted with the glory of our blessed Lord nonetheless. We need to progress—to move toward—His likeness. And how do we do *that?* I see two clues in this passage: (1) prayer, and (2) focusing on the Lord Jesus. We discover here that as Jesus *prayed,* everything about Him, and around Him, was dramatically affected. God's presence and glory shone from His face and from His garments. And the Father proudly said, "This is My Son, whom I have chosen; listen to Him" (v. 35). If you want to see a change in your life and in the things around you, get down to business in your prayer life—and fix your focus on the Lord Jesus Christ. Believe me, my friend, it works!

Small thought here

Tell me something: Have you ever made a list of all the beneficial changes you would like to see occur in your life? As a resource person or Sunday School teacher in your church? Or as a Christian counselor or guide to your friends? You will be ever so much more effective if you know, and are believing God for, those areas which you want to see transformed by His presence and glory.

WHY COULDN'T THEY?

Scripture, Matthew 17:14-20
Then came the disciples to Jesus apart, and said, "Why could not we cast him out?" (Matt. 17:19)

One of the most plaintive questions in all the Gospel records is the one the disciples asked the Lord Jesus after they had failed, so ignominiously, to cast a demon from a demented lad (v. 19). They asked, "Why couldn't we drive it out?" Our Lord said, in effect, "Because of your failure to believe. If you don't believe, it's just not going to work." Jesus went on to tell them that this kind of demon-expelling faith is generated only by prayer and fasting.

"Why couldn't we cast out the demon?" We ask that today, don't we, about some of those stubborn demons that defy our best efforts to dislodge them from some circumstance in our lives? Perhaps a shattered relationship, a troubling illness, or something gone sour in our church fellowship. The key to victory is faith and prayer, and the willingness to set other things aside—like food and sleep. Faith. Prayer. Fasting. This combination will make you invincible over the powers of evil. Hallelujah for that!

Small thought here

It's important to recognize that other people don't have to do things your way. In Mark 9, the disciples said, "Master, we saw a man driving out demons in Your name, and we told him to stop, because he was not one of us" (v. 38). This happens today, doesn't it? Some people say, "You can't possibly be doing God's work because *you aren't doing it my way.* You're not in my denomination. Not in my group." Remember, dear friend, that our blessed Lord reserves the right to use people with whom you and I may disagree.

HOW MANY TIMES?

Scripture, Matthew 18:15-22
Then came Peter to Him, and said, "Lord, how oft shall my brother sin against me, and I forgive him? Till seven times?"
(Matt. 18:21)

Most of us would rather have a prayer meeting than straighten things out with another person, wouldn't we? It's far easier to make a speech to God than to level with your brother and say, "I'm sorry. I've wronged you." And it's easier to pray than it is to forgive someone. The Lord Jesus once discussed that predicament when He said, "When you stand praying, if you hold anything against anyone, forgive him, so that your Father in heaven may forgive you your sins" (Mark 11:25). So there it is.

But Simon Peter got off on a tangent. He asked, "Lord, *how many times* shall I forgive my brother," and the answer, of course, is to forgive and forgive and forgive—not seven times, but seventy times seven. On any given day, that would amount to 490 cases of forgiveness, which seems to be a pretty good standard, doesn't it?

Small thought here

The essence of unforgiveness is a refusal to receive or accept people as they are. The essence of forgiveness is to receive people as they are—*including* their injustice to you. Our Lord Jesus took people as they were and said, "Look, I didn't come to destroy people. I came to save them." Try that on for size, will you? Forgiveness is a matter not of fixing up, or patching up, a relationship—based on something somebody has or hasn't done. Forgiveness is opening your heart wide to another person because the very love of the blessed Lord is being shed abroad in your heart and life.

DOUBLE INVOLVE-MENT

Scripture, Luke 10:1-37
*"Which now of these three, thinkest thou,
was neighbor unto him that fell among
the thieves?"*
(Luke 10:36)

Involvement with God and His work and with people and their needs are essential ingredients in walking with the King. It's not particularly scriptural, or helpful, to pray, "O, Lord, send the sinners in that they may become converted." Yet I've heard that prayer many times, as I suppose you have. The Lord Jesus sent His disciples *out.* That is the scriptural way. Go out and get them. Go out and reach them. Go out and win them. Go out and teach them. Go out and love them. What this means is that you and I should be found sharing the Gospel out *where people are.*

Yes, involvement with God means to get out where people are with the message of our blessed Lord. *It also means meeting people's needs.* To the man who asked, "Who is my neighbor?" our Lord Jesus told a story about two "religious" people who had bypassed their obligations—for a variety of "reasons." In today's jargon, one of the men may have been going to a citywide evangelistic meeting. The other had a special seminar to attend. Each one had his particular alibi, but when the Samaritan came and saw this poor, wretched person lying wounded and robbed on the roadside, he had compassion on him. And he went to him, bandaged his wounds, put him on his own mount, brought him to an inn, and took care of him.

Small thought here
To be involved with people interrupted this man's schedule, made a pedestrian of him, robbed him of a night's sleep, cost him money, and put him in debt. This may well happen to you and to me if we get serious about meeting the needs of people.

LIFE'S GREATEST PRIORITY

Scripture, Luke 10:38—11:36
"But one thing is needful: and Mary hath chosen that good part, which shall not be taken away from her."
(Luke 10:42)

A person can be too busy to be in touch with the Lord. This is illustrated by the story of Martha and Mary. Mary sat at Jesus' feet and heard His word. Martha was too busy doing housework and serving meals. She dashed into the living room finally—sparks coming from her eyes, I imagine—and said, "Lord, don't You care that my sister has left me to do the work by myself? Tell her to help me!" Oh, my, she was irritated. Pause here long enough to realize that you have a choice about what you're going to consider the greatest priority, the greatest concern in your life.

A great servant of our Lord in other days used to say, "No Bible, no breakfast." Martin Luther was heard to remark, "I have so much to do today that I cannot spend less than two hours in prayer." If you want to do four times as much work, pray twice as much. Your work potential increases the square of the time you spend with God. Now, I haven't any Scripture to prove that equation. It's just a "Cookism," but I know it works. Try it!

Small thought here

Tell God what you need—with the expectation that you're going to get it from Him. The key phrases in Luke 11:5 are: "have a friend," "go to him," "say to him, 'friend, give me what I need.'" Make a friend of God so that you don't have to be embarrassed when you approach Him in prayer. Tell Him the exact truth and depend on your Lord to meet your need exactly. He won't give you a stone. He will give you your daily bread (Luke 11:3, 11). He will satisfy your heart. He will meet your need.

THE INSIDE OF THE CUP

Scripture, Luke 11:37—12:12
And the Lord said unto him, "Now do ye Pharisees make clean the outside of the cup and the platter; but your inward part is full of ravening and wickedness."
(Luke 11:39)

I remember how hard it was for me as a small boy—who had to do the dishes as my share of the household chores—to learn to get everything clean. I would tend to wash the part that showed and leave the rest. Little did I understand at that time that clean means *clean*, not partly clean—whether it was the inside of a dish or the backside of your ear. Our Lord Jesus used this same homely illustration to remind people that hypocrisy is really an attempt to get by with less than complete cleansing by God. He went on to tell His disciples to watch out for hypocrisy because it's like yeast. Put a little bit of yeast in bread dough and it expands, permeating the entire mix. I remember when I first tried to bake bread. I was in high school at the time and I was cooking for my father (my mother had been dead for many years). I thought, *one cake of yeast is hardly enough*, so I used three cakes instead! Of course, I had bread dough all over the place, faster than you could tell about it. A little bit of yeast goes a long way.

Small thought here

A little bit of hypocrisy goes a long way. There isn't any future in it, Jesus said. There's no advantage to it. You can't get away with it, so why not be real with God? A very good idea! Specialize, my dear friend, on being the real thing with the Lord and with people.

TWO KINDS OF FRUIT

Scripture, Luke 13:6-21
He spake also this parable: "A certain man had a fig tree planted in his vineyard; and he came and sought fruit thereon, and found none."
(Luke 13:6)

Jesus told the story of the man who became justifiably disgruntled when the fig tree planted in his vineyard failed to produce fruit. What's the point? God looks for fruit. That's obvious. What kind of fruit? Two kinds. First, *the fruit of the Spirit:* love, joy, peace, long-suffering, gentleness, goodness, faith, meekness, and self-control (Gal. 5:22-23). Second, *the fruit of a Christian.* The Lord Jesus said, "You have not chosen Me but I have chosen you, and ordained you, that ye should go and bear fruit, and that your fruit should remain" (John 15:16). What kind of fruit is Christ speaking of here? Well, what is the fruit of a grain of corn? More corn. What is the fruit of an apple seed? More apples. What is the fruit of a Christian? More Christians. Three thoughts here: First, God expects fruit from you (and from me). Second, God gives you time. He's willing to wait until you grow up spiritually. Willing to wait until you learn a few lessons of grace yourself. But, third, God isn't willing to wait forever. The reason some people seem to be completely set aside is that they didn't bear fruit while God was waiting for them. So finally, God said, "All right, that's it."

Small thought here

Think, my dear friend, about the tremendous importance of bearing fruit. Realize that God is patient. He'll wait for you till you mature spiritually and He'll help you along by the Holy Spirit and by His Word. But He *does* expect you to bear two kinds of fruit: *the fruit of the Spirit* and *the fruit of a Christian.*

THE REAL THING?

Scripture, Luke 13:22—14:35

"Then shall ye begin to say, 'We have eaten and drunk in Thy presence, and Thou hast taught in our streets.' But He shall say, 'I tell you, I know you not whence ye are; depart from Me, all ye workers of iniquity.' "
(Luke 13:26-27)

One of the most important spiritual concepts you will ever digest is that God requires reality, especially in your relationship with Him. I think, for instance, of the passage in Matthew 7 that parallels today's text. Our Lord Jesus said, "Many will say to Me on that day, 'Lord, Lord, did we not prophesy in Your name, and in Your name drive out demons and perform many miracles?' Then I will tell them plainly, 'I never knew you. Away from Me, you evildoers!' " We find the same thought here in Luke 13. Professing believers will say, "Lord, open to us," and He'll answer, "I don't know where you're from."

To know *about* the Lord Jesus isn't enough. Ask yourself: Do I really know my Lord or do I merely possess some data about Him? Our Lord insists on a real, working relationship with Himself. Another thought here is that people forget the price of a personal commitment to Christ. "You'd better sit down," He said, "and count the cost" (Luke 14:26-33).

Small thought here

Father, mother, wife, children, brothers and sisters: it's going to cost all you have. It cost our Lord His very life. Oh, you say, that's a pretty big order. Yes, it is. But it doesn't mean that God is going to take everything or everyone from you. It *does mean* that ownership of your life—people, things, your very existence— are going to be transferred to the *Lord* Jesus Christ. If you want to really follow Him—that's the cost. Follow Him, my dear friend, and see, with great joy, how the Holy Spirit of God uses you!

LOST AND FOUND

Scripture, Luke 15:1-32
"Likewise, I say unto you, there is joy in the presence of the angels of God over one sinner that repenteth."
(Luke 15:10)

Whathat is the real nature of what we call Christian separation? That's a thorny one, isn't it? A couple of ideas may be helpful. In today's text, our Lord Jesus told stories of the sheep that was lost due to its own stupidity; of the coin that was lost through carelessness; and of the son who was lost through his own stubbornness and self-will. In each case, something or someone of value was lost. Thankfully, each time someone cared enough to search (or in the lost son's case, to wait faithfully) until the thing or person was returned to a rightful place. Finally, the owners could rejoice because what was lost had been found.

People criticized our Lord because He received sinners and even ate with them. What should you and I do? Well, I think there's a difference between being friendly in order to win sinners and simply choosing unsaved people as your friends. Find your real lifelong friends among believers. Make sure that your life companion is a believer. So too your business partners. Beyond this, each of us has a world with which to share the Good News of the Gospel.

Small thought here

Have you gone out of your way to be kind to any unsaved person recently? This, I think, is the test you and I have to face. Our blessed Lord wants people who do not separate themselves from others, as the Pharisees did. He wants people to live wholly unto God wherever they are, but to care about people in the process.

GOD AND MONEY

Scripture, Luke 16:1-31
"No servant can serve two masters: for either he will hate the one, and love the other; or else he will hold to the one, and despise the other. You cannot serve God and mammon."
(Luke 16:13)

Have you ever said, "Oh, if I only had a break, if I only had a chance to be committee chairman, if I only could become company president or head of my division, or whatever." You know the feeling: "If I just had a little more opportunity, *then* I'd do better." Nothing could be further from the truth. Do your best in what you have and you will be more likely to do well when your horizon is broadened a bit. If you'll be faithful in small things, God will trust you with greater things. If you are careless in small things, you will also be a failure in greater things (Luke 16:10).

Our Lord links faithfulness to the matter of who your master is, specifically whether or not God is lord over your money. Think about this for a moment. Find a person who has made money his god and you'll find a person who is unscrupulous, willing to cut corners, careless with the truth, and unmindful of other people's rights. Find a person who has made God his god—so that money and the things it can buy become subservient to the Lord's will—and you'll find a person who is faithful, considerate, and trustworthy.

Small thought here
Our Lord Jesus said it, and it is an operating principle: Put your money under His lordship and your performance will be faithful, helpful, compassionate, and considerate.

WHAT GOD LOOKS FOR

Scripture, Luke 17:11-19; 18:1-14
And Jesus answering said, "Were there not ten cleansed? But where are the nine?"
(Luke 17:17)

A medical man once told me that many patients he treated had developed certain ailments largely as a result of the frustration that came from not being appreciated or thanked. An interesting concept, isn't it? It hurts when someone fails to say "Thank you," or to appreciate something you've done. Has it ever occurred to you, I wonder, that the Heavenly Father wants you to say "Thank You"? Look at Romans 1, for instance. God's quarrel with the heathen is that they didn't give Him His place as God nor did they thank Him (Luke 17:17-18). Thanksgiving is one of the evidences that the grace of God has done something in our lives. The other is that we pray more effectively. The Lord Jesus said, "Men are always to pray and not to faint" (18:1). Pray past the give-up point. Stay on your knees at least twenty or thirty minutes after you've said to yourself, "I gotta get out of here. I'm going to quit. I have other things I must do." You will find that you'll get much more mileage in prayer by praying *past* your collapse point. It is that extra time of seeking God that brings heavenly results.

Small thought here
God looks for a humble heart. "To this man will I look," God said through the Prophet Isaiah, "to him that is of a humble and contrite spirit, and that trembleth at My Word" (Isa. 66:2). The Pharisee never got anywhere with God because he was proud. The publican was heard, forgiven, and justified because he prayed with a bowed head and a broken heart.

IT'S FOR KEEPS!

Scripture, Matthew 19:1-14
"What therefore God hath joined together, let not man put asunder."
(Matt. 19:6)

Our Lord Jesus made it plain that God never intended for an easy breakup of the marriage relationship. He said, "Moses permitted you to divorce your wives *because your hearts were hard.*" Unfortunately, many men and women today take the marriage vows as though they said, "As long as we find it mutually convenient to live together," instead of the traditional, "So long as you both shall live." Marriage is for keeps. The only thing, however, that can keep it together is the grace of God. A husband and wife cannot only get along, but also be in love, live in love, and enjoy the presence of God if the Lord Jesus Christ is at the center of the relationship.

Two thoughts stand out in today's text: the sanctity of the home and the importance of Christ's touch on a young life. When people brought children to our Saviour, the disciples (who could be counted on to be officious at the wrong time) rebuked those who came and said, "Come on now. Don't do that. Get away! Get away!" But our Lord Jesus said, "No, don't rebuke them. Let them come to Me, for of such is the kingdom of heaven. You have to receive the kingdom as a little child or you don't receive it at all."

Small thought here

I think it's important that children and young people experience, firsthand, biblical truth that you as a parent have shared with them. Such experience may come as they are sharing some very private prayer concerns with the Lord. Or it may come when a specific answer to prayer convinces them that God is *really* interested in how they feel and what they need.

A POOR RICH MAN

Scripture, Matthew 19:16—20:16
Then said Jesus unto His disciples, "Verily I say unto you, that a rich man shall hardly enter into the kingdom of heaven."
(Matt. 19:23)

I remember some of us kidding a friend who had just bought a nice new Chevy. We said, "That's pretty carnal. You're spending a lot of money. You should have put that money into missions." We were giving him a bad time. He said very thoughtfully, "Well, I guess it all depends on whether you have things or whether things have you." Pretty good comment, wouldn't you say? Again and again our Lord Jesus pointed out that how a person is motivated to use his money is an accurate index of where he stands with God. Only when God owns your money and the things it can buy and do for you—only when God controls *that*—will He also control your life. It's very easy to envy someone else's success. It's hard to pray, for instance, for a minister who has more people in his services than you have. Hard to pray for a Sunday School teacher whose class is bursting at the seams while you have difficulty getting new people in. Hard to pray for a person who can afford a new house or a new car or a new wardrobe for his wife, or all three for that matter, while you have difficulty meeting your monthly bills.

Small thought here
It's easy, indeed very human, to envy other people and ask, "Lord, why do You bless him instead of me?" Often when you're aware of another person's faults, you wonder, "God, how can You bless him? Look what he just did!" But if Christ is going to be Lord over your substance, He will also have to be Lord of how much substance you have. Leave the "how much" to God, will you? And be at peace.

HOW DESPERATE ARE YOU?

Scripture, Mark 10:32-52; Luke 19:1-10
And Jesus answered and said unto him, "What wilt thou that I should do unto thee?" The blind man said unto Him, "Lord, that I might receive my sight."
(Mark 10:51)

A man who couldn't see, men who didn't see, and a man who wanted to see. They're all in today's text. Our Lord Jesus asked a strange question of Bartimaeus: "What do you want Me to do for you?" Christ surely must have known that the man was blind and wanted to be helped. Hadn't Bartimaeus been shouting, "Jesus, Son of David, have mercy on me"? (10:47) Why should Jesus ask him again? Because He wanted Bartimaeus to realize his utter desperation.

The same is true of us. God waits for us to decide down deep in our hearts two things: (1) what it is that we absolutely must have from Him and, (2) to realize that we are absolutely helpless without Him. Many a person, myself included, often prays good prayers but without the desperation born of the realization that *only* God can intervene. It is that desperate faith that verbalizes our helplessness to God. Someone has pointed out that it is not our *need* that appeals to God, nor indeed our *request*, and certainly not our *worthiness* (for we have none), but our *helplessness*.

Small thought here

Zaccheus only wanted to be a spectator, but God made him a participator. This notorious tax collector climbed a tree to see the Lord Jesus, but Jesus immediately engaged him in conversation and in activity that changed his life. It isn't what you see about the Lord that counts, but rather your personal involvement with the life-changing Jesus that makes all the difference. Zaccheus found this out and so, my friend, will you.

MIND YOUR BUSINESS!

Scripture, Luke 19:11-22
And he called his ten servants, and delivered them ten pounds, and said unto them, "Occupy till I come."
(Luke 19:13)

Most parables are told to emphasize one truth. But our Lord Jesus' parable recorded in Luke 19 was told with a triple purpose. First, to teach that a long wait must intervene before the kingdom is established. Second, to teach that God expects His people to do business, or to "occupy," until He comes. And third, to teach that severe rebuke awaits those who reject Christ's rule. I'd like to zero in on Christ's use of a certain word here: *talents.* You recall the story of the four servants, one who had ten talents and gained ten other talents, one who had five talents and got five more, one who had two talents and got two more, and one who had one talent but went and buried it. Our Lord Jesus said to this unproductive man, "You are a wicked and lazy servant." Now what does that mean to you and me? Let's say, for example, that you are a gifted singer. Our Lord Jesus' word to you is if you don't sing for His glory and multiply your usefulness, you are being wicked and lazy. Or perhaps you have the ability to manage and to organize. Our Lord Jesus is saying, if you don't use that ability in order to multiple its usefulness for God, you are being wicked and lazy. All of your talents have been given to you to invest for eternity.

Small thought here
The Lord Jesus, who never made a mistake, who never had to say, "Excuse me, please," said that the refusal to invest one's life for God is wicked and lazy. What could I possibly add to that, dear friend?

OPPOR-TUNITY KNOCKS

Scripture, Luke 19:28-44
"Thou knewest not the time of thy visitation."
(Luke 19:44)

What was it that made our Lord Jesus weep as He looked over Jerusalem? I think it was because the people of the nation Israel had missed three essential aspects of life. Jesus said, "If thou hadst known at least in this *thy day* the things which belong unto *thy peace!* But now they are hid from *thine eyes*" (19:42).
• *Thy day.* God's timing. There is a time of opportunity in each life and, it would seem, in the lives of groups and nations. Life is for real. You can't just say, "I didn't mean it." The bitter words, the careless deed, the vicious act create scars. Yes, God's grace can forgive, but life is for keeps.
• *Thy peace.* There is only one way to real peace. It's through making Jesus Saviour and Lord. Yet there He stood, the Lord of Life, outside their city and, tragically, outside their hearts. He said, in essence, "You've rejected the One who can give you peace."
• Then there was this matter of a personal experience with God—*thine eyes.* No one else can see for you. Never lose that deep personal awareness of God.

All of this is so terribly final. Jesus said that because the Jews didn't know the time of God's visitation, their enemies would tear down their walls and destroy their city and nation.

Small thought here
God's day, God's timing, God's perfect peace, and God as a part of your life? What does this mean to you? Make sure that you don't miss God's day of visitation in your life.

EMPTY WORDS?

Scripture, Matthew 21:28-32
"Whether of them twain did the will of his father?" They say unto Him, "The first." Jesus saith unto them, "Verily I say unto you, that the publicans and the harlots go into the kingdom of God before you." (Matt. 21:31)

God accepts and uses unlikely people who really obey Him. In the story of the two sons, one of them said, "I'll go," but he didn't. The other son said, "I'm not going," but changed his mind (repented) and obeyed. It's a common situation in everyday living. There are many people whose profession of religion is excellent, but who somehow never get around to obeying God's will. Here and there, however, are some unlikely people—folks you and I would never view as likely candidates for God's work on the basis of their looks or their promise of performance. But, nonetheless, when they faithfully obey God, *He* teaches them and *He* uses them. "Not many wise men after the flesh, not many mighty, not many noble, are called" (1 Cor. 1:26). I've quoted that Scripture for a purpose, my friend. God blesses people who really put Him first.

Another area of concern is the necessity of giving an account. My father said to me one day, "Boy, I want you to learn to give an account of things. I'll give you an allowance each week to buy the groceries for our meals and I want you to keep a record." I said, "All right, Pop." But day after day I neglected to start record-keeping. After three or four weeks, my father asked, "Boy, where's that record you've been keeping?" "Oh," I said, "I'm not ready. I'll have to finish it up." After supper I brought out my record: stationery, 15 cents; chewing gum, 10 cents, popcorn, 10 cents; miscellaneous, $29.42! My day of accounting had come.

Small thought here

The Apostle Paul said that we'll all stand before the Judgment Seat of Christ and everyone will receive according to the deeds done in the body, whether they be good or bad (2 Cor. 5:10). A day of accounting is surely coming. Are you ready for it?

QUESTIONS AND ANSWERS

Scripture, Matthew 22:15-46
And no man was able to answer Him a word, neither durst any man from that day forth ask Him any more questions. (Matt. 22:46)

The questions that come from the carnal, unsaved heart fall into predictable categories: the proper relationship of man to government, to his wife, to his God, and to his neighbor. Yet the Lord Jesus summed up life's meaning when He asked His disciples: "What think ye of Christ?" (Matt. 22:42) In the final analysis, life's questions and problems are solved quickest and best by relating them to the lordship of Jesus Christ.

Nicodemus came to Christ one day with an inquiring mind and a set of doubts which were summed up by his plaintive question, "How can these things be?" Our Lord Jesus looked at him and said, "Nicodemus, it all depends on who's telling you. Marvel not when I tell you that you must be born from above. You were born once with an earthly nature. Now, Nicodemus, you need to be born again with a heavenly nature." Why did our Lord talk of being born again? Simply for this reason: He was the One who had built human nature in the first place, had provided for the reproduction of the species, and for the miracle we call natural birth. No wonder then, that He would have a right to say, "You need a new birth from above."

Small thought here

The questions of life—questions about relationships to government, the opposite sex, God, and one's neighbor—all tend to fall into place when you settle the one big question: "What think ye of Christ?"

MARKS OF A PHONY

Scripture, Matthew 23:1-39
"Even so ye also outwardly appear righteous unto men, but within ye are full of hypocrisy and iniquity."
(Matt. 23:28)

Matthew 23 gives us a profile of a "phony." Our Lord Jesus used the term *hypocrites*. The first mark of a phony is *noninvolvement*. "I don't want to get involved." Have you ever heard that? The Lord Jesus says of these people that they bind heavy burdens on men's shoulders, but will not move one of their fingers to help (v. 4). Another mark of a phony is *public relations gone to seed*. "All their works they do to be seen of men" (v. 5). "What will people say?" is the giveaway here. Third, a phony is *busy but barren* (v. 15). It may be that you're wearing the same pair of shoes as someone who has been very busy for the Lord, but who is not really experiencing God's blessing. A phony is also *a specialist in trivia*. He majors on minors. "You pay tithe of mint and anise and cummin, and have omitted the weightier matters of the law: judgment, mercy, and faith" (v. 23). "These ought ye to have done" (judgment, mercy, faith), "and not to have left the other undone" (your tithes). Finally, a phony is characterized by *outward shining, but inward sinning*. "You make clean the outside of the cup and of the platter, but within they are full of extortion and excess" (v. 25).

Small thought here

My friend, you and I have to decide whether or not we fit the dreadful definition of the hypocrite, the phony, as presented here by our blessed Lord. There's only one answer to it: Be real with God, be done with the feeble business of the phony, and start today.

THE SON IS COMING

Scripture, Matthew 24:1-44
"Therefore be ye also ready: for in such an hour as ye think not the Son of man cometh."
(Matt. 24:44)

It was business as usual. In Noah's time nobody cared about the future. Sin of every kind was rampant. And God was grieved. Our Lord Jesus said, "As the days of Noah were, so shall also the coming of the Son of man be" (Matt. 24:37).

Noah's generation was given over to pleasure and self-indulgence. Now can you tell me, please, whether there are parallels between that day and our own? Between today and the overt, "pronto," unashamed wickedness of that time? Sociologists say we are in the midst of a *sensate culture*, as people rely on their senses alone. "Don't bother me with thinking," someone has said. Yes, my friend, we don't know *the date*, but we can know we are approaching *the day* when our Lord Jesus said He will return.

Small thought here

Remember that the second coming of Christ will involve drastic separations. Separation at the level of everyday living: two people grinding at a mill, two people working in the field, two people sleeping in a bed, according to another portion of the Gospel record. Ordinary situations. Workaday situations. Domestic situations. The Rapture will likewise produce drastic separations, because only those who are born again, who know the Lord Jesus as their Saviour will be caught up to meet Him.

BE ON THE JOB

Scripture, Matthew 25:1-46
"Watch therefore; for ye know neither the day nor the hour wherein the Son of man cometh."
(Matt. 25:13)

Regardless of the circumstances under which I may be living when our Lord returns, my readiness to meet Him will be determined by what rules my life. If the blessed Holy Spirit, the oil of God, fills my vessel, then I can be sure my lamp will still be burning when the cry is made: "The bridegroom cometh, go ye out to meet Him" (v. 6). Readiness to meet Him also involves the down-to-earth matter of investing my life and talents. The Lord Jesus expects me to use and multiply the gifts and abilities He has given me for His glory. He also says that until He comes I'm to be on the job—meeting the nitty-gritty needs of people—as unto Him. That's what He expects.

When our Lord Jesus one day evaluates your work and service, what stands out will be what you have done for other people as if it were done for Him. So be on the job serving the needs of people as unto Christ. Be ready with your vessel filled with God's Spirit. Be investing your talents faithfully, fruitfully, and sacrificially until He comes. You'll be ready to meet Him. Yes, you will.

Small thought here
God is the God of good business. Have you thought about that? And God is the God of profit. And He is the God of diligent investments and of the conservation of your resources. He believes in these things. He is not the God of "just sit down, do nothing, and let somebody else take care of me."

PILATE'S REVEALING QUESTIONS

Scripture, Matthew 27:1-26
Pilate saith unto them, "What shall I do then with Jesus which is called Christ?"
(Matt. 27:22)

Have you noticed that the questions we ask often show what kind of people we are and frequently indicate the direction and destiny of our lives? Pontius Pilate is a prime example of this truth. His questions had to do with identity: "Art Thou the King of the Jews?" They had to do with reactions to pressure from people: "Hearest Thou not how many things they witness against Thee?" ("Aren't You concerned, Jesus, about what people are saying about You?") Pilate certainly was. He was concerned about being friends with Herod. And he was concerned about keeping peace, so far as he could, with this troublesome minority over which he ruled.

Pilate's questions had to do with seeking the approval of the crowd. "Whom will ye that I release unto you?" You always make a mistake when you ask the crowd what they want. Pilate's questions had to do with his own personal uncertainty. "What shall I do then with Jesus which is called Christ?" And finally, they had to do with his deep rationalization of the whole situation. For in his last dialogue with the crowd, as they shouted for our Lord's crucifixion, he asked, "Why? What evil has He done?" The identity crisis many people talk about stems from their *lack of identity* with God through Christ. Show me a person who is right with the Saviour and I will show you a person whose life has meaning.

Small thought here
Pilate's questions showed him to be insecure, uncertain, and unwilling to face the truth. May the questions you and I ask show us to be people who are willing to face the truth and to *embrace* it in the person of our blessed Lord.

Be thou an example of the believer in word,
in conversation, in charity, in spirit, in
faith, in purity.
(1 Tim. 4:12)

Be a Blessing
IN WHAT YOU SAY!

Have you ever said to yourself, "If only I could keep my big mouth shut"? If so, join the group! So have all the rest of us! Jesus said that "out of the abundance of the heart, the mouth speaketh." Inevitably, what you are inside and the way you feel about things and people is going to come out in your speech. Is there any cure for "foot-in-mouth" disease? Or must you go through life regretting things you say in unguarded moments? "Unguarded"—perhaps that is the key to solving your problem! Paul says that instead of worrying, you should pray about everything. As a result, he says, the peace of God that passes all understanding will keep your heart and mind (the source of what you say) through Christ Jesus. Pray about your words, and be a blessing!

Robert A. Cook

February

You've heard the expression, "He's just a square peg in a round hole!" It's said, of course, about someone who just "doesn't fit" a particular job, group, or situation. Deep down, all of us want to "fit in," don't we? We want to feel accepted, welcomed, and needed. Our meditations this month from portions of Ephesians and related Bible passages begin with the question, "How do I fit in?" We'll discover that God not only *welcomes us* and *works for us,* but He also gives us a heavenly inheritance! Also this month we'll consider some keys to living wisely and learn about the strength God supplies to meet life's demands.

HOW DO I FIT IN?

Scripture, Ephesians 1:1-23
But now hath God set the members every one of them in the body, as it hath pleased Him.
(1 Cor. 12:18)

Let's suppose you are planning a dinner party to honor a celebrity or a dear friend. You go over the guest list carefully, weighing the interests of each person in relation to the others, in order to determine who should sit next to whom. Then you come to John Doe. He is new to your group and to you. You have invited him because your honored guest is staying temporarily in this man's home. Thinking of John you ask yourself, "Will he fit in?" As matters turn out, John Doe shows himself a gracious guest, a fascinating conversationalist, a person keenly interested in his new friends. You say with delight, "Why, he fits right in!"

This matter of "fitting in" is dealt with in God's Word. In several places we find that believers in the Lord Jesus Christ are referred to, corporately, as the body of Christ. Totally unfractured by denominationalism, this happy company includes *all* who declare their faith in the risen Saviour. In this living, spiritual organism, each member has a place and a function distinctly his own. The question now is two-fold: *Where* do I fit in? and *How* do I fit in? The "where" is dealt with in such passages as Romans 12:4-8, Ephesians 4:11-13, and 1 Corinthians 12:18. In the days to come, we'll examine here in Ephesians "how" we fit in. If we confine ourselves only to Ephesians 1, and if for the sake of individual application we use the personal pronoun, we shall see that in these verses God is amazingly at work in the following ways:

God welcomes me, God works for me, God gives to me, and God strengthens me.

Small thought here
As a believer in the Lord Jesus Christ, my induction into the body of Christ, my placement there for service, and my part in the total fulfillment of the divine purpose are all *God's* gracious doing.

GOD WELCOMES ME

Scripture, Ephesians 1:1-23
To the saints . . . faithful in Christ Jesus.
(Eph. 1:1)

The moment you commit yourself to Jesus Christ as Saviour and Lord, God looks upon you as a saint. Unfortunately, not all of us act like saints! Obviously, there is a good deal of refining to be done in each of us, and the Spirit of God addresses Himself to this need on a continual basis.

I have a new relationship. What results will follow? When I am "in Christ," the Holy Spirit positions me where He can use me in a special way. He may take my casual words, or my unplanned attitude, or just the illusive value of my personality and use them for God's glory—all because of this dynamic relationship with Christ that is brought about through the Holy Spirit's dwelling within.

I have a new incentive. What does God want us, His children, to be?

• *Holy.* In His essential character God is holy. He wants us to partake of His nature, to be like Him—to the extent that humankind can share that likeness.

• *Without blame.* God foresaw the fall and ruination of the human race and He made righteous provision for our redemption and freedom from the blame we justly earned.

• *In love.* God envisioned us not as robots, mechanically wound up to do this and that, but as members of a close-knit family, a body bound together by love.

"I am going to accomplish this," He must have said, "through My dear Son Jesus Christ." *And He did!*

Small thought here
It is by this work of God on our behalf—totally apart from any worthiness in us—that we believers in His Son are constituted "the body of Christ" and are welcomed into that blessed fellowship.

GOD WORKS FOR ME

Scripture, Ephesians 1:1-23
And what is the exceeding greatness of His power to us-ward who believe, according to the working of His mighty power. (Eph. 1:19)

We find here at least three ways in which God's gracious work for sinners is made evident.

I am redeemed. From the dawn of Creation, to the provision of animal skins for our sinning first parents, to the singing of the heavenly choirs in Glory in a coming day, the precious message of salvation through the shed blood of Christ is history's constant and timeless theme.

I am forgiven. Only because Christ died can my record be cleared and I be forgiven. I must realize that all I *deserve* is God's judgment. Actually, what the Lord Jesus Christ did was to go into the slave market of sin, so to speak, and find me there. He paid the price of my freedom by giving His life for mine. Then He took me by the hand and led me out saying, "Child, you're free—because you're *Mine.*" He did exactly the same thing for you, if you have trusted Him for salvation.

I am an object of God's grace. The grace of God admits you to the very heart of God, so that you may learn the things that please Him. Grace is not simply a handy formula for getting saved, as we sometimes imply in quoting Ephesians 2:8-9: "For by grace are ye saved through faith . . . ." Oh, no. The grace of God is *Jesus Himself,* the embodiment of God's unexplainable love for poor sinners such as we.

Small thought here

To make Jesus Lord of every detail of our lives, the cohesive center around which everything gathers, we must consciously recognize His ownership and willingly put Him in charge. Just as you exercised faith when you received Him as Saviour, so now are you to trust Him as Lord of all the component parts of your life as they come to your attention one by one.

GOD GIVES TO ME

Scripture, Ephesians 1:1-23
In whom also we have obtained an inheritance, being predestinated according to the purpose of Him who worketh all things after the counsel of His own will. (Eph. 1:11)

Not only does God welcome me into His family and work for me in redemption, forgiveness, and grace, but He also bestows upon me His own unspeakably valuable benefits.

I have an inheritance (Eph. 1:11). We all know that an inheritance, whether temporal or spiritual, requires that the supplicant be a proven member of the family concerned. When you and I came to Jesus for salvation, we were not members of God's family. We were strangers, aliens, wanderers. All this being true, how can we ever achieve inheritance in His family? Paul tells us. We have obtained an inheritance because God has made us members of His family. He "predestinated us unto the adoption of children by Jesus Christ to Himself."

I am enabled to reflect glory (Eph. 1:12). There is nothing anyone can do to brighten the divine image. We can add nothing to it or take anything from it. But God Himself can "turn up the lamp," so to speak, and intensify the brightness. This is exactly what He chooses to do through His redeemed ones. It is important to remember that any glory that is ours is not innate but reflective.

I have the seal of the Holy Spirit (Eph. 1:13-14). My inheritance—and yours too—is already settled. It is made possible by the fact that the Lord Jesus Christ, by His death and resurrection, became both our Saviour and our Elder Brother when we invited Him into our hearts. And by virtue of that relationship we share all that is His.

Small thought here

Have you given any thought lately to whether or not you are reflecting God's glory? The only way to do that is to spend time regularly in the warm glow of the Sun of Righteousness, so that you "soak up" His nature.

GOD STRENGTHENS ME

Scripture, Ephesians 1:1-23
God is the strength of my heart and my portion forever.
(Ps. 73:26)

Beloved, we see the energizing power of God made available to us in three ways:

I am directed in prayer (Eph. 1:17). Paul says in effect: "I pray that you will have the wisdom, the comfort, the reality, and the power of the indwelling Christ—all made possible by the Holy Spirit within you." That should be our prayer too. Look with me at these various components: *Wisdom.* This is more than knowledge. It is the ability to know *what to do* with *what we know. Revelation.* The word is related to our English word *apocalypse* which means an opening of the heavens, an intervention of God in line with His purpose and will on our behalf.

I am enlightened in heart (Eph. 1:18). The word *understanding* in the Greek New Testament means "heart"—the composite of our knowledge, will, and emotions. God wants the eyes of our heart, the total person, to be enlightened. For what reason? To perceive hope, glory, and power!

I am empowered for living (Eph. 1:19-20). Note the expression *according to.* The Greek word suggests "right down the line." In other words, the same power that was in effect at the resurrection of Jesus Christ has come right down the line to you and me. Oh, I rejoice in that! I don't fully understand it, but I see that it is power to save, power to keep, power to endure, power to do more than we ask or think. Hallelujah for that!

Small thought here

God's plan is that you and I should be so filled with His Spirit that our impact on others will reflect the presence and fragrance of our blessed Lord Jesus Christ.

CIRCUM-SPECT IN WALK

Scripture, Ephesians 5:15-21
See then that ye walk circumspectly, not as fools, but as wise.
(Eph. 5:15)

Remember the war years? If you were a soldier who saw combat on enemy ground, you learned the value of concentrated alertness. *Watch out for the mines . . . the traps . . . the barbed wire . . . the snipers.* In today's text the Apostle Paul applies this warning to spiritual warfare. The word *circumspectly* means "to look around, to be alive, to be awake." You don't have to be naive to be spiritual. "The fear of the Lord [that combination of awe, respect, and obedience] is the beginning of wisdom" (Ps. 111:10) and you *can* have it.

We are called to be people who possess God's wisdom. The question is: What is involved in living wisely? In Ephesians 5:16-21 we find our answer couched in several verbs, most of them ending in "ing." To live wisely we are told in these verses to be:

• Wise in the use of time—*"redeeming the time"* (v. 16).
• Wise in perception—*"understanding"* (v. 17).
• Wise in equipment—*"filled"* (v. 18).
• Wise in fellowship—*"speaking . . . singing"* (v. 19).
• Wise in expressing gratitude—*"giving thanks"* (v. 20).
• Wise in submission—*"submitting yourselves"* (v. 21).

We'll look at each of these more fully in the meditations ahead.

Small thought here

Any time you bow your knees and your heart to God, you'll end up a wiser person (James 1:5).

WISE IN USE OF TIME

Scripture, Ephesians 5:15-21
Redeeming the time, because the days are evil.
(Eph. 5:16)

Learn to use your time with eternity in view. That viewpoint will transform your attitude toward even routine and uninspiring tasks. There is nothing religious about emptying the garbage, or scrubbing the kitchen floor, or diapering the baby. But if you think of using time *for God*, it puts His touch of glory on the commonplace.

The next time you have something to do that bothers you (because, as the lady said about housework, "It's so daily," and you're tired of it and bored), look heavenward and say, "Lord Jesus, I'm going to do this for You." You'll be surprised, my friend, at the difference it will make in your own attitude and in the quality of your work.

One of the things you must learn to do in managing your time is to prioritize your schedule of activities each day. The word *priority* means "to give first place, in sequence, to the things to be done."

So make your list, starting with the most important thing. But before that, beloved, look up and say, "Dear Lord, sharpen my mind. Give me Your thoughts about this thing I'm about to do and help me to do it well, for Your glory." Then go from item to item in the same spirit of commitment and expectancy.

Small thought here
Buy up the opportunities. Use them for eternal worth. That doesn't mean you will go around "being religious" all the time. It *does* mean that you can dedicate the whole day, every split second of it, to your Lord and Saviour.

WISE IN PERCEPTION

Scripture, Ephesians 5:15-21
Wherefore be ye not unwise, but understanding what the will of the Lord is. (Eph. 5:17)

Whatever your need, first read and study your Bible. Next, get on your knees and pray about the problem in light of the Word. Be specific. I have found that this method works quickly and well. One time I faced six job options. Following the above rule, I studied the Word for my own soul's sake, not seeking any formula. Then I got down on my knees and began to pray, listing both "pro" and "con" possibilities on a legal pad. You would be surprised at how quickly the Lord screened out certain options. Finally there was just one choice: I made it, and have been glad ever since.

If you really want to know God's will, first look into His Word. Second, talk to the Lord specifically. And third, do what you know *now* to be His will. It's pretty hard to steer a truck that is standing still. It is impossible for God to guide you as long as you procrastinate about that initial step of faith. Don't just stand around, waiting, wondering, and complaining. God leads you as you *move*. Do the thing (small though it may be) that you know *now* to be the will of God. He will show you the next step.

Small thought here

God's will is bound up with faith and obedience. As long as you are willing to obey Him, a step at a time, He is willing to lead you. If a door closes, don't try to batter it down; go to the next one. Very simple! Very glorious!

WISE IN EQUIPMENT

Scripture, Ephesians 5:15-21
Be not drunk with wine, wherein is excess; but be filled with the Spirit.
(Eph. 5:18)

I suppose none of us needs to debate the point that we ought not to get drunk. The excesses that accompany drunkenness are many, among them sadness, violence, selfishness, and lust. Paul says, in effect, "Stay away from anything that leads to these troubles."

You may argue successfully that a glass of sherry before a meal (or a cocktail, or whatever) does no harm. You may also point out that this practice has nothing to do with your salvation, and you would be right. But there could be a potential alcoholic across the table from you who observes that one drink and is pushed right over the cliff into alcoholism, tragedy, and death. I don't think it's worth paying that price, do you?

In the same sentence the apostle continues, "Be filled with the Spirit." What are we to learn from this comparison? Paul's meaning is this: Just as alcohol becomes manager of your reasoning and conduct, so let the Holy Spirit control you. More about that tomorrow.

Small thought here
On the Day of Pentecost the Holy Spirit came to the baby church, at that point just a few believers gathered together in an upper room. A short time later, a great crowd concluded about this same group, "These men are full of new wine!" In other words, "They're drunk!" No, this was not the case, but they were *under the complete control of the Holy Spirit.*

FILLED AND FUELED

Scripture, Ephesians 5:15-21
Be filled with the Spirit.
(Eph. 5:18)

In my opinion, the Holy Spirit does two things that human effort can never duplicate: He produces Christian character and He gives power for witnessing. Look at the first result of this ministry. In Galatians 5 Paul lists qualities called "the fruit of the Spirit"—love, joy, peace, long-suffering, gentleness, goodness, faith, meekness, self-control. Only the Spirit of God can produce such "fruit." Human attempts at spirituality can only produce counterfeits. But to the extent that your life is under the Holy Spirit's control, these good qualities will emerge.

Anything dependent on human effort is subject, in time, to weariness and breakdown. Take a simple illustration: We have all seen children (often our own!) who have been briefed before a visitor arrives: "It's very important that you behave while Mr. So-and-so is here." The children are models of politeness for about the first hour. Then they tire of maintaining that respectable facade and revert to form. They become a little more noisy; perhaps a quarrel erupts between two of them and something is knocked over with a resounding crash. In short, they became *their own selves* when they gave up trying.

Small thought here
We grown-ups, like little children, try to approximate the qualifications and characteristics of the Christian life. For a while we may be able to put up a good front. But then we tire of trying, and at that point the whole effort is lost.

POWER FOR WITNESSING

Scripture, Ephesians 5:15-21
Ye shall receive power, after that the Holy Ghost is come upon you: and ye shall be witnesses unto Me.
(Acts 1:8)

As a born-from-above child of the King, you can experience the continuing miracle of His indwelling Spirit. The moment you received Jesus as Saviour, the Holy Spirit came to live within you to begin His work of producing spiritual fruit—love, joy, peace, and so on (Gal. 5:22-23). No one but the Holy Spirit can accomplish this.

In those early days afer Pentecost, the apostles' witness had a powerful and immediate reaction. In some cases the response was murderous in its intent. (Indeed, Peter and John had several "close calls" and James was put to death by Herod's orders.) In others, it was thoughtful and accepting. ("Men and brethren, what shall we do?") But whenever the Lord's representatives spoke of Him, they were filled with divine power and their witness resulted in a verdict on the part of those who heard.

Paul gives us further insight into this matter of walking wisely as children of God. We'll examine that tomorrow.

Small thought here
Now then, we come back to Paul's command: "Be not drunk with wine . . . but be filled with the Spirit." When your life is controlled by the Spirit of God, your character will be modified heavenward and your witness will be powerful.

WISE IN FELLOWSHIP

Scripture, Ephesians 5:15-21
Speaking to yourselves in psalms and hymns and spiritual songs, singing and making melody in your heart to the Lord.
(Eph. 5:19)

"Speaking to yourselves" has to do with Christian fellowship. You cannot be a recluse and an effective witness for God at the same time. Granted, some of us are solitary by nature. We do not mix easily with a crowd. Others of us are gregarious, happy to be in the center of bustling human activity. Yes, human beings differ in their reactions to others, and there is no point attempting to be someone you're not. But, my friend, you and I, no matter what our personalities, *need each other.* There is something you can say or do—in your quietness or in your enthusiastic outreach—that is capable of making me a better person.

We need to get together as Christians, not simply because we like each other and enjoy companionship, though that may very well be true and ought to be. We also need to join our hearts for the purpose of sharing the things of God and thus strengthening each other in the faith.

How is this done? The apostle suggests several means: psalms, hymns, spiritual songs, and the singing heart. So there you have the formula: *Psalms*—the Word of God. *Hymns*—a worshipful expression of praise to God in music. *Spiritual songs*—what we might call Gospel music. *Heart melody*—praise offered by those of us who cannot carry a tune.

Small thought here
Would you give a little thought today, beloved, to your contact with people, other Christians in particular? Would you ask yourself this question: What touch am I to have, by God's grace, on others—to encourage and strengthen them?

WISE IN GRATITUDE

Scripture, Ephesians 5:15-21
Giving thanks always for all things unto God and the Father in the name of our Lord Jesus Christ.
(Eph. 5:20)

Thanks ... always ... for all things. Oh, that's a big order, isn't it? How can you be thankful for something that breaks your heart? How can you praise God for that occurrence that gives every evidence of being a tragedy? Humanly, I don't think you can!

But by the Holy Spirit's enablement, each of us *can* thank God for fulfilling His sovereign will (though we may not understand it). We can thank Him because, beloved, we know that God will never ask us to do anything that is not *good* or that He will not *help* us to do.

Suppose I have a broken leg. Am I to shout, "Hooray! Look what's happened to me"? No, I can't rejoice in the pain, the inconvenience, the disruption of my plans and the plans of others. But I can— honestly and sincerely—praise God because I know that He means this very circumstance to bring blessing into my life and the lives of others.

As I see it, God is not particularly eager to receive thanks, as such, from us. But He does want us to acknowledge *who He is*—God, the Almighty One. And gratitude to Him is the natural response to such perception and acceptance.

This truth is borne out in Romans 1, where a picture is painted of unregenerate humankind. God's quarrel with the heathen is not that they *are* heathen, but that they refuse to give Him His rightful status as God and (consequently) never thank Him.

Small thought here

The lesson is plain: Let God be God. Acknowledge His sovereignty, yield to His will, rejoice in His working. It is always "for good." If you will do this, there will arise in your heart a lovely spirit of thankfulness with power to strengthen and heal.

HOW TO GIVE THANKS

Scripture, Ephesians 5:15-21
In every thing give thanks: for this is the will of God in Christ Jesus concerning you.
(1 Thes. 5:18)

Years ago, when our children were young, I came home on one occasion after having preached as hard as I could in a very demanding series of meetings. I was bone tired and mentally exhausted. Instead of the quiet renewal that I had yearned for, I came home to find that an accident had befallen one of the children—there was a broken bone to be tended to and things in the household were in bad shape.

I remember saying to the Lord, "Why did this have to happen *now*? I've been doing my best—giving out the Word, going for souls, sparing nothing. I come home dead tired and there is no rest in sight. Why?"

Right then, the faithful Holy Spirit reminded me of this verse, "Giving thanks always for all things unto God and the Father in the name of our Lord Jesus Christ" (Eph. 5:20). I stopped my pacing, my praying, and my complaining, looked up and said, "Dear Lord, I don't like this situation, but by faith I am going to thank You for what You are doing." In that instant my heart was filled with sweetness and love for God and acceptance of the situation, so that I could once again think clearly, seeing exactly what to do next.

Small thought here

Are you bitter about something today, even a little bit? Is there a relationship that has been fractured, a marriage that is breaking up, a tragedy that touches you or your family? May I encourage you to look up to our loving Heavenly Father and say, "Please, for Jesus' sake, give me a spirit of thanks and praise to You, even in this." And He will!

GIVE THANKS IN THE DARK

Scripture, Ephesians 5:15-21
"For I know the thoughts that I think toward you," saith the Lord, "thoughts of peace, and not of evil."
(Jer. 29:11)

The miracle of the Christian life is that every experience that comes your way has God's touch upon it. There are no accidents, no happenstances to those who belong to God by faith in Jesus Christ.

I often think of those five young men who were martyred in the South American jungle many years ago. The entire civilized world began (figuratively) clicking its tongue and saying, "What a pity! What a waste of young talent! Why didn't those fellows stay in the city, where they could be appreciated, and send someone else to the jungle?"

Did God make a mistake in allowing this to happen? Oh, no. The full benefit of the combined sacrifice of those lives will never be known on earth. But already we can trace the result to hundreds of young people who have committed themselves to God for work on mission fields—all because of the challenge of those laid-down lives. Does God know what He is doing? Yes, He does! "Known unto God are all His works from the beginning of the world" (Acts 15:18).

The key to gratitude toward God is twofold: First, realize that you have a loving Heavenly Father who knows what He is doing; and second, commit yourself to His will, even though you may not understand it.

Small thought here
The essence of fallen human nature is rebellion, and the essence of the new nature, obtained through faith in Christ, is submission and obedience: "Giving thanks always for all things unto God." Contrary to the views of modern intellectuals, we are not dealing simply with the forces of the universe, but with a Person who is *God!*

GIVE THANKS FOR THE FATHER

Scripture, Ephesians 5:15-21
Blessed be God, even the Father of our Lord Jesus Christ.
(2 Cor. 1:3)

God is not only the creator and maintainer of the universe, but also a loving Heavenly Father. Obviously, it is not two persons but two aspects of the divine character that are in view in Ephesians 5:20. To His followers Jesus spoke of God as "your Father in heaven." He said that the pattern of their praying (and ours) needs to begin with an acknowledgment of the Father/child relationship: "Our Father which art in heaven, hallowed be Thy name."

O beloved child of God, get hold of this. God is your *Father*. Our Lord Jesus said concerning Him: "If ye then, being evil, know how to give good gifts unto your children, how much more shall your Father which is in heaven give good things to them that ask Him?" (Matt. 7:11) Earlier in the same sermon Jesus drew a picture of loving, caring parents by asking a series of questions: If your child wanted bread, would you give him a stone? If he was hungry for fish, would you offer him a viper instead? If he asked for an egg, would you give him a scorpion? The answer, of course, is "No, no, no!" Why? Because it is the nature of a true father to give *good* things to his children.

Small thought here

You have a Father in heaven. He cares for you and will give you only what is best for you. That being the case, you can honestly and sincerely thank Him for what He gives, though you may not understand the reason for it or relish the taste of the "medicine" at the time.

GIVE THANKS FOR JESUS

Scripture, Ephesians 5:15-21
Giving thanks always for all things unto God and the Father in the name of our Lord Jesus Christ.
(Eph. 5:20)

What is it that connects you, a finite human being, with infinite providence and the compassion of the Heavenly Father? The last phrase of our verse contains the answer: your relationship to the Lord Jesus Christ. As your Saviour, He pleads your cause before a holy God. As your Redeemer, He snatches you out of the slave market of sin and empowers you to "stand fast ... in the liberty wherewith Christ hath made us free" (Gal. 5:1). He is the One who, by means of the indwelling Holy Spirit, can produce the kind of life that honors and glorifies God.

If you have never made Jesus Christ your Saviour and Lord, remember that all it takes to establish this relationship is a call on your part. "Call unto Me," God says, "and I will answer" (Jer. 33:3). And Isaiah wrote, "Seek ye the Lord while He may be found, call ye upon Him while He is near" (Isa. 55:6).

In this moment, look up and ask Jesus Christ to become your Saviour and Lord. Commit yourself to Him in faith and love, and watch Him transform your life.

Small thought here
Thank God for Jesus! He makes all of this possible. What is the next step in living wisely? Submission! This may come as a shock, but we'll talk more about that tomorrow.

WISE IN SUBMISSION

Scripture, Ephesians 5:15-21
Submitting yourselves one to another in the fear of God.
(Eph. 5:21)

"**S**ubmitting" is an interesting word. In the original Greek it means "to place under." Paul's implication here is that submission is something we must do in relation to other people. We hear a great deal about standing up for our rights, but little about foregoing them.

After I had grown up and dared to ask my father some questions never posed when I was younger, I said to him one day, "Pop, you have a very forceful personality. You call it your 'positive nature.' (And I chuckled.) How in the world did you and my mother get along so well, as everyone says was the case? Didn't you ever quarrel?"

He thought a moment. "No, Boy, I don't think we ever did quarrel. When I said or did anything that she disagreed with, she would explain to me, very carefully, how she felt, and then she would add, 'Whatever you want, dear,' and I'd end up doing it her way." That was a very wise lady!

Of course, not every "explanation" has that kind of result. But I can tell you this: the person who is *willing* to yield suffers far less trauma than the one who is not.

People say to me rather belligerently, "Do you want me to be a doormat?" No, not that. I am only urging you to put in perspective the things that really count. Some things you must not yield. But thousands of other issues in daily life are not worth quibbling about. In dealing with *these* things, explain your point of view lovingly, clearly, and without heat. Then be willing for whatever outcome may follow.

Small thought here

The willingness to cheerfully go out of your way to help other people, without being asked to do so, is one of the great trademarks of Christian faith in action. This may require you to take a back seat, to play second fiddle, to let the other person have his way—all to the end that Jesus Christ may be honored and glorified through your life.

THE ULTIMATE SUBMISSION

Scripture, Ephesians 5:15-21
Let this mind be in you, which was also in Christ Jesus.
(Phil. 2:5)

You and I are not under each other's authority but under God's. The result of this relationship is that our heavenward stance—submission to the Lord—produces flexibility in our relationships with people. Ephesians 5:21 speaks of the "fear of God." This is not cowardice and abject dread, but holy respect and awe. With such an attitude, the everyday contacts you have with people will reflect the perfections of the Lord Jesus Christ—perhaps in small but certainly significant ways.

Finally, in this matter of submission you need to be willing for the other person's advancement. If you're truly serving God, then you'll make room in your thinking and attitudes for the other person to get a little more exposure than you do, a little more praise. Instead of saying, "Lord, get him out of my way," you'll learn to beseech the Father for His blessing on people who seem better off than you. You will be surprised at what this kind of praying will do for the temperature of your own soul.

Small thought here
Now that we have concluded our meditations on Ephesians 5:15-21, I pray that each of us, freshly aware of the dear Saviour's nearness, the faithful Holy Spirit's enablement, and the firm grasp of the Father's hand on our own, may learn more and more each day what a joy it is to walk wisely.

STRENGTH ENOUGH FOR ANYTHING

Scripture, Ephesians 6:10-17
Finally, my brethren, be strong in the Lord, and in the power of His might.
(Eph. 6:10)

Everyone wants to be strong enough to deal satisfactorily with the particular situation he faces. Suppose you are a child, tugging at a big box which contains toys you want. Your little fingers pry the heavy latch, but it does not move. You are not strong enough to open it. Or you are a teenager. Peer approval means more to you than anything else. You did not expect heavy drinking at this party. But suddenly, there it is. You need strength to resist the temptation to yield. Or you are a business person, a working mother, a newly bereaved spouse. Each of you (and persons in uncounted other categories) needs strength of a particular nature.

In Ephesians 6:10-17 a special kind of strength is described, an enablement that *everybody* can use. The passage suggests and answers four questions which we will study the next four days:
• *What is the strength I need?* (v. 10)
• *How do I get the strength I need?* (vv. 11, 13)
• *Why do I need this strength?* (v. 12)
• *What are the evidences of this strength?* (vv. 11-17)

Small thought here
Some of you are carrying heavy burdens, the weight of which threatens to crush you. Others have the pain of heartbreak as your constant companion. Still others have problems related to home, school, or career. Bring your need to God, dear friend. Appropriate *His* strength. Depend on "the God who is there" and who answers prayer. "Be strong in the Lord and in the power of His might."

WHAT IS THE STRENGTH I NEED?

Scripture, Ephesians 6:10-17
I am not ashamed of the Gospel of Christ for it is the power of God unto salvation. (Rom. 1:16)

The two key words of Ephesians 6:10 are *power* and *might*. Paul's emphasis is twofold: Let your life be filled with the dynamic staying power of God that—like the sun—never gets tired, never wears out, never gives up. Let it be marked also by supernatural achieving power, bulldozer strength that levels every obstacle in its way. Mark this: It is *God's* power. No man can create it. Nonetheless, it is real, observable, and measurable.

Can God's power be real and measurable at times of bereavement, pain, and crisis, as well as in the tedium of your daily routine? Oh, yes, it can, beloved! You can see the footprints of your blessed Lord's nail-pierced feet as you follow the path of obedience marking His perfect will. You can *know* that He is ever working for your good and for His glory. How? Because the moment you became a Christian, the Holy Spirit came to live within you. You have, then, the privilege—the *command*, if you believe Ephesians 5:18—to be "filled" with the Spirit, the One controlling your very life and thoughts. That being so, the potential is there for an unlimited demonstration of His power, making the promise of Ephesians 3:20 operative in your life: "(God) is able to do exceeding abundantly above all that we ask or think, according to the *power* that worketh in us."

Small thought here
Everything that God can do through human flesh can be done in and through *you*, His child.

HOW DO I GET THE STRENGTH I NEED?

Scripture, Ephesians 6:10-17
Put on the whole armor of God that ye may be able to stand against the wiles of the devil.
(Eph. 6:11)

Perhaps you are the parent of a school-age child and are incensed by the propagation of secular humanism in the public schools. You *should* be! What is secular humanism? It is that world philosophy that says: You can better yourself by leaving out God ... by substituting modern beliefs for rock-firm, Bible-based values ... by supposing the universe began by some great "accident," not by divine fiat ... and by viewing yourself as a mere animal (made highly intelligent, of course, through millennia of evolution), having no need to be governed by One who is higher. God-denying and God-defying propaganda is being taught worldwide, polluting the minds of young people by the millions. We ought to get behind any movement that seeks to bring an awareness of God's Word into the classroom. We ought also to let our dissenting voices be heard in any dialogue that aims at undervaluing that Word. But in the last analysis, our conflict is not with the science teacher, or the principal, or the president of the university, or the school board. They and their staffs are not our targets. We must recognize that they are tools of Satan, and our quarrel is with *him*.

How do we protect ourselves and our children from his advances? By teaching them reverential trust in God and reverence for His Word. "Thou shalt teach them diligently unto thy children, and shalt talk of them when thou sittest in thine house, and when thou walkest by the way, and when thou liest down, and when thou risest up" (Deut. 6:7).

Small thought here

O beloved, familiarize yourself with the enemy's methods. Steep yourself in God's Word to protect against his wiles. Remind yourself that thus outfitted, you *can* be victorious every time!

WHY DO I NEED GOD'S STRENGTH?

Scripture, Ephesians 6:10-17
We wrestle . . . against principalities, against powers, against the rulers of darkness of this world, against spiritual wickedness in high places. (Eph. 6:12)

The Christian life is not child's play. Indeed, the Apostle Paul wrote, "Be sober, be vigilant, because your adversary, the devil, as a roaring lion, walketh about, seeking whom he may devour" (1 Peter 5:8). Nevertheless, many a Christian has experienced defeat because he failed to take into account the seriousness of the warfare. Satan is a defeated foe because of Christ's triumph. But the battle—that is, the mopping up—is still going on. That is where we come in. We need to realize that our encounters with Satan are only one phase of the campaign. The time is coming when there will be full demonstration of the Saviour's right to reign, when every knee shall bow and tongue shall confess that Jesus is Lord (Phil. 2:10-11). In the interim, our blessed Lord "causes us to triumph" as we appropriate *by faith*—day after day after day—the benefits of His finished work.

You may have heard the story of the orphan boy who was adopted by a rich gentleman and all of a sudden had a palatial home, new clothes, and a room of his own. "Whatever you want," said the gracious benefactor, "just ask for it. I have put $10,000 in the bank in your name and you can draw from it any time. Here is the bankbook." The lad was thrilled but somewhat incredulous. At the bank he told a teller, "I would like to withdraw some of my money." Do you know how much he withdrew? *Just ten cents.* Never before having had a dime to call his own, he was going to have one now—the limit of his idea of riches.

Small thought here

In a spiritual sense many of us are like that adopted son. If we are to have "strength for anything," we must give up our miniscule notions and *by faith* appropriate the strength of Almighty God which is always available to us.

EVIDENCES OF SPIRITUAL STRENGTH

Scripture, Ephesians 6:10-17
Stand therefore, having your loins girt about with truth, and having on the breastplate of righteousness, and your feet shod with . . . the Gospel of peace; taking the shield of faith . . . and the sword of the Spirit. (Eph. 6:14-17)

M any a Christian bemoans his inability to do spectacular things for God. We hear: "I can't pray like Mrs. So-and-so." Or, "I never had any training in personal witnessing so I can't speak to others about Christ." These are flimsy excuses when placed alongside the equipment with which every believer in the Lord Jesus Christ is endowed.

• *Ability to stand.* My friend Ken Taylor puts it this way: "To do this you will need the strong belt of truth." In other words, commit to memory those passages of God's Word that emphasize His operating principles—and the whole Bible does that. Rely on those divine values essential to spiritual strength.

• *Ability to resist.* God's righteousness stands against all of Satan's fiery darts, and absorbs, as it were, their force without allowing you to become a victim. But remember, it is a righteousness that must be appropriated *by faith.*

• *Ability to move forward.* Your feet carry you into different situations every day. As they do, make sure that you have on "Gospel shoes," ready to share with others the Good News that brings peace with God.

• *Ability to rejoice in full protection.* Notice the prominent verb in the verse we are considering: "*taking* the shield of faith . . . *take* the helmet of salvation, and the sword of the Spirit." Take! *You* do it. If you are going to be protected, you must avail yourself of the means of protection. God will not do that for you.

Small thought here

Strength enough for anything? Yes, dear child of God, you *can* have it. It is God's strength. He gives it. It becomes yours just in the measure that you actively appropriate the provisions your loving Father has made for your weaknesses and needs. Launch out—*by faith* —and "be strong in the Lord and the power of His might."

HOW DO YOU SEE YOURSELF?

Scripture, Ephesians 6:18-24
I am an ambassador in bonds: that therein I may speak boldly, as I ought to speak. (Eph. 6:20)

Suppose that Angela Benson (or someone you know) is sitting at a big mahogany desk across from the personnel director of the XYZ Company. Her children are grown and gone from home and she yearns now to reenter the job market. The company official looks carefully at her application. Finally he says, "This is a very good report, Mrs. Benson, but where have you worked the past twenty-five years?" "Oh," Angela replies, "I've been at home. Just a housewife." Yet this woman may have, with the cooperation of her husband, reared sons who are now launched on their own careers. As the boys were growing up she may have been active in the community and been a source of strength and help to her church. But today she sees herself as "just a housewife." Did she get the job? We don't know. Usually other people see us the same way we see ourselves. What is infinitely more important than the outcome of this imagined incident is how you and I, as believers in the Lord Jesus Christ, envision ourselves. We are highly placed in God's economy. We ought to delight in this fact and express it to others. The Apostle Paul held such a perspective. Here he was, languishing in a cold, foul-smelling Roman prison, handcuffed to cruel guards, his ministry aborted, his missionary travels ended. He could very well have moaned, "I'm nothing any more. Just a prisoner." Instead, we can hear him proudly proclaiming, "I am an *ambassador* in bonds" (Eph. 6:20), a representative of the King of kings and Lord of lords. Do you see yourself with the same blessed privilege?

Small thought here
We are challenged in Ephesians 6 to be men and women who pray, who care, who speak up, and who share. May our Lord help us, by His grace, to meet this challenge.

BE A PRAY-ER

Scripture, Ephesians 6:18-24
In everything by prayer and supplication with thanksgiving let your requests be made known unto God. And the peace of God . . . shall keep your hearts and minds through Christ Jesus.
(Phil. 4:6-7)

If we are to be men and women of prayer, we must follow definite guidelines.
• *Be constant.* God wants the best for us, His "born ones," and the more constant our prayer life becomes the more we shall be able to recognize His divine purposes on our behalf. Certainly, prayer embodies praise, confession, and petition, but underneath all this is the tremendous concept of God Himself talking through you and me, as we pray, thus completing the cycle of real fellowship. Of ourselves we are unable to maintain this relationship, but the Holy Spirit can. He breathes through you and me the kind of prayer that is exactly in line with what God Himself wants to bestow! Make no mistake: this kind of prayer is different from "emergency calls" ("Lord, help me!"), though that kind of petition has its place.
• *Be specific.* There is nothing unspiritual about asking God for specific things. Much of our praying, it must be admitted, is so general that only God Himself can interpret what we want, and of course He does. But if we are growing in grace and long for lives of real effectiveness in prayer, we must learn to be definite in our dealings with the Almighty. Many a person's prayer is just a routine moment of thanking God that He is still on the job. You remember the prayer attributed to a little boy at bedtime, "Lord," he said, "take care of Yourself because if anything happens to You, we're all sunk." Let your prayer be to-the-point. Let it be a combination of worship, adoration, and praise, of confession, petition, and intercession.

Small thought here
To cure every form of worry, pray about everything.

DO YOU CARE ABOUT OTHERS?

Scripture, Ephesians 6:18-24
When He saw the multitude He was moved with compassion on them.
(Matt. 9:36)

Have you noticed how many times in the Gospel record we read that Jesus "had compassion"? In its simplest terms, compassion is *uncritical caring*. Though the crowds that followed Jesus included those with sharp tongues and disbelieving hearts, He cared about them. And what about Job? Once the criticism leveled against the patriarch by his visitors had ended and his own questions were silenced, Job's tormenters were told to repent and offer burnt offerings. At this point, addressing these men, God said: "My servant Job shall pray for you, for him will I accept" (Job 42:8). From your own experience, would you say that Job found it easy to pray for these troublemakers? But look what happened when he prayed: "And the Lord turned the captivity of Job when he prayed for his friends; also the Lord gave Job twice as much as he had before" (v. 10). Though Eliphaz, Bildad, Zophar, and Elihu are here designated "friends," they certainly had not behaved in friendly fashion. Yet God said, "Job, pray for them!"

There are some people for whom it is hard to pray and care. Oh, they may be believers in the Lord Jesus Christ, all right, just as we are. But their dispositions are thorny, rough, and abrasive. They leave us lacerated and wounded. Nonetheless, Paul tells us to pray for *all* the saints. Will you try this little experiment? Seek out, honestly, the good in someone particularly troublesome to you. Start praying for God to *bless* that life (remember: no complaints, no suggestions). Two things will happen. God will answer your prayer and will bless that individual. And in the process He will bless *you* as well.

Small thought here
Oh, beloved, let the Spirit of God clothe your life with a compassionate, uncritical attitude. For your own soul's sake (as well as theirs) pray for "all the saints." This is the highest form of caring.

SPEAK UP FOR THE LORD

Scripture, Ephesians 6:18-24
Praying . . . for me (Paul) . . . that I may . . . speak boldly as I ought to speak. (Eph. 6:18-20)

A re you surprised that one with the intellect, background, spiritual maturity, and outstanding teaching skills Paul had should yearn for the prayer support of fellow believers? Notice that Paul did not seek prayer for his deliverance or comfort. He did not say, "Dear fellow Christians, ask God to get me out of here." He was thinking of his needs in an entirely different context. What he wanted was, first, "that utterance may be given me." *Utterance*—the ability to open one's mouth and say something for God's glory—has to be part volitional (what *you* do) and part miracle (what God does). It involves your everyday speech as well as your witness for Christ.

Do you realize that you can glorify God in even the so-called nonreligious conversation of daily life? This kind of talk has nothing to do with pious speech; it has everything to do with allowing God to control every split second of your life. If you are a believer in the Lord Jesus Christ, the Holy Spirit lives within you. He is there to direct, to teach, to comfort. One of His ways of working is to *not* speak of Himself but to magnify Christ—through you. You can trust Him to put His words in your mouth, so that what you say has eternal significance. Your words may have no claim to eloquence, but God's touch will be upon them. Indeed, our Lord said to His disciples, "It is not ye that speak, but the Spirit of your Father which speaketh in you" (Matt. 10:20).

Small thought here

When my life is controlled by the Holy Spirit, what I say is impelled and authorized by Him. How do you see yourself? Are you *one who speaks up?* God wants you to be.

OPEN YOURSELF TO OTHERS

Scripture, Ephesians 6:21-22
That ye also may know our affairs . . .
Tychicus shall make known to you all things.
(Eph. 6:21)

Most of us are too well insulated from other people's concerns. We fear becoming vulnerable. We don't want to be hurt. Yet Paul admonishes us to open ourselves to others, not in terms of a long recital of personal ills, but by acknowledging our common frailties.

Don't try to hide your hurtful feelings, but let the Lord Jesus Christ live through you in those troublesome situations. Because you are human, you can't help getting tired, but you can avoid becoming a victim of despair. Because you are human, the rough edges of life may cut and bruise you, but you need not incubate those hurts until they fester in your soul. Your honest admission of pain to another person will carry healing balm for both of you.

Imprisoned in Rome, Paul wanted fellow Christians to know what he was up against. Tychicus was sent to tell them. What kind of person can be counted on to share another's burdens? Speaking of his friend, Tychicus, the apostle cited three important characteristics. First, he was "a beloved brother." He knew how to give and to receive that all-embracing affection that every Christian owes every other believer. Second, he was a "faithful minister." And in Colossians 4:7 he is described as a "fellow servant." What a challenge to us, wouldn't you agree?

Small thought here

Each of us is a long way from perfection—in praying, in caring, in speaking up, and in sharing. But each of us born-again ones has God's Spirit and God's Word to plug us into His almightiness. Hallelujah for that!

Be thou an example of the believer in word, in conversation, in charity, in spirit, in faith, in purity.
(1 Tim. 4:12)

Be a Blessing
IN YOUR LIFESTYLE!

"Be thou an example of the believer," Paul says, in your "conversation," an old English way of saying "manner of life." What are some ways in which your lifestyle can be a blessing? You can be *confident* and assured in God. Paul's confident assertion, while standing on the deck of a sinking ship, brought encouragement to all the passengers and crew. "Sirs," he said, "I believe in God!" You can be *committed* to God's will. This need not be a constant pious pronouncement, but rather a quiet willingness to put God first in any situation. You can be *concerned* for others because of your love for God. "The love of Christ constraineth us," Paul said. People will be blessed when they sense that because you love the Saviour, you are concerned for them as well.

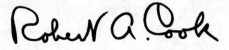

March

An interesting exercise used at management training seminars is to have groups brainstorm what they would do if stranded on a remote island with . . . (this part varies) as their only resources. Usually the groups are pitted against each other and given a time limit. It is amazing what ideas are generated in such a context! But what a contrast, dear friend, to come this month to Philippians, and related Bible passages, and to learn of the *limitless resources* we have in our blessed Lord Jesus! All that He is—for all that we need. We'll also be looking into precious truths from 1—2 Thessalonians, and into Romans 14 for some tips on how to get along with others.

CHRIST SUPPLIES MY NEEDS

Scripture, Philippians 1:1-30
For to me to live is Christ, and to die is gain.
(Phil. 1:21)

Christ is the very stuff of which life is made. Unfortunately, the great amount of burn-out among Christian workers is a tragic indication, it seems to me, of ignorance on this point. In what ways is Christ my life? Paul answers this question in 1 Corinthians 1:30: "Christ is made unto us wisdom, righteousness, sanctification, and redemption."

Wisdom is knowing what to do with what you have. *Righteousness* is the demonstration of God's character and life through you. *Sanctification* is being set apart for God's special use. *Redemption* is the process which begins with God's purpose for you and ends in His eternal glory—when you become Exhibit "A" up yonder.

You can look heavenward at any given moment and say, "Lord Jesus, be my wisdom!" You can lift your heart in a whispered prayer when you are under the pressure of testing, temptation, or heartbreak and say, "Lord, be my righteousness!" In the world about us, where secularization and godlessness is everywhere, you can look up and say, "Lord Jesus, be my sanctification. Keep me specially set apart for Your own use!" And as you rejoice in His final completed purpose, you can exclaim even now with joy, "Lord, be my redemption!"

Small thought here

Harry D. Loes summed it up so well in his song, "All Things in Jesus I Find": "All that I want is in Jesus; He satisfies, joy He supplies; life would be worthless without Him; all things in Jesus I find." Hallelujah for that, dear friend!

CHRIST HELPS ME CARE

Scripture, Philippians 1:1-30
For God is my record, how greatly I long after you all.
(Phil. 1:8)

When Christ is in your life, you will find that you have a deep concern for and wholesome confidence in other people. But these qualities do not spring forth, full bloom. As a pastor, I was one time distressed about a brother in my church who was causing a lot of ill will. He would announce to his Sunday School class, "Well, fellows, I certainly have been faithful to the Lord this week, and I've been so blessed." He would tell at length what happened and then add needling words like these, "Now if you had been faithful to the Lord, you would have been blessed too." This fellow was born in the accusative case, you might say. I told myself, "I am going to pray this man right out of my church!" I went down on my knees and really besought the Lord to promote this brother to greener pastures elsewhere. But I got absolutely nowhere in my praying: no blessing, no heavenly dew, nothing! Then it dawned on me that I should pray for the man himself. As I did, God began to reveal to me my own need, the depth of my resentment. (Resentment is hatred with a tuxedo on, you know.) Once I repented of my own shortcomings, I was enabled to leave in God's hands the matter of my brother's annoying ways. You know what happened? The Lord gave him a series of preaching assignments away from our church, and he was so happy winning souls that he had little time for accusation.

Small thought here
It isn't enough to cope with people as though they were problems to be solved or to manipulate them as a means to an end. It isn't enough to work with people as the stuff of which a great ministry is made. It's only enough when you love them as Jesus loved them, with compassion and concern, that maturity comes and God is pleased.

CHRIST SHAPES MY OUTLOOK

Scripture, Philippians 1:1-30
According to my earnest expectation and my hope, that in nothing I shall be ashamed, but that with all boldness . . . Christ shall be magnified.
(Phil. 1:20)

Some people are so concerned with what is going on here and now that they forget that the Bible has a good deal to say about God's plan for the future. Others are like a deacon in a church where I ministered who said to me, "Now young man, we are all saved here. We don't need sanctifying. So I wish you would preach a good sermon on prophecy." But if Christ is your life, He keeps the whole picture before you. There is a perfect balance between the here and now and the sweet by and by.

The Apostle Paul wanted the Lord to be honored and magnified in everything he did "that in nothing I shall be ashamed." Do you know why people become ashamed? Because they feel guilty, or inferior, or like failures because they haven't reached an objectve. Thankfully, as a Christian, you can have a different outlook. First, realize that be you ever so beautiful, or gifted, or intelligent, someone will always come along who is better in that particular area than you are. So lift up the Lord Jesus instead. Brag on what He can do. And what about failure, those times when you've tried your hardest, run your fastest, studied your best, but haven't reached your objective? Do you quit? No, you keep on, because there are *no failures* to the person who walks in the will of our blessed Lord. Hallelujah for that!

Small thought here
Let's think for a moment about guilt, inferiority, and failure. If you have something on your conscience, repent of it, turn from it, then go on—cleansed, restored, and unashamed.

CHRIST SOOTHES MY SUFFERING

Scripture, Philippians 1:1-30
In nothing terrified by your adversaries . . .
for unto you it is given in behalf of Christ,
not only to believe on Him but also to
suffer for His sake.
(Phil. 1:28-29)

Every person's pain is different, be it physical suffering, emotional trauma, or harassment from the godless world we live in. For some it may even mean giving up life itself. For John and Betty Stam, who went to China as missionaries in the early 1930s, it meant parting from their beloved infant daughter, and then kneeling on a hillside to be beheaded for Christ's sake.

A young Korean man, a vital soul-winner whose story Bob Pierce has told, was similarly tested. When the Communist invasion occurred, this strong Christian was captured and subjected to trial by violent leaders. A great crowd gathered. Over the loud speaker the command rang out, "Confess that you are a capitalistic spy!"

The Korean could see in the audience the eyes of people with whom he had prayed for salvation, people looking at him and wondering what he would do next. He held up his hand for silence. The crowd quieted. The cold muzzle of a .45 pressed against his skull.

"You want me to confess?" he cried. "Then I *will*. I confess that Jesus Christ is my Lord and Saviour. He is the King of kings and the Lord of lords. There is no other way of salvation but through Him." Moments later, that devoted young man lay shot to death, but his spirit had gone to be with Christ "which is far better."

You and I may not be shot at sunrise, as some of God's dear people are, but other testings face each of us every day. They all call for a display of divine victory, if we are to make an impact on our generation.

Small thought here

The world will determine just how real Jesus is to you. People judge Christianity as they see how you handle pressure, as they see how you face the heartaches, the suffering, the total price of living for God.

CHRIST GIVES ME PEACE

Scripture, Philippians 1:1-30
But I would that ye should understand, brethren, that the things which happened unto me have fallen out rather unto the furtherance of the Gospel.
(Phil. 1:12)

Human nature being what it is, you will always find people who do not see things your way. Not all will treat you as well as you deserve to be treated. You may be a threat to them psychologically or socially, and they may oppose you even though you are doing a great work.

When I was in Chicago years ago, I was given responsibility and leadership in Youth for Christ. Not everyone believed in what we as an organization were trying to do. Now and then I would receive a hot letter—generally anonymous or signed "Your friend in Christ." The biting criticism really hurt. One day I went to see Dr. H.A. Ironside who was at that time pastor of Chicago's Moody Memorial Church. He was my friend, loyal to the point of standing by me even when it wasn't advantageous to do so. Dr. Ironside sat back in his office chair, folded his hands on top of his capacious middle, just above the big gold watch chain that extended from side to side, and patiently listened as I told him my troubles. When I paused for breath, he looked at me intently and with that famous voice and fatherly tone he said, "Well, young man, if what your critics are saying about you is true—mend your ways. If it is not true, forget it and go on serving God."

Small thought here

You can have complete victory over circumstances, critics, and competition. Why? Because you've settled your objectives. God is still saying, "Ask what I shall do for thee." He waits for you to say what means the most to you.

CHRIST AS LORD OF MY FEELINGS

Scripture, Philippians 2:1-30
Consolation in Christ . . . comfort of love . . .
fellowship of the Spirit.
(Phil. 2:1)

As a child I used to be afraid of the dark. Motherless lad that I was, I had the dubious privilege of being welcomed into different homes and staying for sometimes lengthy periods of time. Once I lived in an Ohio farmhouse with an aunt and uncle—wonderful people though very frugal and unsentimental. The house had electric lights, but they were used only for "company." Electricity was regarded as too expensive for everyday use. So we resorted to kerosene lamps or candles. Each night someone would put this little six-year-old to bed, close the door firmly, and be gone. Outside the old farmhouse grew a pine tree and when the wind blew, its branches would scratch against the side of the house—and groan. If the moon shone through those gnarled branches, the worst kind of shadows would appear on the wall. I would lie there, whimpering until someone would come stomping up the stairs—generally my Uncle Frank—and fling open the door and shout, "Now, Robert, you shouldn't be afraid! You're nearly seven now." Then—slam! He was gone. Though quiet, I was still scared.

When my father would come from Cleveland to visit (as often as work allowed), I would catch sight of him as he plodded down the old dirt road, swinging his battered suitcase. He would see me and we would run to greet each other. Then we'd have supper together that night. At bedtime, my father would lie down beside me in the big four-poster bed, in the very same dark room that had terrified me before. But you know something? I wasn't scared at all! A *person*, my dad, made the difference.

Small thought here

If you want a difference in the way you feel about things—whether it's fear or resentment, sorrow or jealousy, greed or pride, lust or anger—it takes a *person* to effect that change. His name is Jesus. You must make Him Lord of your feelings.

CHRIST AS LORD OF MY RELA- TIONSHIPS

Scripture, Philippians 2:1-30
Fulfill ye my joy, that ye be like-minded, having the same love, being of one accord, of one mind.
(Phil. 2:2)

As believers in Christ, you and I may not agree about everything, but we can be of one mind about the things that really matter. In a word, we believe in the historic, orthodox doctrines of the Christian faith. We are "like-minded" on these issues. That being the case, we do well to avoid trivia. Indeed, when we stick to the main issues we shall find that God will bless, regardless of small differences.

Take a hypothetical situation. Say that you belong to a Scandinavi- an family with certain time-honored traditions such as preparing lutefisk at Christmas. For you, Christmas would not be Christmas without it. Now your son, Sven, falls in love with Lucia, a fine Italian girl. Her people have well-loved traditions too. At Christmas their specialty is not lutefisk but baccala—similar in kind, but for each family strikingly different. Imagine that Sven and Lucia marry and face a real crisis. Do you all get together and argue about your distinc- tive Christmas customs? No, of course not. As parents you agree: "We love those kids. We're willing to mortgage our house, to take care of their kids, to do *anything* to help them." You are "like- minded" on the main issues. Love is your common motivating force.

Small thought here
When you love the Lord Jesus Christ supremely, that relationship makes possible a blessed drawing together of those of like faith, regardless of differences in culture, custom, or viewpoint.

CHRIST AS LORD OF MY MIND

Scripture, Philippians 2:1-30
Let this mind be in you which was also in Christ Jesus.
(Phil. 2:5)

Almost any business magazine you pick up today will have an article on the value and availability of computers. But do you realize that you have, between your ears, a computer far more complex and efficient than anything that industry will ever be able to build? Your "computer" has the ability to communicate between the billions of electrical contacts that God has built into your brain. More than that, it has the expertise to reason and to draw conclusions based on that reasoning—and that is something a manufactured computer cannot do.

Paul says, "Let this mind (the mind of Christ) be in you," that is, "Put Him in charge of your computer." There is a saying among computer programmers that is represented by four letters: GIGO—"garbage in, garbage out." It is likewise true that what you put into your mind will later show up in your life. Many of God's people are feeding their minds mainly on the garbage of this world. Then they are surprised when, under pressure, that kind of worthlessness is their only resource.

Don't expect God to do a miracle in upgrading the contents of your mind. He has left that task to you. But as you become willing, He will reciprocate with exceeding faithfulness.

Small thought here
If I have meditated on, memorized, and obeyed God's Word, it is His responsibility (and I say it reverently) to provide a satisfactory "printout" for any given life situation.

CHRIST AS LORD OF MY MOTIVES

Scripture, Philippians 2:1-30
Let nothing be done through strife or vainglory; but in lowliness of mind let each esteem other better than themselves. Look not every man on his own things, but every man also on the things of others.
(Phil. 2:3-4)

Every now and then you ought to back off from what you are doing and ask, "Why am I doing this?" If you are honest, you will often be amazed at the answer that comes. Paul admonished, "Don't do anything through strife"—to gain the upperhand by arguing. Likewise, "Don't do anything through vainglory"—to make yourself look better by making comparisons.

Do you want to get along better with other people? Learn to think in these terms: What does this person really *need?* If he finds that you are interested in what interests him, he will feel safe with you. I learned this truth the hard way one day when I complained to a friend about what I thought was going on in my job situation. When I paused for breath, he replied, "Oh, Bob, it's wonderful how you understand just what I'm going through." He hadn't heard a word I said *about myself* because he was too busy thinking *about himself.* The Apostle Paul implied, "Don't do that! Don't just think about yourself. Other people have needs too."

Small thought here

Every person you meet will be hurting somewhere. Find out where that painful spot is and if you can, apply the healing balm of God's love and grace. If you follow this course, your relationships will be easier and more effective. In your daily prayer time, ask God to make you want things for *His* reasons. Make Him Lord of your motives.

CHRIST AS LORD OF MY LIFESTYLE

Scripture, Philippians 2:1-30
Do all things without murmurings and disputings: that ye may be blameless . . . in the midst of a crooked and perverse nation, among whom ye shine as lights in the world, holding forth the Word of life. (Phil. 2:14-16)

Occasionally your peers may misinterpret your intentions. But what they say about you again and again over the course of time is probably very close to the truth. The way you live, talk, and act with other people is directly affected by your relationship with Jesus Christ. I daresay that the closer a person gets to the Lord, the easier he is to live with.

We are to "shine as lights in the world, holding forth the Word of life." Our biggest job iot to succeed, but to *shine*. Not to be praised, or to make x-number of dollars, or to be considered the greatest soul-winner since Billy Sunday—but to shine for God.

How are you doing at the job of holding forth the Word of life? Remember, your "shine" will be dimmed when you give place to murmurings, disputings, blame, and harmful actions. Ask God to show you the things that keep you from shining brightly for Him.

Is Jesus really Lord of the key areas of your personality: your mind, feelings, relationships, motives, and lifestyle?

Small thought here

"For to this end Christ both died, and rose, and revived, that He might be Lord" (Rom. 14:9). That's what He wants. That's what He waits to be. Give yourself wholly to Him.

CHRIST AND MY DECISIONS

Scripture, Philippians 3:1-21
I count all things but loss for the excellency of the knowledge of Christ Jesus my Lord . . . that I may know Him.
(Phil. 3:8, 10)

Is the Lord Jesus Christ—the One with whom I am identified and the One for whom I am living—worth what He costs? The answer calls for a value judgment. Each of us is making that kind of appraisal, in many different areas, every day. You young women make a value judgment when that tall, dark, and handsome young man invites you for a date. His father is rich; Junior drives a Mercedes. You ask, "Where are we going tonight?" He tells you, "Oh, I thought we'd go to my favorite nightclub. It's a little bawdy, but there's a good floor show, and we can have a drink or two." What flashes through your mind? "Shall I tell him I'm on a different wavelength? Shall I give up the possibility of snaring him? Or shall I tell him where I stand?" That's a big choice. It calls for a value judgment.

A decision of another kind had its setting in a Florida church where I conducted a series of evangelistic meetings. In the inquiry room was a lady whose clothes and manner marked her as a person of some means. She had a problem. "Mr. Cook," she said, "my husband has told me that if I ever become a Christian he will divorce me immediately. I simply cannot face that eventuality." She picked up her mink stole and walked out the door to the new Cadillac waiting at the curb. She had made a value judgment, alas a poor one with eternal implications.

Small thought here
What decisions have you made regarding your values? To Paul, Christ was the constant marvel, the perfect role model, the impeccable example, and to know Him—really *know* Him—was the ultimate achievement for any Christian.

CHRIST AND MY CONCEN- TRATION

Scripture, Philippians 3:1-21
That I may know Him and the power of His resurrection, and the fellowship of His sufferings, being made conformable unto His death.
(Phil. 3:10)

Do you *really* have divine power in your life? Or are you just talking about the Christian life? Believe me, power is needed—and neither you nor I can produce it. Only God's power will suffice. A young man whom I approached after a meeting in Los Angeles told me frankly, "You couldn't do a thing for me, Preacher." "Well," I told him, "I know that as well as you do. But Jesus can do something for you. Do you want to talk to me about Him, or not?" "Yeah," he said, "I'll talk to you." So he did. This was his story: Then a boy of sixteen, he had already been mixed up with car theft, liquor, drugs, and sex. What do you do with a boy like that? Give him John 3:16 . . . Romans 10:13 . . . Acts 16:31. I have news for you. That boy had just won the privilege of two weeks at a camp for having learned, letter perfect, 500 Bible verses. His mind was full of Scripture. But his heart was full of sin. Thankfully, we were able to get him in touch with the all-powerful Saviour, and He made a difference in that boy's life. Christ turned him completely around.

Power with Christ is a by-product of knowing Him. Another evidence of that relationship is compassion. Suffering souls are longing for love, for intelligent caring. It is not enough to say, "Let the Red Cross do it; let the police do it; let the pastor do it." Compassion is not just feeling bad. It is sympathizing enough to *act*.

Small thought here
Power, compassion, resemblance to Christ—these are the marks of the yielded believer who is being "conformed to the image of His [God's] Son."

CHRIST AND MY INCENTIVE

Scripture, Philippians 3:1-21
*Forgetting those things which are behind,
and reaching forth unto those things
which are before, I press toward
the mark for the prize of the high calling
of God in Christ Jesus.
(Phil. 3:13-14)*

The expression "press toward the mark" paints a mental picture—of a sprinter in the 100-yard dash or of a distance runner nearing the tape. Every muscle is strained. Every effort is focused on winning the race. What goal is in view for the apostle and for us? It is "the high calling of God in Christ Jesus." It is the realization of His highest purpose for each of us. Jesus has plans that are particularly for you, specifically tailored to your personality. He has purposed that you should be the kind of person to honor and glorify Him in a special way throughout eternity. Each of us has gifts "differing according to the grace that is given unto us" (Rom. 12:6). Some have the gift of helps, others of hospitality, still others of teaching, of preaching, of giving, and so on.

To develop your gifts, I invite you to do two things: first, take inventory of what you have—all the characteristics, skills, and abilities you possess. Second, become a competitor instead of a spectator. Write down the things you do well and also those you do poorly or not at all. You may be surprised to find areas of usefulness that you never dreamed you had. Pray over this list and watch for God's leading. Then, do *something*. Life is a warfare—get in and do your part.

Small thought here
Remember this, dear friend: The Lord has laid hold of you. He has you in His mighty hand. He is not about to let you go. If you persist in wanting your own way, He will discipline you, but He "will never leave you nor forsake you" (Heb. 13:5).

CHRIST AND MY INTER-PERSONAL NEEDS

Scripture, Philippians 4:1-23
*But my God shall supply all your
need according to His riches in glory
by Christ Jesus.
(Phil. 4:19)*

If Christ is the supply for *all* our needs, that abundance must surely be put to use in our dealings with *people*. Did you know that 90 percent of Christian work (or any work, for that matter) involves getting along amicably with others? What are some specific ways for improving human relations?

• *Notice the other person.* That is, see him; be aware that he is there. Joe Ankerberg, now with the Lord, at one time had the largest boy's Sunday School class in the Chicago area. Someone asked, "What's the secret of his tremendous following of kids?" One of his own youngsters gave the answer: "Mr. Ankerberg will notice something about every one of us, even if it's only one new shoelace."

• *Then, listen.* Look behind the facade for the *real* source of this person's confusion or pain. Every psychiatrist can differentiate between the *presenting* cause (the verbalized, spoken complaint) and the *actual* cause, which lies far deeper. Once someone has spoken, repeat to him, in your own words, what you think he has said. That will tell him you have really been listening.

• *Finally, try to bring your listener into God's presence.* There are times when it is not your right to lead in prayer; to do so would be inappropriate. But on many occasions you can say, "Let's just talk to the Lord about this." Be brief. In thirty seconds you can commit the situation to God, and the person at your side will be aware that heaven has been brought into the equation.

Small thought here

People may be difficult to get along with. But they will be less so if you notice them, listen to them, and get them into the Saviour's presence.

CHRIST AND MY FREEDOM FROM WORRY

Scripture, Philippians 4:1-23
Be careful for nothing; but in everything . . . let your requests be made known unto God. And the peace of God . . . shall keep [garrison] your hearts and minds through Jesus Christ.
(Phil. 4:6-7)

All of us have heard about freedom from worry and some of us have even preached sermons about it. Yet none of us are worry-free. The fact remains, however, that worry is both definable and conquerable. Worry has been defined as the absence of an organized plan. It follows then that the only way you can obtain an organized plan entirely sufficient for any given situation is by turning the whole matter over to God who already knows the score. "Known unto God are all His works from the beginning of the world" (Acts 15:18).

When I am upset about something I find it helps to write down what I am worrying about. Many times when I make that effort I see immediately the fallacies in my thinking and a way out of them. Try it yourself the next time you start to fret. Next, tell God about your problem, point by point. Finally, wait on Him. When you really pray about what is bothering you, God, in His faithful way through the Holy Spirit, will always give you one step of obedience that you can take immediately.

Small thought here

When you take that first step, the pressure flees and the worry dissipates because you *know* you are now walking in the direction of God's perfect plan for you. His peace will come to you and guard your heart and mind like a garrison of soldiers.

CHRIST AND MY THOUGHT LIFE

Scripture, Philippians 4:1-23
Whatsoever things are true, whatsoever things are honest, whatsoever things are just, whatsoever things are pure, whatsoever things are of good report . . . think on these things.
(Phil. 4:8)

How will you manage your thoughts? Here is a formula to follow. Take the attributes of the Lord Jesus Christ as revealed in His Word and "program" them into your mind. Then the faithful Holy Spirit will bring them to your attention as you need them.

Obviously, you don't always have the thoughts that you wish you had. Random, or unworthy, or evil thoughts will undoubtedly flash through your mind on occasion. And when they do, you tend to become frustrated and say to yourself, "I can't help it!" And you know, you're right! Even though you're a Christian, you're still human.

But when you yield your mind to your blessed Lord and find that you can program into it the truth of God's Word and the essential attributes of your dear Saviour, then you have a "managed mind," because *He* is in control.

When something unworthy invades your stream of consciousness, at that moment say, "Lord Jesus, You are my Saviour. I want You to control my thoughts—all of them, now. Control my reactions: to circumstances, to people, to life itself." He will!

You don't have to be a victim of errant, prodigal thoughts. You can think in line with God's will—oh, yes, you can. Let Him do it.

Small thought here
Our blessed Lord has His divine supply ready to match our every need—even those that involve our thought life.

CHRIST AND MY STRATEGY FOR LIVING

Scripture, Philippians 4:1-23
Those things, which ye have both learned, and received, and heard, and seen in me, do; and the God of peace shall be with you. (Phil. 4:9)

By this command the Apostle Paul was not at all setting himself up as a perfect example to be followed. Rather, he was implying that God's work within in any individual is worth studying and learning from.

So how do we develop a strategy for living? An excellent method is to study the persons whose lives are preserved for us in God's Word. Examine their characteristics and experiences. Analyze their strengths and weaknesses. Find how surprisingly human they were and yet how lovingly and faithfully God led. In these sacred pages are principles for living.

There is a sense also in which our learning reaches into the future. As a Christian, you look into God's Word and find Him telling you how to live *today* in light of *eternity*. Great changes are taking place all about us. If our Lord Jesus tarries, the electronic revolution is going to produce a lifestyle and a type of employment entirely different from those of the present. God, however, will never be taken by surprise. He will prepare you *now* for your tomorrows.

Small thought here
Perhaps, dear friend, you have lived long enough to see in your own life, as I can see in mine, how wisely God has led in many different kinds of ministry, each of them contributing to the next in His own continuing plan.

CHRIST AND MY CONTENT- MENT

Scripture, Philippians 4:1-23
For I have learned, in whatsoever state I am, therewith to be content.
(Phil. 4:11)

I've never heard anybody say, "Oh, goodie, I have to go to the dentist!" We all go, without complaining (not much, that is), because we know that something beneficial is being done for us. In a much greater sense, we can trust God and realize He is working on our behalf, even though we sometimes don't understand His ways. Indeed, the secret of contentment is knowing that God is on the job, ordering everything that comes into your life, ensuring that "all things work together for good." When you believe that in your heart, you can relax. You have yielded to your blessed Lord; henceforth the responsibility is *His*. "It is *God* which worketh in you both to will and to do of *His* good pleasure" (Phil. 2:13).

Yes, Christ Himself is the source of true contentment because He is the One who meets every need. When the Lord Jesus is the center of your life, the focus of your love, the implementer of the divine will in and through you, the strengthener of your feeble human efforts, then you can rejoice! He always completes what He begins. For you—for each of us who trusts Him—there are no "loose ends." There are no unfinished symphonies.

Small thought here

Christ is the Divine Supplier for my interpersonal needs, my freedom from worry, my thought life, my strategy for living, and my contentment. By God's grace and the Holy Spirit's enlightenment, these truths are attainable and gloriously life-changing!

THESE THREE THINGS

Scripture, 1 Thessalonians 1:1-10
Remembering without ceasing your work of faith, and labor of love, and patience of hope in our Lord Jesus Christ.
(1 Thes. 1:3)

Have you noticed how many threes there are in the Bible? See how many you can find here in 1 Thessalonians 1 and note how they relate to each other. For instance, in verse 3 you have the work of faith, the labor of love, and the patience of hope. Then in verse 5 Paul says, "Our Gospel came not unto you in word only, but in power, and in the Holy Ghost, and in much assurance." That's another triad of truth. There's another one in verse 6: "Ye became followers of us, and of the Lord, having received the word in much affliction, with joy of the Holy Ghost." Followers, afflictions, joy in the Holy Ghost. And yet another in verses 9-10: "Ye turned to God from idols to serve the living and true God; and to wait for His Son from heaven."

Stop here, will you, to realize that faith is no good unless work is tied to it. Love is no good unless it's costly. Hope is no good unless it's combined with patience. Work of faith, labor of love, patience of hope. Christian ministry is made valuable by three things: the power that comes from God, the Holy Spirit who speaks the truth, and the assurance of a person who knows he has had a real experience with the Lord.

Small thought here
Think of some examples in your life when real assurance has come because God did something in you or in the life of a friend or family member. The connection between such encouragement and dynamic Christian service and witness is plain to see!

WHAT DO YOU REMEMBER?

Scripture, 1 Thessalonians 2:1-23
We were willing to have imparted unto you, not the Gospel of God only, but also our own souls.
(1 Thes. 2:8)

When I was just a boy I sometimes stayed at my aunt's and uncle's farm in Ohio. An elderly lady lived with my relatives, and though she had become blind, she still maintained the indomitable Prussian spirit that was her heritage. Whenever people would say they had done this or that, she would chime in, "I used to do that lots of times." You could never get the best of her. She had already done it. Well, you know, many a person reveals his insecurity by what he remembers about himself.

Notice in 1 Thessalonians 2:2 what Paul remembered about himself and his ministry: *We suffered; we were bold in our God.* And in verse 4: *We were put in trust with the Gospel.* Then in verses 5-6: *We didn't use flattering words.* Verse 7: *We were gentle as a nurse.* Verse 10: *We behaved holily and justly and unblameably among you.* (Someone has said, "You ought to behave what you believe." And I agree, don't you?) Verse 11: *We exhorted and comforted and charged every one of you, as a Father doth His children.*

Look back on your life thus far and profile your memories. What you remember is a good indication of what you are really like. How can you change what you are if you don't like all you see? By applying God's Word to your life every day throughout the day!

Small thought here
The psalmist said, "I thought on my ways and turned my feet unto Thy testimonies." If you really want to be different, put the Word of our blessed Lord in your unconscious mind by way of memorization, meditation, and obedience. If you do, I promise that God will change you.

MARKS OF CHRISTIAN CONCERN

Scripture, 1 Thessalonians 3:1-13
Night and day praying exceedingly that we might see your face, and might perfect that which is lacking in your faith.
(1 Thes. 3:10)

What are some of the marks of genuine Christian concern? We find several here. First is *a mindset that risks personal cost in order to help someone else*. You and I can't begin to understand what that meant to the Apostle Paul. He was an outgoing person who cherished the fellowship of other believers. Nonetheless, despite his physical impairment and the fact that he was "understaffed," he kept on keeping on. Indeed, to be left alone in the midst of thoroughly heathen cultures, with very few around him who knew the Lord, really meant personal sacrifice.

Another mark of Christian concern is *action*. In more precise language, true caring means sharing. Paul wrote that he "sent Timotheus, our brother and minister of God ... to establish you and to comfort you" (1 Thes. 3:2). A third mark of real concern is *focused attention on the continued well-being of another person* (vv. 3-7). Paul didn't just start the church in Thessalonica and leave it helpless. Though he couldn't always be with the believers in person, he was with them in spirit.

What really gives you fulfillment? What do you really enjoy? If you're walking closely with your blessed Lord, your concern is going to be the joy, the large charge (as they say) that comes from seeing other people grow in grace (v. 8). And finally, of course, if you're really concerned, you're going to *keep on praying*—night and day (v. 10).

Small thought here

A genuine Christian concern for other people *doesn't* mean going around with a long face. It *does* mean that the focus of your interest and energies is others-oriented and that you are willing to let your concern cost you something.

WHAT REALLY COUNTS?

Scripture, 1 Thessalonians 4:1-18
Ye have received of us how ye ought to walk and to please God.
(1 Thes. 4:1)

The question of one's morality needs to be examined, not from the viewpoint of "What will people say?" or even "What will the church think?" One's concern, rather, ought to be how to live each day in a way that pleases God. That is the true basis for Christian morality.

How do you please God? Here are a few of ideas from 1 Thessalonians 4. First, a clean sex life. This means not only fleeing immorality, but also ordering your life apart from the usual, "I want what I want when I want it." We live in a day when moral permissiveness is the rule rather than the exception. Make sure your heart attitude and relationships with the opposite sex are above reproach. Second, you can please God by showing an awareness that you have been called, not to uncleanness, but to holiness. Third, you can please God by being quiet, industrious, and honest. And finally you can please God by having the upward look, waiting expectantly for His coming.

Small thought here
Notice what 1 Thessalonians 4 says about pleasing God: it starts with the inward look, ends with the upward look, and in between is the lordship of Jesus Christ in every step of life. Look in, look up, and in between look to our blessed Lord.

YOU WON'T REGRET IT

Scripture, 1 Thessalonians 5:1-28
The very God of peace sanctify you wholly; and . . . your whole spirit and soul and body be preserved blameless unto the coming of our Lord Jesus Christ.
(1 Thes. 5:23)

If you had to sum up in a few words God's purpose for your life, what would you say? Obviously, His plan is not simply to get you to heaven. If it were, He could have easily translated you as soon as you were born again. No, He leaves you here for a purpose. And what is that purpose? That your whole being—your spiritual, emotional, psychological, and physical life—be preserved blameless till our Lord Jesus Christ comes again (1 Thes. 5:23).

The word *sanctify* means "set apart for God's use." If God has all of you, you won't have any regrets. Indeed, the only time you'll have regrets is when you decide to use your life yourself, when you insist on doing things your way. But if God has you to use as He sees fit—the use of your spirit to worship Him, the use of your emotions to enjoy Him and to sense His nearness, the use of your body to implement His will toward others—He will preserve you blameless as you await Christ's promised return.

Small thought here
How does God preserve us? He makes us awake (v. 6). He makes us aware (vv. 4-5). He arms us against the enemy (v. 8). Awake, aware, and properly armed. That's how God proposes to work out His purpose in your life.

FAITH'S THREE ADDITIVES

Scripture, 2 Thessalonians 1:1-12
We pray ... that our God would ... fulfill the work of faith with power.
(2 Thes. 1:11)

Three interesting combinations occur in 2 Thessalonians 1. The first is *faith with love* (v. 3). Next is *faith with patience* (v. 4). The third is *faith with power* (v. 11). Why all of this? In order "that the name of the Lord Jesus Christ may be glorified in you, and ye in Him" (v. 12).

How do you glorify God? Faith with love. One of the hardest jobs you will ever face is showing real Christian love to a fellow church member who bothers you and aggravates you. But without love, faith is just talk. Faith also has to be combined with patience if it's going to endure testing. You see, it isn't just being able to survive troubles; it's being able to wait until God brings you through them and glorifying Him in the process It's knowing, in other words, that your troubles are not just happenstances but that God has allowed them for His own purposes. And then there is the work of faith with power. God wants to make your life an extension of His almightiness.

Small thought here
Most of us are poverty stricken spiritually. We don't begin to exercise the power that is ours. Here's an idea. Take a seemingly impossible situation in your life and risk it to God's ability to see you through. You'll be amazed at what He'll do. That's *faith with power!*

THE WORST ONE OF ALL

Scripture, 2 Thessalonians 2:1-17
They received not the love of the truth, that they might be saved.
(2 Thes. 2:10)

I was a pastor for eighteen years. During that time I made about three calls a day, a thousand calls a year—talking to people about the Lord, calling on the sick, counseling those in trouble and in sorrow. Of them all, I think my saddest conversations were with people who were self-deceived and rejected the truth. I called on a lady, for instance, whom I knew was dying of a terminal malignancy. But she had convinced herself that nothing was wrong. Time after time, I called on this dear lady. Oh, yes, she was getting better; she just knew it. And then one day we buried her. Well, you say, she was just keeping up a brave front. No, I've met people who were keeping up a brave front. I know the difference. This dear woman had rejected what the doctor had told her and made up her mind what she thought was the truth, and that was that. Perhaps it was easier for her that way. But when it comes to the truth of God, my friend, it's a pitiful thing to see people who are deluded because they will not accept it.

Small thought here
On the other side of the ledger, life's greatest consummation is to receive Christ and realize that He has chosen us from the very beginning, and that He will comfort our hearts and establish us in every good word and work.

TASTE IT FOR YOURSELF

Scripture, 2 Thessalonians 3:1-18
The Lord is faithful, who shall stablish you, and keep you from evil.
(2 Thes. 3:3)

Do you ever despair of growing up spiritually? Do you ever say, "I wonder if I'll ever be as good a Christian as So-and-so"? Don't be discouraged. God's faithfulness is your guarantee that you're going on with Him. Hallelujah for that. Not only does He establish you because He's faithful, but He directs your heart toward His love and the hope of Christ's return (2 Thes. 3:5).

How much do you really depend on God to motivate you? Have you asked God to help you love Him more? Have you asked Him to direct your heart, your mind, your desires toward a closer walk with Him? He wants you to experience that deep fellowship. And He also wants to direct your heart toward an attitude of patient anticipation of Christ's coming. I can't tell you, honestly, that I've met many people who are praying to be ready for the Second Coming. A lot of folks talk about it, to be sure. But are they truly prepared for the Lord's return? And in the middle of all this, Paul brings up the work ethic. He says if a person won't work, don't let him eat. Interesting.

Small thought here

The work ethic is part of the Christian's horizon. The love of God, the direction of God, the blessing of God, the second coming of Christ, and right in the middle of it: Get to work! Isn't that great? Try these truths on for size, will you, and discover how they will bless you and help you to be a blessing.

HOW TO GET ALONG WITH OTHERS

Scripture, Romans 14:19
Let us therefore follow after the things which make for peace, and things wherewith one may edify another. (Rom. 14:19)

Have you ever noticed that in most human confrontations peace is the object in view? It may be "my way" against "your way," but the mutual goal is to settle the disagreement and achieve harmony. Where do we begin? First, to be peacemakers we must be sure we are right with God: "Being justified by faith, we have peace with God through our Lord Jesus Christ" (Rom. 5:1). Isn't it true that most of our heated discussions, arguments, and disputes can generally be traced to a discomforting sense that something isn't quite right inside? We need to yield to God through Christ.

I find that when I am spiritually dry and fruitless because of having neglected my blessed Lord, I tend to be more demanding of others, more disparaging in my remarks, and more brittle in my relationships. But when I have taken time for prayer, repentance, and heart-searching, I am far less judgmental, critical, and insistent on having my own way. In other words I am, it seems to me, a little easier to get along with. Peace *with* God and the peace *of* God become the basis for interpersonal peace. "Things that make for peace" begin at God's mercy seat, dear friend, and they begin with us individually. More about getting along with others tomorrow.

Small thought here

When God's grace operates in one's life there is humility, patience, understanding, and spiritual insight. All these things contribute to living amicably with others.

PUSH FOR PEACE

Scripture, Romans 14:19
Follow after the things which make for peace.
(Rom. 14:19)

The Apostle Paul provides us four workable ways to achieve success in our interpersonal relationships. We are to push for peace, to be builders, to learn to edify, and to practice patience.

The Greek word translated *follow after* means "to pursue as a hunter stalks his quarry." Christians are to work for peace with that kind of intensity. Years ago a church deacon in LaSalle, Illinois gave me a set of management books. One of them, which dealt with conflict resolution, advised asking yourself in any negotiation: What does the other person want? What do I want? and How can we get together? "The things that make for peace" are often rooted in a willingness to look at an issue from the other person's viewpoint.

A friend once told me about a visit he made to a farm where a number of leghorn hens, enclosed in a wire coop, began to fight. (Birds and animals are like people: they pick on each other for no good reason.) The farmer took in the situation at a glance. Picking up a spading fork, he stepped inside the enclosure and turned over a few forkfuls of earth—revealing the succulent worms and grubs that chickens enjoy. What happened to the fighting? It suddenly ended. The hens were agreed on one thing: it was dinnertime. The farmer looked at my friend and said, "Reverend, I'll tell you something. If you want people to stop fighting each other, get them scratching for something—together."

Small thought here
When we are united in prayer, in Bible study, in witnessing, and in caring for the needs of others, there is precious little time for bickering. We are free to experience and enjoy God's peace.

BE A BUILDER

Scripture, Romans 14:19
Follow after the things which . . .
edify another.
(Rom. 14:19)

To *edify* means to "build up," as one builds a house, from its foundation to its finish. Barnabas was a builder. He took John Mark, an acknowledged misfit, and, by God's grace, brought him to where he was "profitable to [Paul] for the ministry" (2 Tim. 4:11). This truth is also important for parents, because in a sense we "build" our children—not by dominating them or dictating their futures, but by exercising an active concern for their spiritual development. My father used to say, "It would be easy for me always to say yes to you, my boy. But I can't do that. I'm responsible to God for you. I have to *build your life.*" So give priority to this business of "equipping the saints," will you? It works in family matters, in church affairs, and in one-on-one relationships.

But what do you do if you see a weakness in another person that needs correction? Prayerfully, humbly, and carefully seek God's guidance about that person's need. *Don't preach.* No one is more odious than the person who disguises a spiritual lecture as an invitation for coffee. Watch for an open door. If the other person asks, "What do you think I should do about thus-and-so?" perhaps that is your opportunity to express yourself. And don't forget to do your share of listening—with an open mind and heart. Most importantly, it is God—not you—who is responsible for changing lives.

Small thought here
How do you deal spiritually with a person who has been feeding on the junk food of the world and whose inner life is flabby and weak? By encouraging a different diet for his soul. Show him, by your own example, how to feed and delight in God's Word.

LEARN TO EDIFY

Scripture, Romans 14:19
Edify [one] another.
(Rom. 14:19)

You can strengthen another person by giving yourself to him. This is more than merely offering time, though the two undoubtedly go together. It is sharing your unique, God-given personality and the lessons He has taught and is teaching you. If you and I are too busy to give of ourselves in this way, well—then we're too busy. I remember the encouragement I received while attending Wheaton College. As a student pastor, I would often preach or teach as many as five or six times each Sunday—in different locations. By Sunday night I was completely exhausted. But Monday morning was sure to arrive, and I had an eight o'clock Greek class! Sometimes I became so tired and discouraged I thought I couldn't make it.

But those Monday mornings somehow became easier to face after a man on his way to catch a train into Chicago befriended me near the campus. Almost forty, he had sold his farm in Wisconsin, moved his family to Wheaton, and taken a job in the city so that he could go to school to prepare for full-time Christian ministry. When he saw me, invariably he would put his strong farmer's hand on my shoulder and give me the full expression of his warm heart, encouraging this neophyte (me) to keep on with God. I'll always remember that man. I felt more able to face the day, more determined to amount to something for God, after I had met my friend.

Small thought here
You can have a similar impact, sometimes by just giving yourself to another person in complete attention, compassion, and concern, even if only for a moment.

PRACTICE PATIENCE

Scripture, Romans 14:19
Him that is weak in the faith, receive ye.
(Rom. 14:1)

Based on Romans 14:19, we've discovered Paul's counsel to push for peace, to be builders, to learn to edify, and finally to practice patience. But for a moment I want to reach back to Romans 14:1 because it contains a final suggestion for helping us to get along with and edify others. In effect, Paul counsels regarding the "weak" brother: Let him in. Don't throw him out. Don't turn him away from the Lord and the truth of God's Word.

Returning now to verse 19, Paul presents two concepts. The first concerns peace, about which we've spoken. The second concerns building up the weaker brother by means of "things wherewith one may edify another." That requires patience, but what can you do to develop it? One way is to be gentle. If you want to build up another person, involve him or her with you in productive Christian activity and ministry.

Take your friend with you on home or hospital visitation. Perhaps the person you visit will receive Christ through your Spirit-led witness. Even though your friend may say nothing the entire call, it will be a tremendous learning experience for him and he will be touched immeasurably by God's power and your brotherly concern.

Small thought here

Your friend is thrilled because he was involved—albeit silently—in something of eternal worth. You have gently spurred his growth in grace. In this matter of helping the one who is "weak," remember that the same lesson may need to be presented again and again. So *practice patience.*

Be thou an example of the believer in word, in conversation, in charity, in spirit, in faith, in purity.
(1 Tim. 4:12)

Be a Blessing
IN CALVARY LOVE!

"Be thou an example of the believer," Paul commanded, in "charity"— another word for love. This, however, is a very special kind of love. The Greek word *agape* is used in John 3:16 and elsewhere in the New Testament to refer to God's redeeming love in Christ and the divine love that is placed in the believer's heart by the Holy Spirit. "The love of God," we read in Romans 5:5, "is shed abroad in our hearts by the Holy Ghost." People feel safe with this kind of love and respond to it. There is no ulterior motive, no desire to get—only to give, to help, to point to Christ. Let God fill your heart with His Spirit and express His great heart of Calvary love through you.

Robert A. Cook

April

Someone has said that the Psalms contain "a song for every mood" of our lives. That's a good way to describe these up-close, personal expressions of the human heart! Throughout this month that is known for "showers," we want to shower our hearts with the refreshing water of God's Word. Starting in Psalm 1, a truly *blessed* place to begin, we'll meditate our way through thirty selections from this popular, precious portion of the Bible. As we do, dear friend, ask our lovely Lord to lift your heart heavenward by the perfect "Law of the Lord" which is the only power that can transform our intellect, will, and emotions. And He will!

GOD'S BLESSED MAN

Scripture, Psalm 1:1-6
Blessed is the man that walketh not in the counsel of the ungodly, nor standeth in the way of sinners, nor sitteth in the seat of the scornful. But his delight is in the Law of the Lord.
(Ps. 1:1-2)

W hat precious blessings are promised to God's blessed man! How delightful to be like a fruitful, unwithering tree, planted in God's special place by His special design, and watered continually by the refreshment of His eternal Word! But these blessings are not without their price, my friend. There are three lifestyles we must avoid.

Walking in the "counsel of the ungodly" is living with the attitude, "I can do better for myself without God." This is Satan's ancient lie, which has remained unchanged through the centuries. We must beware of trying to better ourselves outside of God's will. Adam and Eve tried it and the action cost them Eden, innocence, the fellowship of their Creator, and life itself.

Standing in the "way of sinners" is characterized by a "me first" mindset. The world's dictum is "Nice guys finish last." But the Apostle Paul said, "Look not every man on his own things, but every man also on the things of others.... In honor preferring one another" (Phil. 2:4; Rom. 12:10).

Sitting in the "seat of the scornful" is thinking or saying, "I am better than you." We need to remember that we are all level at the Cross. Wendell Loveless used to say, "Everything outside of the lake of fire is pure grace!"

The positive side of God's requirements for His blessed man is preoccupation with and delight in His Word. The only permanent way to modify human character and conduct is to subject it to the Bible. Leland Wang used to say, "No Bible, no breakfast." He would not eat until he had been with his Lord in the Word for a heart-satisfying time.

Small thought here

There are unlimited blessings available to you and to me, all purchased by Christ's precious blood shed on Calvary. But they are only available if we face up to God's requirements: the Word in our lives, producing a different walk, a different stance, and a different attitude.

THOU VISITEST HIM!

Scripture, Psalm 8:1-9
What is man . . . that Thou visitest him?
(Ps. 8:4)

Here is a truth so great that it will take all eternity to understand and appreciate it: God visited our planet! He "made Himself of no reputation, and took upon Him the form of a servant, and was made in the likeness of men; and . . . became obedient unto death, even the death of the cross" (Phil. 2:7-8). This glorious visit by our Saviour has answered forever the questions in every human heart. Paul lists some of them in Romans 10:6-10.

• *What is God like?* Answer: God is like the Lord Jesus Christ. Jesus said, "He that hath seen Me hath seen the Father."

• *What is it like to die?* Answer: Christ has already been there and come back, a victor. We have nothing now to fear!

• *What shall I do about my sinful heart and my untamed tongue?* Answer: The word of faith, "Jesus is Lord!" and the commitment of faith makes us new creatures in Christ!

Just as we cherish for years the memory of a visit from some outstanding person or loved one, even so—but in a larger sense—all creation has felt the impact of that divine visitor. Because He came, lived, died, and rose again, we are free from condemnation, forgiven, adopted into God's family, and able to come boldly into the presence of the Almighty and find it a "throne of grace."

The ultimate thrill in understanding this truth comes when we realize that because of that divine visit, the presence and power of God are here, now, spread throughout the world in the lives of believers. Jesus in essence said, "When He, the Spirit of Truth is come, He will convince the world *through you* of sin, righteousness, and judgment" (John 16:8-9).

Small thought here

God wants to visit some life through you . . . today. He knows who is ready, whose heart is hungry, who will respond. As you bow to pray, commit yourself to Him, to work in some needy life.

DO YOU KNOW HIS NAME?

Scripture, Psalm 9:1-20
And they that know Thy name will put their trust in Thee: for Thou, Lord, hast not forsaken them that seek Thee.
(Ps. 9:10)

Alexander Cruden, in the concordance that bears his name, points out 134 names used in Scripture to refer to the Lord Jesus Christ.

One name, however, stands out in the heart of the believer. "Wherefore, God also hath highly exalted Him, and given Him a name which is above every name: that at *the name of Jesus* every knee should bow ... and every tongue should confess that Jesus Christ is Lord" (Phil. 2: 9-11).

There is conviction in that name. Peter, preaching to the crowd on the Day of Pentecost, said, "God hath made that same Jesus, whom ye have crucified, both Lord and Christ" (Acts 2:36). The Scripture record goes on to remark that "when they heard this, they were pricked in their heart" (2:37)—in other words, convicted.

There is transforming power in that name. Peter took the lame man by the right hand, saying, "In the name of Jesus Christ of Nazareth rise up and walk" (3:6). Immediately, we read, His feet and ankle bones received strength, and he ... entered with them into the temple, walking, and leaping, and praising God" (3:7-8). Later, as Peter addressed the crowd, he said, "Faith in His name hath made this [lame] man strong" (3:16).

There is no other way to God except through that name. Peter, responding to the threats of the rulers, stated flatly: "Neither is there salvation in any other: for there is none other name under heaven given among men, whereby we must be saved" (4:12).

Small thought here

Do you know His name and its mighty power? And have you committed yourself to Him as Lord of all? Today's text exhorts you to do two things in this connection: *trust Him* and *seek Him*. Seeking God means spending time with Him in prayer and in His Word. Trusting Him means turning the details of your life over to Him. And be assured of this: He will never turn you away.

WHAT CAN THE RIGHTEOUS DO?

Scripture, Psalm 11:1-7
If the foundations be destroyed, what can the righteous do?
(Ps. 11:3)

This Scripture has often been used to describe the hopeless condition of a nation or society which has allowed its foundations to be eroded through sin and neglect. Certainly, there have been times when people went too far in their wickedness, and not even the prayers of God's people could save them. Three times, Jeremiah was commanded, "Pray not thou for this people ... for I will not hear thee."

When we look at this psalm as a whole, however, we see it as an answer to the despair forecast by the prophets of gloom and doom. They say, "Flee as a bird to your mountain! For lo, the wicked bend their bow, they make ready their arrow ... that they may shoot at the upright in heart" (vv. 1-2).

Believers, on the other hand, always face such situations with complete trust in God. In troubled times, we can turn to God. In making decisions, we can ask for the divine wisdom that is given to all men liberally. In coping with heartaches, we can lean hard on the everlasting arms. When we start with God, the victory is already assured!

Nor is this blind, unthinking trust—far from it. Look at the rationale for the psalmist's faith (vv. 4-7): God's *character* hasn't changed. He is still holy. God's *authority* hasn't diminished. He knows what's going on. God's *justice* hasn't changed. He is still the God of judgment. God's *love* hasn't changed. "The righteous Lord loveth righteousness; His countenance doth behold the upright."

Small thought here
This is no time to give up, my friend! Instead, look up and trust the God who is there and hasn't changed.

IN THY PRESENCE

Scripture, Psalm 16:1-11
Thou wilt show me the path of life: in Thy presence is fullness of joy; at Thy right hand there are pleasures for evermore.
(Ps. 16:11)

This affirmation of faith is based on the statements that precede it. Let us look at them: (1) God controls my future, my present, and my place in society (vv. 5-6); (2) God gives me His counsel when I need wisdom (v. 7); (3) God fills my horizon, so I am unshakable (v. 8); (4) God gives me hope beyond the grave (vv. 9-10).

"Show me the path of life": what a wise prayer for any believer to pray! God has a plan for each of our lives. But achieving His plan comes only by trusting Him. It is precisely because He controls me, counsels me, steadies me, and gives me hope, that I trust Him to work out His perfect plan for my life. You don't have to agonize over getting God's guidance, dear friend! Just begin to trust Him and obey the promptings of His Holy Spirit.

"In Thy presence," the psalmist says, "is fullness of joy." How much do you know about the presence of God? Such a condition goes beyond our best prayers and the emotional uplift that sometimes accompanies them. Here we are in the holy of holies . . . quiet, relaxed, humbled, cleansed, satisfied . . . with God. Practicing the presence of God" takes time, to be sure. And it is costly, in the sense that God will reveal Himself only to those whose hearts are honest before Him. But when, by faith, you take your place with your risen Saviour, trusting in His shed blood, His perfect righteousness, and His never-failing promises . . . ah, friend, there is fullness of joy!

Small thought here
Help yourself to a blessing by setting aside time just to be with God. You'll be a holier, happier person as a result!

GOD'S WORD: PERFECT

Scripture, Psalm 19:1-14
*The Law of the Lord is perfect,
converting the soul.
(Ps. 19:7)*

The only way to move a person's character heavenward is by the impact of God's Word on his intellect, emotions, and will. "Wherewithal shall a young man cleanse his way?" the psalmist asks (Ps. 119:9). The answer comes back immediately: "By taking heed thereto according to Thy Word." Plow God's Word into your mind and memory and you will be kept by the power of His truth: "Thy Word have I hid in mine heart, that I might not sin against Thee."

For the fainthearted and wavering, the Word is settled in heaven (119:89). For the bored and jaded, God's Word is "sweeter than honey" (v. 103). For the thin-skinned and easily offended, the Word is protection for their feelings: "Great peace have they which love Thy Law: and nothing shall offend them" (v. 165). For those needing guidance, "Thy Word is a lamp unto my feet, and a light unto my path." (v. 105). For the scatterbrained, the Word will teach "good judgment and knowledge" (v. 66). For the discouraged, there is "hope in Thy Word" (v. 81). For the chronic backslider, the Word of God is a cure: "Before I was afflicted I went astray: but now have I kept Thy Word" (v. 67).

Make up your mind that the Bible is the ultimate source book, the last court of appeal, the absolute rule for your faith and conduct. You cannot improve on it, and you court disaster when you attempt to get around its plain teachings. It is perfect.

The Bible *does* make a difference. I guarantee that your regular Bible reading, and the prayer which that reading inspires, will make a perceptible difference in those needy areas of your life and personality!

Small thought here
Dare to risk the decision-making situations of life on the plain teachings of God's Word. See for yourself the difference it can make.

GOD'S WORD: SURE

Scripture, Psalm 19:1-11
The testimony of the Lord is sure, making wise the simple.
(Ps. 19:7)

Scripture's *prophecies* are sure. The shining example of this truth is found in the record of our Saviour, the Lord Jesus Christ—from the Virgin Birth to Calvary. Jesus Himself foretold the total destruction of Jerusalem, and the temple in particular, saying that not one stone would be left on another. Years later, Roman soldiers, knowing that the stones of the temple were encrusted with gold, literally took the building apart as they searched for the precious metal.

Scripture's *warnings* are sure. God warned His chosen people that they would be scattered abroad if they forsook Him, and that is exactly what happened. God's warnings against immorality are also very plain, and down through the centuries people have learned the tragic results of sin. It indeed "will find you out."

Scripture's *promises* are sure. What comfort and assurance the believer finds in trusting the precious promises of God's Word! The Apostle Peter remarks, "Whereby are given unto us exceeding great and precious promises, that by these ye might be partakers of the divine nature, having escaped the corruption that is in the world through lust" (2 Peter 1:4). The preciousness of the promises, and of the Saviour who gave them to us, is made real only when we believe (i.e., commit ourselves to them). The world says, "Show me, and I'll believe." God says, "Believe, and I'll show you."

Small thought here
You are wise in direct proportion to how well your presuppositions work. When you depend on the sure Word of God, you become truly wise, because it always works!

GOD'S WORD: RIGHT

Scripture, Psalm 19:1-14
The statutes of the Lord are right, rejoicing the heart.
(Ps. 19:8)

What is the secret of a rejoicing heart? "The statutes of the Lord." A statute involves an obligation of some kind, a command or a prohibition issued by a governmental authority. Human nature routinely resists obeying statutes. Take highway speed limits, for example. How few there are who defend them, and how many there are who grumble about them and seek to circumvent them! Each of us considers himself the exception to the rule, resisting compliance as long as possible.

The Christian outlook on God's commands is entirely different. Christ, of course, is our pattern. He said, "I delight to do Thy will, O God; yea, Thy Law is within My heart" (Ps. 40:8). Because the Holy Spirit indwells each believer, we can rejoice with the Apostle Paul, "It is God that worketh in [us], both to will and to do of His good pleasure" (Phil. 2:13).

The simple fact is that when you accept Jesus Christ as your Lord, and trust Him as your Saviour, you are committing yourself to the concept that God's statutes—in other words, those things He asks you to do—are equitable and just. None of God's laws are what the law courts call "capricious and arbitrary." All of His commands are reasonable, right up to His request for the use of your whole life—body, soul, and spirit (Rom. 12:1). Paul says this is "your reasonable service."

Small thought here

Will you make up your mind today that what God commands in His Word is absolutely right, equitable, and just? When you pass that volitional milestone, you will suddenly find yourself feeling happier about your compliance with His will. It's great to be right!

GOD'S WORD: PURE

Scripture, Psalm 19:1-14
The commandment of the Lord is pure, enlightening the eyes.
(Ps. 19:8)

The chronic malady of the unsaved is that they are spiritually blind. Paul says that "the god of this world hath blinded the minds of them which believe not." When an unbeliever impatiently says to you, "I just don't see it!" he is acting true to form. The fact is, he can't see God's truth until his "eyes of understanding" are enlightened by the Holy Spirit. What is the point at which this blindness begins to be removed? It is precisely the point at which God's pure Word enters the human mind for serious and honest consideration. "The entrance of Thy words giveth light" (Ps. 119:130). Other diluting concepts are excluded. Human philosophy is superceded. Tradition and prejudice are set aside. As a new Christian once told me, "I knew about God for years. But it was not until I really got serious about the Scriptures that I decided to commit myself to Christ. God's Word convinced me of my lostness without Christ, and I cried out to Him to save me."

There is also a blindness that affects God's people. It is the blindness of unbelief, in other words, lack of faith. A classic example of this truth can be found in 2 Kings 6:17. Dothan, the town where the Prophet Elisha lived, had been surrounded during the night by Syrian armies. When Elisha's servant saw this display of military hardware, he cried out, "Alas, my master! How shall we do?" Elisha's answer was both a statement of faith and a prayer. The statement was, "They that be with us are more than they that be with them." The prayer was, "Lord, I pray Thee, open his eyes that he may see." Then, for the first time, the servant became aware of "the mountain . . . full of horses and chariots of fire round about Elisha."

Small thought here

The cure for both kinds of spiritual blindness is God's Word, applied to your heart. If humanly you just cannot see the answer, go to the Bible and let the Holy Spirit shed light on the situation.

GOD'S WORD: SATISFYING

Scripture, Psalm 19:1-14
More to be desired than gold . . . sweeter also than honey . . . by them is Thy servant warned . . . and in keeping of them there is great reward.
(Ps. 19:10-11)

Anyone who has lived long enough knows that sin leaves the human heart unsatisfied and soiled at the points of greatest hunger and need. And every believer knows—or ought to know—that God's Word touches those same points with power and satisfaction.

Occasionally I will ask an audience to help me list "the things people worry about," thus revealing what is most important to them. Invariably, money ("gold" in our text) is first on the list. While there is nothing sinful in making, saving, or investing money, the tragic possibility exists that money will move in and control your life. When that happens, you realize that you never seem to have enough of it and are always unsatisfied.

Sensual pleasures, as epitomized by the phrase "sweeter than honey," have the same capacity to disappoint and mock you. No human experience, by itself, ever satisfies that "God-shaped vacuum" in your soul.

All ofhich brings us to the question, "Is there any real satisfaction in life or is it just a mockery?" The answer: Yes, satisfaction and contentment can be found, but only through God's Son as revealed in God's Word. God's Word has value . . . more than gold. God's Word provides a thrilling taste that will never sour on your lips. God's Word provides warnings sufficient to keep you from stumbling. And God's Word has its own built-in reward for the obedient soul!

Small thought here
If you know that sin mocks and frustrates you, and if you also know that God's Word guides, satisfies, and rewards you, doesn't it make sense to get serious about obeying it . . . today?

THE LORD IS "MY" SHEPHERD

Scripture, Psalm 23:1-6
He leadeth me . . . Thou art with me.
(Ps. 23:2, 4)

The world is full of people who are comfortable with generalized, indefinite references to God, but who either panic or bristle when words like "yours" or "mine" are used in religious conversation. The progress of thought in Psalm 23 describes this difference in attitudes quite clearly, it seems to me.

First of all, you are never really ready to speak intelligently about your Lord until you can say, "The Lord is *my* shepherd." When you own Him as your Shepherd, you also commit yourself to all the wonderful things He does for His sheep. The green pastures and still waters (His nurturing Word), the restored soul (His indwelling Spirit), the paths of righteousness (His gentle guidance)—all are yours when you say, "*My shepherd.*"

Even at that, your relationship with God may still be somewhat theoretical and academic. It is only when you sense the presence of your dear Shepherd in the valley of the shadow and in the midst of your warfare with God's enemies that you can say, "Thou art with me."

Even when there are no still waters, no refreshment, and seemingly no shining pathway of guidance—only gloom, threats, and dire forebodings—your trusting heart can rest in these promises: "*Thou* art with me; Thy rod and Thy staff they comfort me. *Thou* preparest a table before me in the presence of mine enemies: *Thou* anointest my head with oil." Not "He" any longer, but "Thou"!

Small thought here
Make the transition today from an indefinite, impersonal relationship with God to that personal commitment of love that allows you to say amid the deepest gloom, "Thou art with me."

WHO GETS THE BLESSING?

Scripture, Psalm 24:1-10
He that hath clean hands and a pure heart; who hath not lifted up his soul unto vanity, nor sworn deceitfully. He shall receive the blessing from the Lord.
(Ps. 24:4-5)

God reveals the way to blessing in four basic principles: clean hands, a pure heart, a humble attitude, and honest words. Disarmingly simple truths, yet profoundly moving, if you take them seriously.

Despite the "only believe" school of thought, it would seem that God expects us to exercise our faith in His mercy and grace. Look, for example, at Isaiah 1:16-18. "Wash you, make you clean; put away the evil of your doings from before Mine eyes; cease to do evil; learn to do well; seek judgment, relieve the oppressed, judge the fatherless, plead for the widow. . . . Though your sins be as scarlet, they shall be as white as snow." Clearly, God waits until you and I are ready to deal with what we know to be wrong in our lives and to change what we can change before He applies the beautiful promise of scarlet guilt cleansed white as snow. Saved by grace, through faith, plus nothing— of that we are sure; but it must be a vital, honest faith dealing with all that grieves God's heart.

There is something to be said for honesty before God and with people. In the same Isaiah passage, God complains that His people's dishonest worship and their many prayers are just a source of weariness to Him! It might be an excellent exercise to review our prayers and see how many of them are in the class of mere routine, patently dishonest because they are not offered in earnest to our Lord. In other words, we didn't really mean what we said.

Small thought here
To be honest, humble, and clean: this is what God asks of us when we come in faith to claim the merits of Christ's sacrifice on Calvary. We can't save ourselves, nor can we cleanse our hearts or consciences; but God asks us to be honest with Him so He can work His will in us. Tell God the truth today.

THE SECRET OF THE LORD

Scripture, Psalm 25:22
The secret of the Lord is with them that fear Him; and He will show them His covenant. (Ps. 25:14)

Two facts stand out in this matter of secret things. One is that God knows and holds all the secrets of the universe. "The secret things belong unto the Lord our God" (Deut. 29:29). Even our Lord Jesus, God incarnate, said, "But of that day and that hour knoweth no man, no, not the angels of heaven, but My Father only" (Matt. 25:36). By voluntarily limiting Himself in His incarnation, Christ gladly left certain secrets with God the Father. Secondly, God loves to reveal His secrets to those who seek Him. Look at our text again: "The secret of the Lord is with them that fear Him." Daniel spoke of the God "that revealeth secrets." "Eye hath not seen," said Paul, "nor ear heard, neither have entered into the heart of man, the things which God hath prepared for them that love Him. But God hath revealed them unto us by His Spirit" (1 Cor. 2:9-10).

To learn the secrets of God, one must enter into His covenant. "He will show them His covenant," says the psalmist. The writer to the Hebrews takes up this same theme and speaks of a New Covenant, one based on the death and resurrection of our Lord Jesus Christ. Indeed, the way into the very secrets of God is now open to every believer because our Lord Jesus opened it for us when He died and rose again. A powerful motivator, it would seem to me, for us to spend more time in God's Word and in prayer, so we can learn those wonderful heavenly secrets!

Small thought here

Jesus said that we are to pray to the Father who "seeth in secret." The way to appreciate God's secrets is to share yours with Him!

CURE FOR FAINTING SPELLS

Scriptures, Psalm 27:1-14
I had fainted, unless I had believed to see the goodness of the Lord.
(Ps. 27:13)

David is such an easy person to identify with! Look at the sources of his faintheartedness: wicked people, enemies, war, trouble, loneliness and being forsaken, false accusations, cruelty. Sound familiar? The solid fact is that any one of these experiences is enough to make you and me want to run away; and when several of them arrive together, they can be devastating. Indeed, David wrote, "I really would have given up had I not believed that God is good."

A focus like David's can keep us from collapsing too! Once we have made up our minds that God's goodness is in operation, we will have far less difficulty in coping with the events of everyday life. Since He is in control, and since He is a good God, we can relax in His care. The Prophet Isaiah said, "Thou wilt keep him in perfect peace whose mind is stayed on Thee, because he trusteth in Thee" (Isa. 26:3).

In many a heart there is the lurking suspicion that God really doesn't want a good life for people, that He is somehow out to punish us and deprive us of enjoyment. This is, of course, the devil's ancient lie. Satan used it in the Garden of Eden and has not changed his approach since. The truth is, God wants to give good things to His children. Jesus said, "If ye then, being evil, know how to give good gifts unto your children, how much more shall your Father which is in heaven give good things to them that ask Him?" (Matt. 7:11)

Small thought here
The way to become convinced of God's goodness is to spend time with Him. "Wait on the Lord . . . and He shall strengthen thine heart." Get alone with God, and you'll get over your fainting spell!

GOD'S BLESSED MAN: FORGIVEN!

Scripture, Psalm 32:1-11
Blessed is he whose transgression is forgiven, whose sin is covered.
(Ps. 32:1)

There are four aspects of blessedness which result from the way God deals with our sins: (1) forgiveness; (2) covering; (3) no iniquity imputed (reckoned), but rather God's own righteousness; and (4) an honest, guileless spirit.

David dealt with the last item first. He was evidently full of guile and duplicity just before he wrote this psalm. At first, he kept silent. He found to his dismay, however, that such conduct only got him into more trouble. Finally, he decided to acknowledge his sin before God, and at that point obtained forgiveness.

God's covering mercy is another precious fact. David wrote, "Thou art my hiding place!" When we have leveled with the Lord and have nothing unconfessed, we can depend on Him not only to forgive, but also to cover us.

God also gives us His righteousness instead of preserving the record of our sins and shortcomings. Notice His gracious offer, when forgiveness has been obtained: "I will instruct thee and teach thee in the way which thou shalt go: I will guide thee with Mine eye" (Ps. 32:8). And from the New Testament: "Abraham believed God, and it was counted (reckoned) unto him for righteousness (Rom. 4:3). Paul wrote these marvelous words not for Abraham's sake alone, but for us also, to whom it (i.e., righteousness) shall be imputed, if we believe on Him that raised up Jesus our Lord from the dead (Rom. 4:23-24).

Small thought here

Forgiveness is great; positive righteousness is better. God offers both to you if you level with Him and commit yourself to Him in faith!

FORMULA FOR A LONG LIFE

Scripture, Psalm 34:1-22

What man is he that desireth life, and loveth many days, that he may see good? Keep thy tongue from evil, and thy lips from speaking guile.
(Ps. 34:12)

I was joking with a friend one day and remarked, "I expect to live to be 93, and then they'll probably have to shoot me!" He replied, "Why stop at 93? I can tell you how to live to be 100!" "That interests me!" I said. "How do you do it?" "Well," he said, "first, you get to be 99. Then . . . be very careful!"

Be that as it may, the fact is that there are some divine promises relating to long life. The fifth commandment says, "Honor thy father and thy mother, that thy days may be long upon the land which the Lord thy God giveth thee" (Ex. 20:12). To the person who dwells in "the secret place of the Most High," God promises, "With long life will I satisfy him" (Ps. 91:16).

Today's text indicates other factors in the longevity of life: our speech, conduct, and motives. Because God's Word tells us that "out of the abundance of the heart the mouth speaketh," it is necessary to submit our hearts to the blessed Holy Spirit, so the right words will come from our lips. Conduct is divided into two sides, positive and negative. We are to depart from evil, putting distance between ourselves and the sources of temptation and sin. There is a time to pray and there is also a time to run away. As we experience this truth, we are more likely to do good as a by-product of God's grace in our lives (Eph. 2:10). Finally, our motives must be rooted in God's Word to ensure personal "peace that passeth understanding." God's peace takes care of situations that would otherwise produce king-size ulcers!

Small thought here

Everything starts with desire. If you *want* God's blessing over a long span of years, start living Psalm 34!

CURE FOR WORRY

Scripture, Psalm 37:1-40
Fret not thyself because of evildoers....
Rest in the Lord, and wait patiently for Him.
(Ps. 37:1, 7)

John Houtkamp, my star deacon during the 1930s, used to point to Psalm 37:1, look seriously at me, and say, "Remember, Preacher, it says, 'Fret not thyself.' When you fret about something, who gets fretted? You do!"

Whenever God gives you a command, He makes it possible for you to understand enough to obey it. This passage is a case in point. "Don't worry!" is the command. Why not?

• Troubles and troublemakers don't last. This too shall pass (v. 2).

• Simple trust in God, plus obedience, opens the door to His miraculous provisions for you (v. 3).

• When you bring your desires and delights in line with God's will, you can have whatever you want! (v. 4)

• Commitment—the willingness to leave the situation to God—allows Him to bring your dreams to reality (v. 5).

• Resting in the Lord means relaxing because He is in control (v. 7). When He is piloting life's frail craft, you can wait patiently for the outcome of His plans, because He never fails!

• God actually controls your steps! (v. 23) Someone pointed out to me that steps must of necessity mean stops. Besides, "Though [you] fall, [you] shall not be utterly cast down, for the Lord upholdeth [you] with His hand" (v. 24).

God is greater than any trouble you may face. He will still be there when the tempest is past . . . and so will you! He delights to give you what you want, if you will begin specializing in His will. He promises to hold on to you even when you falter and stumble along the road of life. So why worry?

Small thought here

The process of being freed from worry begins with *trust* and culminates with *rest*. Trust says, "I am going to leave this situation to God." Rest says, "I'm so glad I did!"

HOPE IN GOD

Scripture, Psalm 42:1-11
Why art thou cast down, O my soul? And why art thou disquieted within me? Hope thou in God!
(Ps. 42:11)

Questions, questions! And none of them seem to be answered. The hungry heart asks, "When is God going to satisfy my longings?" The cynical critic asks, "Where is there any evidence that your God is real?" The discouraged heart asks, "Why has God forgotten me?"

Job was in the same predicament. With his fortune vanished, his immediate family wiped out, and his health gone, he sat in an ash heap, a pitiful and miserable sight, and asked, "Why was I born? Why didn't I die at birth? If I had only died then, I would not have lived to see this day of sorrow and suffering." No answers came to these and other questions that Job raised. Finally, when God spoke to him, Job said, "I will lay mine hand upon my mouth." In other words, "I have said too much already!" Later, at the end of God's conversation with Job, the patriarch exclaimed, "I have heard of Thee by the hearing of the ear: but now mine eye seeth Thee. Wherefore I abhor myself and repent in dust and ashes" (Job 42:5-6).

What Job needed—and what you and I need—were not answers to the "why" questions but a new revelation of God. Indeed, God is the only source of hope. Everything human fails and decays. This is the rationale behind Paul's benediction found in Romans 15:13— "Now the God of hope fill you with all joy and peace in believing, that ye may abound in hope, through the power of the Holy Ghost." By believing God, committing yourself to His promises, and risking the next step on His revealed will, you can have hope. And it is a hope that grows and reduplicates itself. Discouragement is also contagious. For every discouraged Simon Peter who says, "I go fishing," there are several more who say, "We also go with thee." But when hope fills your heart, you will produce hope in other lives as well!

Small thought here

Hope relates, not to things or circumstances, but to a wonderful Person! "Hope thou in God, for I shall yet praise Him!"

BE STILL AND KNOW

Scripture, Psalm 46:1-11
Be still and know that I am God: I will be exalted among the heathen, I will be exalted in the earth.
(Ps. 46:10)

"I never really thought deeply about God until I landed here in the hospital. Then, flat on my back, with nowhere to look but up, I began to get serious with my Lord!" This, the testimony of one who learned to "be still and know. . . ."

It does seem that God sometimes has to bring us to a screeching halt in order to get our attention. Only when we become still (because everything we *thought* was important has ceased), does He speak to us, taking His rightful place in our lives as Lord and King.

What do we learn from the stillness? That God is a refuge and hiding place; that God is our strength, the One who sees us through impossible situations; and that because He is God in our lives, we need not fear. *We need not fear physical circumstances.* Earthquakes, floods, and tidal waves are just samples of the physical conditions that cause fear. No need to fear: God is on His throne! *We need not fear people.* "The heathen raged, the kingdoms were moved," wrote the psalmist, but "He uttered His voice" and the earth trembled. Enjoy today the luxury of not having to merely "cope" with people. Let God rule in your relationships and see what a difference He makes! *We need not fear war.* You and I live under the threat that some madman will pull the trigger on a nuclear war, thus incinerating most of the human race. While it is true that this sinful world has never been without conflict, it is also true that in the midst of our warring human race, God has a way of using His children to carry out His divine purposes. The reason we don't fear war is not that we are brashly defying injury and death, careless of the consequences—far from it. We can be confident in a warring world because we know that amid the strife, God is expressing His love to others through us!

Small thought here

The first step in knowing God better is to be still. The next step is to enthrone Him in every relationship of life. In relation to circumstances, people, and conflict, make Him Lord!

RESTORED JOY

Scripture, Psalm 51:1-19
*Restore unto me the joy of Thy salvation;
and uphold me with Thy free spirit.
(Ps. 51:12)*

One of the immediate results of salvation is joy. Peter remarked, "Whom having not seen, ye love; in whom though now ye see Him not, yet believing ye rejoice with joy unspeakable and full of glory" (1 Peter 1:8). Isaiah wrote confidently, "Therefore with joy shall ye draw water out of the wells of salvation" (Isa. 12:3). Our Lord Jesus said plainly, "These things have I spoken unto you that My joy might remain in you and that your joy might be full" (John 15:11). According to Paul, the fruit of the Spirit is joy (Gal. 5:22). It should be obvious to us, therefore, that true joy depends on a right relationship with the Saviour and on an ungrieved Holy Spirit.

Unfortunately, because we are sinful, faulty human beings, we get out of line, failing both God and each other. When that happens, suddenly the joy seems to vanish from our hearts. We no longer look forward to prayer and devotion, no longer hurry into activities of Christian service. At that point, we must run to the mercy seat! "Let us come boldly unto the throne of grace, that we may obtain mercy and find grace to help in time of need," admonished the writer to the Hebrews (Heb. 4:16). "If we confess our sins," wrote John, "He is faithful and just to forgive us our sins and to cleanse us from all unrighteousness" (1 John 1:9).

It may be helpful here to remind ourselves that there are some things which we need to guard against. Paul exhorted, "Grieve not the Holy Spirit of God. . . . Let all bitterness, and wrath, and anger, and clamor, and evil speaking, be put away from you, with all malice, and be ye kind . . . tenderhearted, forgiving" (Eph. 4:30-32).

Small thought here

The joy returns when you come back to Him and cease to grieve His Spirit. God hasn't moved. Come back and rejoice!

POWER, AND MERCY ALSO!

Scripture, Psalm 62:1-12
God hath spoken once; twice have I heard this; that power belongeth unto God. Also unto Thee, O Lord, belongeth mercy.
(Ps. 62:11-12)

Hundreds of Bible references speak of God's power. There is power to save: God's "dynamite" power as demonstrated in the Gospel. There is Spirit-given power to witness with the authority of the One who said, "All power (authority) is given unto Me in heaven and in earth. Go ye therefore" (Matt. 28:18-19). There is power to go beyond our fairest hopes and dreams. He is "able to do exceeding abundantly above all that we ask or think, according to the power that worketh in us" (Eph. 3:20). We gladly become "partaker[s] of the afflictions of the Gospel according to the power of God" (2 Tim. 1:8)—His power makes us victors over the opposition of a wicked world! All of this is ours through the Lord Jesus Christ, who becomes through faith, "Christ, the power of God and the wisdom of God" to us who open our hearts to Him (1 Cor. 1:24).

Now comes this divine afterthought: "Also unto Thee, O Lord, belongeth mercy." For all the promises in Holy Writ, and for all the outpoured power of God which is ours by grace, we give thanks. But as we kneel at the Cross, you and I know that, first of all, we are supplicants for God's mercy. Before He uses us by His power, He must save and cleanse us through His mercy and grace (Titus 3:5). Thank God for the "also" phrases in the Bible. Power, yes indeed! More power than we will ever use. But mercy also!

Small thought here

Jesus said to the disciples, "Tarry ye in the city of Jerusalem until ye be endued with power from on high" (Luke 24:49). While there is only one Pentecost in the historical sense, the divine order is the same today: wait on God for His mercy and His cleansing, and then enjoy and use the power of the Holy Spirit!

WHO, ME?

Scripture, Psalm 69:1-36
O God, Thou knowest my foolishness; and my sins are not hid from Thee. Let not them that wait on Thee, O Lord God of hosts, be ashamed for my sake: let not those that seek Thee be confounded for my sake. (Ps. 69:5-6)

God knows all our failings. "All things," wrote the writer to the Hebrews, "are naked and opened unto the eyes of Him with whom we have to do" (Heb. 4:13).

People who know us are aware of our failings also! And our failings affect them in two ways. First, those who are waiting on God, that is, walking closely with Him and seeking to obey Him, are ashamed when they see us doing or saying something that does not square with His Word. It is not that they resent us, but just that they are embarrassed to have the world see Christians living in an unchristian manner. What the psalmist really was saying was, "Lord, don't let me embarrass any of Your saints!" Second, our failings confuse those people who are really trying to understand the Gospel and experience God's grace. How often we have heard someone say, "I thought I knew what God's will was in this matter, but since I met So-and-so, I'm confused." So the psalmist in essence prayed: "Lord, don't let either some foolish word or action or some downright sin on my part confuse a person who is really seeking You!"

Now let's return to Hebrews 4:13-16. Immediately after saying that God knows all about us, the writer reminds us that we have a Great High Priest, our Lord Jesus Christ, who has been tested as we have and who knows how we feel. The answer to human failings is to run to the throne of grace for mercy and help. God writes *finis* over our failings when they are covered by Christ's righteousness!

Small thought here

Neither believers nor unbelievers will ever be embarrassed or confused about you if they know that you are honest about your failings and doing something constructive about them through God's transforming grace.

HOW TO GET PROMOTED

Scripture, Psalm 75:1-10
For promotion cometh neither from the east, nor from the west, nor from the south. But God is the judge: He putteth down one, and setteth up another.
(Ps. 75:6-7)

Joseph, some would say, was the perfect example of a "spoiled" boy. Scripture says plainly that Jacob loved Joseph more than any of his other sons. Indeed, envy was inevitable. And Joseph's tales of dreaming that his brothers were bowing down to him certainly did not help matters. Then came the day when the jealous brothers sold Joseph to a band of traveling tradesmen, who in turn sold him to Potiphar in Egypt. At this point, who was responsible for Joseph's predicament? The obvious answer would be his rascally brothers! Yet years later, when Joseph, now a ruler in Egypt, faced his brothers once more, did he blame them for their shameless and cruel treatment? Not for one moment. Listen to what he told them: "God sent me before you to preserve you a posterity in the earth, and to save your lives by a great deliverance. So now it was not you that sent me hither, but God" (Gen. 45:7-8).

God's sovereign placement of His servants is a fact of life. The Prophet Nathan reminded King David, "Thus saith the Lord of hosts, 'I took thee from the sheepcote, from following the sheep, to be ruler over My people, over Israel: and I was with thee . . . and have made thee a great name' " (2 Sam. 7:8-9). Paul pointed out believers' differing gifts, mentioning among them prophecy, ministry, teaching, exhortation, giving, supervision, and showing mercy (Rom. 12:6-8). Thus, if you are born from above, what you are, where you are, the work in which you are engaged, and the circumstances surrounding that work are all part of God's perfect plan for you at this time. Don't fight them. Thank God for them and minister through them!

Small thought here

The secret of promotion is not just doing your best; it is doing your best *as unto the Lord!* (Col. 3:23)

HAS GOD FORGOTTEN ME?

Scripture, Psalm 77:1-20
Hath God forgotten to be gracious? Hath He in anger shut up His tender mercies? (Ps. 77:9)

We can identify with Asaph in this psalm because he is so human! First, he waited until he was in trouble to start praying. Second, when he did pray, he complained to God. Third, when he considered his present difficulties, he longed for the "good old days" when blessings were more numerous and things were better. And finally, he became a victim of the idea that God had cast him aside.

Looking at the psalmist from the perspective of history, it is easy to see what went wrong. We pray when we become aware of a heartbreak, and we expect immediate answers. What we often forget is that most heartaches do not suddenly come into existence, full-grown, as it were. They have been developing for months, sometimes years. One of the most important procedures attached to praying is to give God time . . . time with other people, and time with ourselves. Faith trusts God for the answer even though it has not yet arrived.

I suspect that even in his distress, the psalmist knew the answers to his questions. "Will the Lord cast off forever . . . favorable no more?" Answer: "I will never leave thee nor forsake thee!" "Is His mercy clean gone forever?" Answer: "His mercy endureth forever!" "Doth His promise fail forevermore?" Answer: "There hath not failed one word of all His good promise." "Hath God forgotten to be gracious?" Answer: "Can a women forget her child? Yea, they may forget, yet will I not forget thee."

The turning point for the psalmist—and for you and me—is when he turned from his miseries to God. Yes, God hasn't forgotten you, dear friend! Go to Him in prayer and let Him tell you so.

Small thought here
There is no substitute for talking things over with God. Verbalize the situation to Him, just as you would to your dearest human friend. That's what Asaph did, and he could report, "I cried unto God with my voice, and He gave ear unto me."

LIVING IN GOD'S SECRET PLACE

Scripture, Psalm 91:1-16
He that dwelleth in the secret place of the Most High shall abide under the shadow of the Almighty.
(Ps. 91:1)

God's secret place turns out to be more of a relationship than a specific location. Elsewhere the psalmist wrote, "The secret of the Lord is with them that fear Him" (Ps. 25:14). "His secret," said Solomon, "is with the righteous" (Prov. 3:32). Obviously, then, if we are ever to know God's secret, we must establish a right relationship with Him . . . one based on godly fear and reverence, as well as righteousness obtained by faith in Jesus Christ. The closing verses of Psalm 91 make this clear. Note five phrases: (1) he hath set his love upon Me (v. 14); (2) he hath known My name (v. 14); (3) call upon Me, and I will answer (v. 15); (4) I will deliver him and honor him (v. 15); (5) with long life will I satisfy him (v. 16).

The first key to dwelling in God's secret place—loving Him with all our heart—is only possible through the indwelling Holy Spirit. "The love of God is shed abroad in our hearts through the Holy Ghost which is given unto us" (Rom. 5:5). Second, to know His name means to know His saving power and to accept Him as Lord of our lives. To know His name means a life commitment, not merely an intellectual exercise. Third, to live in God's secret place means relying on prayer and its miracle answers. When the psalmist prayed, he received an answer. That answer was, first of all, realizing that the living God was right there with him! The answer also meant deliverance and honor (because he first honored God). And finally, because he was dwelling in God's secret place, life itself became a long, fulfilling adventure instead of a series of crises and catastrophes!

Small thought here

Most self-help books somewhere contain this thought: "Every day, plan some solitude for yourself." For the Christian, that solitude is found, not just in aloneness, but in drawing aside and entering into God's secret place.

A PACKAGE OF PRAISE

Scripture, Psalm 103:1-22
Bless the Lord, O my soul; and all that is within me, bless His holy name.
(Ps. 103:1)

We praise God for what He does. He forgives; He heals; He redeems; He crowns with loving-kindness and tender mercies; He satisfies with good things; He renews; He judges; and He reveals Himself to His people.

We praise God for what He is: merciful, gracious, and slow to anger. He deals with us in grace, not according to what we deserve. "As the heaven is high above the earth, so great is His mercy. . . . As far as the east is from the west, so far hath He removed our transgressions. . . . The mercy of the Lord is from everlasting to everlasting upon them that fear Him" (Ps. 103:11-12, 17).

We praise God because He is God! "The Lord hath prepared His throne in the heavens; and His kingdom ruleth over all" (Ps. 103:19). All the hosts of hell and all the turbulence of earth do not shake His throne. He is God Almighty and we are His!

One somber note is sounded in this anthem of praise. Verses 14-16 declare that our time here on earth is very short, and life itself is as precarious as a blade of grass . . . here today and gone tomorrow. This reminds us of two truths: God will be just as real, and we will come to know and serve Him far better in the tomorrows of eternity. And second, precisely because life is short and uncertain, we had better do our praising while we can! Today, let some wandering, discouraged soul hear you praising your Lord.

Small thought here

Praise ought not be a halfhearted activity. *All* that is within me," said the psalmist. A halfhearted compliment is a slur; and halfhearted praise is an insult. When you praise God, involve your whole being— body, soul, and spirit.

WHEN PRAYER REALLY COUNTS

Scripture, Psalm 107:1-43
Then they cried unto the Lord in their trouble, and He delivered them out of their distresses.
(Ps. 107:6, 13, 19, 28)

It is axiomatic that, given enough trouble, pressure, or danger, people pray. Psalm 107 profiles prayer-producing situations and the results that accrue when true prayer goes heavenward.

The prayer of the wanderer. The chronic loneliness of the human spirit has no cure apart from God. "They wandered . . . they found no city to dwell in . . . their soul fainted in them. *Then* they cried unto the Lord" (Ps. 107:4-6). Note the twofold answer to this prayer: it involves being led in the *right* way *and* it provides a heavenly destination—a city of habitation!

The prayer of the willful. "They rebelled against the words of God, and [despised] the counsel of the Most High" (Ps. 107:11). When willful people repent, God mercifully brings them out of darkness, breaks their chains, and frees them to obey His will. The truth about insisting on your own way is that you become enslaved to it; the truth about yielding to God's way is that you are set free to live for Him!

The prayer of the worthless. "Fools because of their transgression . . . are afflicted. . . . Then they cry unto the Lord in their trouble" (Ps. 107:17, 19). There is some comfort in the fact that God even hears the prayers of those who lack the common sense to stay out of trouble! Perhaps that statement includes more of us than we would like to admit. The answer to a scatterbrained person's prayer is not more advice, but a generous helping of God's Word (v. 20), the application of that Word by the Holy Spirit, and the continuing miracle of Christ being "made unto us wisdom" (1 Cor. 1:30).

Small thought here
If you pay attention to these things, wrote the psalmist, you will understand the loving-kindness of the Lord (Ps. 107:43). The principle involved here is this: God answers prayer by sending His mercy and love to operate in needy hearts.

HOW TO MODIFY CHARACTER

Scripture, Psalm 119:9-16
Wherewithal shall a young man cleanse his way? By taking heed thereto according to Thy Word.
(Ps. 119:9)

People don't change. They merely become more set and more obvious in their ways. Unless, that is, they have a life-changing contact with the Word of God. God's Word can make a difference!

If you want to be different, where do you start? "By taking heed according to God's Word." Start reading the Bible with a notebook and pen or pencil nearby. Whenever God's Spirit speaks to your heart, write down those thoughts, and use them as the basis for meditation and prayer. Think and pray honestly about your faults and weaknesses and look for biblical truths that apply to your particular needs. Most certainly, this process doesn't allow any halfway surrender to God's will. "With my *whole* heart have I sought Thee," wrote the psalmist (Ps. 119:10). God will not do it for you!

The Word in your heart is a sure protection against slipping into sin. Use that computer between your ears to store God's Word, so the Holy Spirit can bring into your consciousness the exact Scripture passage you need to reinforce your faith at a critical time. And check your value system. Many a person strays from God's will because his values became twisted. "I have rejoiced in the way of Thy testimonies, as much as in all riches," declared the psalmist (Ps. 119:14). Which means more to you: advancement, money, acceptance by your peers, personal pleasure, *or* the will of God?

Small thought here

What you think about constantly becomes the fabric of your life and the basis for your decisions. Notice the word *meditate* in verse 15. Take time every day to think about God's Word and fill the empty moments with portions of Scripture. While you are waiting for a friend or while you are on "hold" during a telephone call, meditate on a favorite verse. You'll be delighted at the blessing this simple procedure brings each day!

CURE FOR APATHY

Scripture, Psalm 119:25-32
My soul cleaveth unto the dust: quicken Thou me according to Thy Word.
(Ps. 119:25)

T wo problems plague the soul that would get going for God. One is the stick-in-the-mud syndrome. "My soul cleaveth unto the dust" may well be the complaint of millions who would like to serve God, but just never seem to get started. The second problem turns out to be the cause of the first. To *quicken* means "to give life." Unfortunately, by nature, we are dead to God, as well as to all the wonderful initiatives He can provide. We need quickening!

The solution to these problems, of course, begins at the Cross. "You hath He quickened," wrote Paul, "who were dead in trespasses and sins" (Eph. 2:1). The soul that is committed to the Lord Jesus Christ is indwelt by the blessed Holy Spirit, whom Paul calls "the Spirit of life in Christ Jesus" (Rom. 8:2). What a glorious experience to be blessedly alive, in Christ!

Many of us are good starters but poor finishers. The psalmist recognized this fact when he remarked, "My soul melteth for heaviness: strengthen me according unto Thy Word (Ps. 119:28). This is the case of the deacon or Sunday School teacher who says to the minister, "Don't nominate me for this work next year. I'm tired." Or perhaps it is the case of a believer who has tried without success to win someone to the Lord and who is about to give up, or the case of one who had resolved to read the Bible daily, but found his soul "melting for heaviness." The Word of God understood (v. 27), honestly applied (v. 29), and kept before one's mind as a guide (v. 30) will make the difference. You'll be alive and moving forward in the will of God!

Small thought here
"I will run . . . when Thou shalt enlarge my heart," said the psalmist. Much of our apathy stems from constricted spiritual arteries. Spending time with God and His Word will enlarge your spiritual capacity and allow the free flow of spiritual power.

CURE FOR DISCOUR-AGEMENT

Scripture, Psalm 119:81-88
My soul fainteth for Thy salvation: but I hope in Thy Word.
(Ps. 119:81)

Here are the causes of discouragement as listed in this passage: exhaustion (v. 81); delay (v. 82); neglect by other people (v. 83); postponed answers to prayer (v. 84); malicious conduct by others (v. 85); and persecution (vv. 86-87). A formidable list, you'll admit!

Discouragement often hits when you are physically and emotionally exhausted. Elijah went through this experience, you'll recall (1 Kings 18—19). He even prayed that he might die! God's answer was to rest him, feed him, and reveal Himself in the "still small voice" that gave renewed courage and vision. Rest, nourishment, and a new meeting with God will take care of 90 percent of all your discouragements!

Postponed answers to prayer are also hard to take. The implied criticism in Martha's greeting to Jesus, as recorded in John 11, was, "Lord, You didn't answer soon enough. You didn't get here in time to keep Lazarus from dying!" But in the case of Lazarus, our Lord wasn't thinking of healing. He had something far greater in mind: presiding at a resurrection! God's delays are always the precursors of greater things! Once you learn this lesson, the discouragement of delay will have been mastered forever.

The psalmist had to learn the difference between "they" and "Thou." When attention is focused on what others are doing, it is possible to become quite discouraged, even bitter. But when attention is centered on God, His Word, and His will, discouragement flees and faith begins to soar.

Small thought here
The more you think about yourself, the more miserable you will become; but the more you meditate on God's love and mercy on your behalf, the more you will be impelled to faith, praise, and action!

May

Most of us would rather *give* advice than
get it, isn't that true? Down through time a
lot of advice has been both given and
gotten. And a lot of it has often been
dispensed with more *candor* than *concern*.
It is also a fact that, more often than not,
advice is greeted with a kind of resolute
disregard, not to mention "ignortion," as my
good friend Lloyd Cory is wont to say!
Based on everything from the entrails of a
chicken to a Ouija board to the constellation
Capricorn, all sorts of advice can be freely
obtained. How refreshing to have God's
"more sure Word of prophecy," this month
as we meditate together in Proverbs. Think
of it as thirty-one days to a new you!

BEGIN RIGHT!

Scripture, Proverbs 1:1-9
The fear of the Lord is the beginning of knowledge, but fools despise wisdom and instruction.
(Prov. 1:7)

To be successful in this life, you must be wise; and to be truly wise, you must know God . . . must fear Him, in the sense of reverential trust, obedience, and love. "The fear of the Lord" is a phrase calling to mind the total humiliation which occurs when a sinful creature is confronted by his holy Creator. Daniel said, "[I] saw this great vision, and there remained no strength in me: for my comeliness was turned in me into corruption" (Dan. 10:8). Isaiah cried out upon seeing a vision of God's holiness, "Woe is me, for I am undone!" (Isa. 6:5)

The fear of the Lord will keep you straight morally. Joseph, when pressured by temptation from Potiphar's wife, said, "How then can I do this great wickedness, and sin against God?" (Gen. 39:9) The fear of the Lord guarantees that you will be secure amid the most dangerous circumstances! "The angel of the Lord encampeth round about them that fear Him, and delivereth them" (Ps. 34:7). And the fear of God lets you in on His secrets, thrilling your heart as you become attuned to His plans and purposes. "The secret of the Lord is with them that fear Him; and He will show them His covenant" (Ps. 25:14).

There is just one way to start right in life: by beginning with the fear of God. Put Him first in everything. If you have difficulty doing this, pray until the Lord has revealed Himself to your heart and until your will has said yes to Him. Then go on, trusting and obeying.

Small thought here
The great hindrance to a wholesome fear of God is what the Bible calls *idolatry* . . . putting someone or something in the place of God where your life's priorities are concerned.

LEARN TO WALK

Scripture, Proverbs 2:8-9, 20
*Then shalt thou understand righteousness,
and judgment, and equity; yea,
every good path.
(Prov. 2:9)*

Solomon urges that those who fear God "walk in the way of good men, and keep the paths of the righteous." What are those ways? They are, simply stated, the steps of faith. "The just shall live by faith," Habakkuk declared (Hab. 2:4); and his statement is three times quoted in the New Testament. Paul said, "As ye have therefore received Christ Jesus as Lord [i.e., by faith], so walk ye in Him" (Col. 2:6).

Living by faith is like breaking pieces off a loaf of bread, one by one. You don't live a whole day at a time, but a moment at a time, a situation at a time, a temptation at a time, a heartache at a time. Each step is to be lived by faith, in complete dependence on the One who saved you.

Living by faith results in righteousness, judgment, and equity. Righteousness is outward behavior in line with the divine righteousness imputed (reckoned) to you the moment you trusted Christ. Judgment is the inner motivation to right conduct. "I will put My law in their inward parts, and write it in their hearts," God said through Jeremiah (Jer. 31:33). Equity has to do with consistent living. Without a doubt, many a Christian's effectiveness has been sharply reduced or even canceled because of some glaring inconsistency in his life. Our goal as believers, as we walk by faith through this world, is to bring honor to the One who has called us out of darkness into His marvelous light.

Small thought here
Failure in matters such as thoughtfulness, courtesy, ethical business practices, and personal integrity can destroy a lot of so-called "witnessing for Christ."

KNOW THE WILL OF GOD AND DO IT

Scripture, Proverbs 3:1-35
In all thy ways acknowledge Him, and He shall direct thy paths.
(Prov. 3:6)

Look at the commands found in the early verses of this chapter: "Mercy and truth . . . *write them* on the table of thine heart. *Trust* in the Lord with all thine heart. *Lean not* unto thine own understanding. In all thy ways *acknowledge* Him. *Fear* the Lord and depart from evil."

God's Word *in your memory* will insure the guidance of the Holy Spirit. "[He] shall bring all things to your remembrance," the Saviour said of the Comforter who was to indwell each believer (John 14:26). Scripture in your mind means God in your thoughts and grace in your conduct. *Trust* is the willingness to leave the situation to God's will, wisdom, and power. While you may not know God's will about everything in your future, enough has been revealed to you to keep you busy obeying Him. *Lean not unto thine own understanding* means just what it says. "There is a way that *seemeth* right unto a man," Solomon warned (Prov. 14:12). "It seemed like a good idea at the time," mused a convicted Watergate planner. Test *your* ideas by God's ideas. *In all thy ways acknowledge Him.* How do you do this? Start where God starts: "That every knee should bow . . . and that every tongue should confess that Jesus Christ is Lord" (Phil. 2:11). Walking surely in God's will is based on constant awareness of His sovereign control. Make Him Lord of all. What's more, "Rest in the Lord and wait patiently for Him" (Ps. 37:7). That's hard to do, when you are impatient and eager for action, but it's the only wise course.

Small thought here
"Pray your way through the day," I often urge my friends. You'll never go wrong when you are praying, "Jesus, guide me now!"

DON'T PRO-CRASTINATE

Scripture, Proverbs 3:1-35
Withhold not good from them to whom it is due, when it is in the power of thine hand to do it.
(Prov. 3:27)

The tendency to put things off is native to us all. Every son and daughter of Adam will at some time say, "Not now, but later." The fact that something is human nature, however, doesn't make it right. Every time we put off doing the right thing, we are voting against it, and by so doing, Solomon says, "devising evil against [our] neighbor." For the most part, we do not postpone matters which we consider really important. The key, therefore, to overcoming this tendency to delay is to reconsider life's *priorities*, find out what is really important, and decide to do something about them *now*.

It is a God-ordained duty to do good. "What doth the Lord require of thee, but to do justly?" (Micah 6:8) The Apostle Paul echoed this truth when he remarked, "For we are His workmanship, created in Christ Jesus unto good works, which God hath before ordained that we should walk in them" (Eph. 2:10). We all have the ability to do good. "It is in the power of thine hand to do it," Solomon says. Excuses will not suffice here. Even the most limited human being can find something good to do. Furthermore, God holds us responsible for doing the good of which we are capable: "To him that knoweth to do good, and doeth it not, to him it is sin" (James 4:17).

Small thought here

Learn and begin to use the technique of "prioritizing" your life. List your duties and opportunities in order of importance, then take up the most important thing first and get at it immediately.

HOW TO GET GOOD BREAKS IN LIFE

Scripture, Proverbs 4:1-27
Keep thy heart with all diligence; for out of it are the issues of life.
(Prov. 4:23)

W hat an awesome truth: *the success or failure of your outer life will ultimately be decided by your inner life!* But how do you "keep" your heart? First, make sure your inner life belongs to Jesus Christ and is under His control. Paul says that we are to bring "into captivity every thought to the obedience of Christ" (2 Cor. 10:5). Second, fill your conscious mind and memory with God's Word. It is impossible for you to concentrate on two concepts at once. When the Word of God fills your mind, no room will be left for other, less worthy thoughts. Third, when you are aware that some unworthy thought or desire has alighted, like an ugly bird, in your mind, turn immediately to Jesus and ask Him to cleanse your heart and mind. You may not be able to keep stray thoughts from wandering into your mind, but you need never keep them there! Fourth, work at thinking good things, first, about your Lord, and then about the people around you. This is a matter of the will . . . something you can decide to do. Indeed, no matter whom you meet, you can always discover a worthwhile thought to think about him or her. You will be surprised and delighted at the change in the interpersonal weather when you "keep your heart with all diligence." And remember: good breaks—the "issues of life"— come from good relationships!

Small thought here
Of the godless fool, the psalmist wrote, "God is not in all his thoughts" (Ps. 10:4). Turn that statement around and see for yourself how life is enriched when your Lord can say of you, "God is in all his thoughts."

A STORY WITH NO HAPPY ENDING

Scripture, Proverbs 5:1-23
And thou mourn at the last, when thy flesh and thy body are consumed.
(Prov. 5:11)

Dr. John R. Rice used to say, in one of his famous sermons, "All the devil's apples have worms!" Notice the contrasts in this passage. The temptress uses words sweet as honey and smoother than oil. The end of the relationship, however, is bitter as wormwood and sharp as a two-edged sword. "Stolen waters are sweet," is the enticing message; but of the victim, Solomon said, "He knoweth not that the dead are there; and that her guests are in the depths of hell."

Now what about all this? First, remember that temptation is always presented as being pleasant and profitable. Satan's approach in the Garden of Eden was to convince Eve and Adam that the forbidden fruit was good to eat, pleasant to the eyes, and that eating it would make them as wise as God. The result? Lost innocence, the curse, sin, sorrow, and death. Second, there is never a happy ending to the story of disobedience, short of God's grace. Several insights come to the tragic victims of sin. Unfortunately, they all come too late:

• Sorrow: "Thou mourn at the last" (v. 11).
• No more potential: "Flesh and body . . . consumed" (v. 11).
• It was a heart matter: "My heart despised reproof" (v. 12).

What to do? Note the phrase in Proverbs 5:6—"Ponder the path of life." "I thought on my ways," wrote the psalmist, "and turned my feet unto Thy testimonies" (Ps. 119:59). How does a person change his ways, his behavior? "By taking heed thereto according to Thy Word" (Ps. 119:9). Think: If I go on this way, where will it end? Is that what I want to do with my life?

Small thought here

Disobedience, compromise, and sin can only purchase for you a basket of heartache and woe. Go God's way for a happy ending! "Mark the perfect man, and behold the upright: for the end of that man is peace" (Ps. 37:37).

WHAT'S WRONG WITH WORK?

Scripture, Proverbs 6:1-35
Go to the ant, thou sluggard; consider her ways, and be wise.
(Prov. 6:6)

To all appearances, it would seem that today's definition of work is "something to get out of." The average job applicant is apt to ask questions such as, "What are the fringe benefits? How much vacation do I get? and How soon can I retire?"

What does the Bible say about work? God ordained it and planned that it should be pleasant and rewarding. He placed Adam in the Garden of Eden to dress and keep it. But after the Fall, mankind associated work with the curse of sin and through the centuries it has tended to frustrate and discourage him. Our blessed Lord, however, was a worker and had a good attitude about it. He said, "I must work the works of Him that sent Me while it is day: the night cometh, when no man can work" (John 9:4). The Apostle Paul knew the divine energy provided by the Holy Spirit. He said, "I also labor, striving according to His working, which worketh in me mightily" (Col. 1:29). The crowning dignity of human labor is to be associated with the Almighty: "We are laborers together with God!" exclaimed Paul (1 Cor. 3:9).

Furthermore, the work we do in this life will be evaluated at the Judgment Seat of Christ. "Let every man take heed how he buildeth," Paul warned (v. 10). "If any man build upon this foundation gold, silver, precious stones, wood, hay, stubble; every man's work shall be made manifest: for the day shall declare it, because it shall be revealed by fire" (vv. 12-13).

Small thought here
Work turns out to be something which, when done for the Lord and in the power of the indwelling Holy Spirit, has a link to eternity and promise of a heavenly reward!

DEFEATING THE DEVIL

Scripture, Proverbs 7:1-27
My son, keep my words, and lay up my commandments with thee.
(Prov. 7:1)

Watch a professional sports team in action and you will notice that each play is carefully recorded on videotape. People carrying on this procedure may be employed by the team itself, but more than likely they are competitors, scouting the opposition. The idea, of course, is that *if you know how your opponent works, you stand a chance of defeating him.*

Our opposition is Satan and his hosts. The important consideration, therefore, is to become familiar with his *modus operandi*, so as to confront him successfully and win. Satan's approach in temptation has not changed since the Garden of Eden. He pointed out to our first parents that the forbidden fruit was palatable, pleasing, and powerful—that it would make them as wise as God! The Apostle John called it the lust of the flesh, the lust of the eyes, and the pride of life.

Solomon's illustration has to do with sex and morals, but is typical of every tempting approach Satan makes—pleasing, progressive, and plausible. When we at last yield to the temptation, our fall is precipitous and sudden. The end of the story is always the same: death and hell.

The only way to win over Satan's temptations is to have a reservoir of inner power greater than any force from without. That power comes from God's Word. "Thy Word have I hid in my heart, that I might not sin against Thee," said the psalmist (Ps. 119:11).

Small thought here
Realize that Satan always goes for your three points of human weakness: the flesh, the eyes, and the pride of life. Awareness of his tactics combined with dependence on God's Spirit and His Word will defeat the devil every time.

KNOW WHAT TO HATE

Scripture, Proverbs 8:1-36
The fear of the Lord is to hate evil.
(Prov. 8:13)

One mark of the unsaved heart is hatred . . . for people. Paul describes the condition as follows: "We ourselves also were . . . living in malice and envy, hateful, and hating one another" (Titus 3:3). *Hateful* means "hate-filled," a reservoir of bitterness with no particular object.

The glory of Christ's salvation is that He takes away the hatred we have had for people and replaces it with His Calvary love! (Rom. 5:5) If we love God, we will hate that which insults and rebels against Him, that is, all sin. Pride says, "I am better than others and as good as God." Arrogancy says, "I have to be recognized, to be first in line." The evil way says, "Sin is fun and nice guys finish last." The froward mouth says, "Don't tell me what to do. I don't take orders from anyone, not even God!" If we wrap these all together, we have a pretty good description of today's world.

The important thing is to hate evil without rejecting the sinner. Our Lord Jesus is the prime example of this virtue. How tenderly He spoke to those who had fallen and how graciously He received them when they repented! His scorn and rebukes were reserved only for those who, even while their lives were full of sin, professed to be righteous and thus in no need of redemption.

Small thought here
Spend time with your Lord, until your heart is filled with His love. Christian love is tough love, but it has the tenderness of the Saviour.

LEARN FROM CRITICISM

Scripture, Proverbs 9:7-10
Give instruction to a wise man, and he will be yet wiser: teach a just man, and he will increase in learning.
(Prov. 9:9)

The first thing to do about criticism is to expect it. Your enemies will criticize you because they dislike you; your friends, because they love you and wish to see you do better. In either case, there is no profit in getting angry about criticism. Listen to the comments of others; there might be the glimmer of a new idea in what is being said.

Second, remember that you can always profit by considering criticism against the backdrop of your past experiences. Notice the phrasing in Proverbs 9:9—"wise man . . . yet wiser: just man . . . increase in learning." The key question to ask is, "What can I learn from this conversation?" *not* "How can I get back at this person?"

Third, form the habit of sharing all criticism, good or bad, with your Lord. King Hezekiah's experience provides a beautiful illustration of this truth: Rabshakeh, the Assyrian, sent a threatening letter to Hezekiah, saying in effect that it would do no good to trust in God, because all the other people who trusted their gods had already been conquered. How did the king respond? "Hezekiah received the letter of the hand of the messengers, and read it; and Hezekiah went up into the house of the Lord, and spread it before the Lord" (2 Kings 19:14). The thrilling answer came from Isaiah: "He [the king of Assyria] shall not come into this city, nor shoot an arrow there, nor come before it with shield, nor cast a bank against it. . . . I [God] will defend this city" (vv. 32, 34). That night, the angel of the Lord brought death to 185,000 Assyrian soldiers!

Small thought there
Remember, it is God's name and reputation at stake, not just your own. Instead of fighting back at your critics, share the sting of criticism with your Lord. He'll heal your wounded spirit and help you learn from the experience.

SPIRITUAL SURE-FOOTEDNESS

Scripture, Proverbs 10:1-32
He that walketh uprightly walketh surely.
(Prov. 10:9)

Steady, surefooted behavior in a slippery world is no accident. Unfortunately, most people begin to consider this subject when it is too late, prompting Solomon to emphasize the importance of having and maintaining a right relationship with one's parents (v. 1). Young readers would do well to remember that a direct relationship exists between your treatment of your parents and your destiny. "Honor thy father and thy mother" is still in the Book!

Nonslip behavior depends on a nonskid value system. "Treasures of wickedness profit nothing, but righteousness delivereth" (v. 2). Make no mistake about it: that which you value most will determine your destiny. Jesus said, "Where your treasure is, there will your heart be also" (Matt. 6:21). Stability of conduct also depends on whether you have decided that God is all He claims to be and that He will not fail you. Indeed, "The Lord will not suffer the soul of the righteous to famish" (v. 3). Someone has said that when you have nothing left, you may for the first time become aware that God is all you need.

There is a lot of just plain good sense in Christian living. Proverbs 10:4-7 bears this out. Carelessness leads to poverty, and contrariwise, diligence leads to prosperity. Surefooted behavior is built on willingness to learn from others and to take advice (v. 8). No one can lead who has not first learned to follow a leader.

Small thought here
An "upright walk" means a life where Jesus is Lord of all. When He is in control, you can depend on God's promise that He orders your steps (Ps. 37:23).

HOW TO AVOID REGRETS

Scripture, Proverbs 10:1-32
The blessing of the Lord, it maketh rich, and He addeth no sorrow with it.
(Prov. 10:22)

W hat riches there are in the blessing of God!

There is the blessing of forgiven sin. "Blessed is he whose transgression is forgiven, whose sin is covered" (Ps. 32:1). "In whom we have redemption through His blood, the forgiveness of sins according to the riches of His grace" (Eph. 1:7).

There is the blessing of concentration on the Word of God. Lovers of God's Word can agree with the psalmist who exclaimed, "Blessed is the man whose delight is in the Law of the Lord; and in His Law doth he meditate day and night" (Ps. 1:2).

There is blessing in simply trusting God! "Blessed are all they that put their trust in Him" (Ps. 2:12). Trust involves *persons, situations,* and *outcomes.* First, we place ourselves in His hands (2 Sam. 24:14). Then we trust Him to work out problem situations (Prov. 16:7). And finally, we leave the outcome to Him. Daniel's three-times-a-day prayer schedule landed him in the lions' den, but we have no indication that his faith faltered. In the morning, he was able to say, "My God hath sent His angel, and hath shut the lions' mouths, that they have not hurt me" (Dan. 6:7).

And of course, the Beatitudes (Matt. 5:1-12) remind us of the blessing of a Christ-filled character. Our wonderful Lord epitomizes the virtues extolled in this list of "blesseds."

Small thought here

There are no regrets in the blessing of God! Far too often, the accomplishments we enjoy in this world leave a sour aftertaste. But the Lord's blessing is pure joy, unflawed and unalloyed. "He addeth no sorrow with it."

THE LAW OF GENEROSITY

Scripture, Proverbs 11:1-31
The liberal soul shall be made fat: and he that watereth shall be watered also himself. (Prov. 11:25)

The law of generosity involves three things. First, when you give freely as unto your Lord, He promises you'll have something left over. Notice verse 24: "Scattereth, and yet increaseth." Some years ago, a church member stood up during the midweek service and said, "I have to admit that I have been upset with the pastor's preaching about tithing. After all, I only make a few dollars a week, and there is never enough money to go around as it is. I thought it was impossible to give God a tenth of my income. Last week, though, I got to thinking about it, and the idea came to me that God deserves a chance to prove Himself. So I thought, I'll try it for one week. When payday came, I took one tenth of the money and laid it aside for the Lord's work. Folks," he said with a smile, "I can't tell you how it happened, but when we got done paying our bills, we had a little money left!"

Second when you are generous, you will be more influential and significant, with an air of spiritual health about you (v. 25). And third, when you are generous, you will be perceived by others as a source of blessing! (v. 26) What an inducement to give generously for our Lord's glory!

Small thought here

Try giving to God off the top of your paycheck rather than after every other obligation has been paid. God says, "Them that honor Me, I will honor" (1 Sam. 2:30).

SAY THE GOOD WORD!

Scripture, Proverbs 12:5-25
Heaviness in the heart of a man maketh it stoop: but a good word maketh it glad.
(Prov. 12:25)

Scripture repeatedly confirms the vital connection between one's thoughts and words. In today's Scripture, for example, we see thoughts (v. 5), words (v. 6), and results (v. 14) are all interrelated. Thus if we are to say a good word, we must have good thoughts and trust God for a good result which "showeth forth righteousness."

It may come as a surprise to some of us that we actually decide what to think about another person—good or bad. This, it seems to me, is Paul's intent when he exhorts believers, "In lowliness of mind let each esteem other better than themselves. Look not every man on his own things, but every man also on the things of others" (Phil. 2:3-4). When we think critically about others, we create an atmosphere of distaste which communicates itself without a word being spoken.

But we are talking about words . . . the *good* word. How do we manage that? Clearly, if our thought patterns have been overhauled in line with Paul's command, we will have little difficulty in saying something that is sincerely uplifting and encouraging. Here are a few pointers that may help:

• Notice something about the other person that is worth complimenting. People said about a famous Sunday School teacher of another generation, "Joe would notice something about a boy, even though it were only one new shoelace!"

• Comment with appreciation when you know that someone has worked especially hard on a project.

• Be alert for symptoms that indicate the other person may be "hurting" and offer encouragement (not advice!) and love.

Small thought here

The good word is a word of recognition, appreciation, empathy, and love. All of them come from within, from a heart filled with the love of God, shed abroad in our hearts by the Holy Spirit.

THE POWER OF COMPANIONSHIP

Scripture, Proverbs 13:1-25
He that walketh with wise men shall be wise: but a companion of fools shall be destroyed.
(Prov. 13:20)

There are many proverbs about the power of companions to change one's character and behavior. Back on the farm in Ohio they used to say, "If you play with a skunk, you'll smell like him!" From Spain comes the saying, "He who runs with the wolves ill certainly learn to howl!" And before flea powder provided for the comfort of man's best friend, the saying was, "If you lie down with the dog, you'll rise up with fleas." Scripture has much to say on the subject as well. God's blessed man, we are told in Psalm 1:1, "walketh not in the counsel of the ungodly." Moses warned his people against getting friendly with the pagans around them (Ex. 23:32-33). The Apostle Paul wrote, "If any man that is called a brother be a fornicator, or covetous, or an idolater, or a railer, or a drunkard, or an extortioner; with such a one no not to eat" (1 Cor. 5:11).

God's directive is: find wise individuals and walk with them. How do you do this? *Choose Christians.* Unsaved people may be shrewd, smart, able, even geniuses. But if they do not know your Lord, they will ultimately hinder you. Choose Christians who pray for and who receive God's wisdom (James 1:5). And choose Christians with good sense who are using it to succeed in their chosen vocation.

Small thought here

Choose as your friends Christians who are growing as persons . . . reading, learning, expanding their horizons constantly. Your own outlook will be enriched by the association.

BITTERNESS AND JOY

Scripture, Proverbs 14:1-35
The heart knoweth his own bitterness; and a stranger doth not intermeddle with his joy.
(Prov. 14:10)

Bitterness is the normal reaction of a heart that is frustrated, disappointed, unsatisfied, or out of fellowship. Esau missed the patriarchal blessing, and "cried with a bitter cry." Hannah longed for a child, and not having one, "was in bitterness of soul." Family matters can often lead to bitterness. Paul wrote "Husbands, love your wives and be not bitter against them" (Col. 3:19). And even the church is not immune to bitterness! The writer to the Hebrews said, "Looking diligently lest any man fail of the grace of God; lest any root of bitterness springing up trouble you, and thereby many be defiled" (Heb. 12:15).

The source of bitterness, of course, is in one's heart. "But if ye have bitter envying and strife in your hearts, glory not, and lie not against the truth" (James 3:14). *The cure for bitterness* is twofold: peace and holiness (Heb. 12:14). When one follows Paul's directions in Philippians 4:6-7, turning everything over to the Lord in prayer, it is impossible to remain bitter about anything, because He is in control. Faith fills the believer with hope, peace, and joy (Rom. 15:13). And when the Holy Spirit fills one's life with Himself, Ephesians 4:31-32 becomes a blessed reality: "Let all bitterness, and wrath and anger, and clamor, and evil speaking, be put away from you, with all malice: and be ye kind one to another, tenderhearted, forgiving."

Small thought here

The monitoring of the believer's heart is his own responsibility. The command is quite clear: "Follow peace ... and holiness ... looking diligently lest any root of bitterness spring up." God will provide grace. You must provide the attention and the will.

SAYING THE RIGHT THING

Scripture, Proverbs 15:1-33
A soft answer turneth away wrath: but grievous words stir up anger.
(Prov. 15:1)

Does "a soft answer" involve craven fear, compromise, and a loss of self-respect? No! The soft answer of which the Bible speaks denotes respect for one's opponents and critics, acknowledgment of the possibility of error, and the need for righting wrong. It is a calm, loving statement of the facts as one sees them. Gideon was faced with some irate countrymen. They were angry because it was only after the enemy army from Midian began to flee that they were asked to take up positions to cut off the retreat. What was Gideon's "soft answer"? "God delivered into your hands the princes of Midian, Oreb, and Zeeb. And what was I able to do in comparison of you?" Then, Scripture says, their anger was abated toward him.

What about "wholesome words"? Using wholesome words means using knowledge in the right way (v. 2)—especially to enrich others (v. 7). Wholesome words have a dynamic quality capable of bringing life and hope to some needy heart! (v. 4) Wholesome words are timely words, "spoken in due season" (v. 23). Look for times when your words to another person can encourage, revitalize, bring joy, and renew faith. "The words of the pure are pleasant words"(v. 26). One need not be like a human bulldozer, riding rough shod over the feelings of others.

Small thought here
People will enjoy your words when they feel safe with you; and they will feel safe with you only when they know that your heart is pure. Anything less, be it ever so carefully phrased, is mere manipulation—you will know it, and so will your hearers!

MOTIVES UNDER CONTROL

Scripture, Proverbs 16:1-33
Commit thy works unto the Lord, and thy thoughts shall be established.
(Prov. 16:3)

The hardest task for a human being is to control inner feelings and motives. A believer soon learns that though he may act like a Christian, he does not always feel like one!

The first step toward control of motives is to realize that the prepared heart and the ready answer both come from God (v. 1). Paul reminds believers, "It is God which worketh in you both to will and to do of His good pleasure" (Phil. 2:13). Realize with joy that before you were mystified, or perplexed, or irritated by some situation, God was already there and had the answer!

The second step toward successful monitoring of motives is to learn to distrust them until they have been brought before the Lord in prayer (v. 2). There is a good reason for the injunction, "Everything by prayer." Your motives will always be tinged with selfishness until they have been to Calvary.

The third step involves talking the situation over with God in terms of possible actions. Talk to God about your job, your family, and your schoolwork. Talk to Him about matters of the heart, the checkbook, and the future. Commit your works—that is, things you want to do—to the Lord. When you do, He will direct your thoughts so that your motives are pure and your procedure for action is clearly outlined.

Small thought here

The key word in godly motivation is *better*. Right is *better* than rich (v. 8). Wisdom and understanding are *better* than gold and silver (v. 16). Inner strength is *better* than muscle (v. 32). A frugal meal with peace is *better* than a Thanksgiving dinner with strife (17:1).

THE BEST MEDICINE

Scripture, Proverbs 17:1-28
A merry heart doeth good like a medicine.
(Prov. 17:22)

Three verses in Proverbs deal with the happy, joyful heart. Proverbs 15:13 says, "A merry heart maketh a cheerful countenance." Verse 15 of the same chapter remarks that "he that is of a merry heart hath a continual feast." And our text says that a merry heart does good like a medicine.

Now let us see where the merry heart originates. Salvation brings joy. "I will joy in the God of my salvation" (Hab. 3:18). There is the joy of the Saviour's word (John 15:11). There is the joy of answered prayer (John 16:24). There is the joy of active faith. "The God of hope fill you with all joy and peace in believing" (Rom. 15:13). There is the joy of the fruit of the Spirit: "Love, joy, peace" (Gal. 5:22-23). There is the joy of leading someone to Christ, for Paul spoke of the believers at Philippi as "my joy and crown" (Phil. 4:1). There is the joy of being tested. "Count it all joy when ye fall into divers temptations" (James 1:2). And there is the supreme joy of knowing and loving the Lord Jesus Christ. "Whom having not seen, ye love; in whom, though now ye see Him not, yet believing, ye rejoice with joy unspeakable and full of glory" (1 Peter 1:8).

With this God-given joy in your heart, then, it is no wonder that there are certain visible results in your life and in the lives of others. A happy look, a truly satisfied heart, and a beneficial influence on others all flow from God's joy within.

Small thought here
Specialize in the kind of spontaneous joy that makes others better! People ought to say "Thank God, you've come!" rather than, at your departure, "Thank goodness, he's gone!"

LEARN TO LISTEN

Scripture, Proverbs 18:1-24
He that answereth a matter before he heareth it, it is folly and shame unto him. (Prov. 18:13)

For believers, this whole matter of listening starts with our relationship with God. "Be still," He says, "and know that I am God" (Ps. 46:10). We need to master the art of waiting on God, of being quiet in His presence, and of identifying and following the promptings of the Holy Spirit, if we are to learn anything of Him. In the learning process, this is the order to follow: first, we must fill our minds with God's Word. Then we must pray on the basis of that Word, depending on the Holy Spirit for aid; and what help He gives!

What we listen to is important. Our Lord said, "Take heed what ye hear" (Mark 4:24). This is a noisy, high decibel age. Is it possible, we wonder, in the din and hubbub of everyday living, to choose to hear anything in particular? How can God tell us to be careful what we hear, when our eardrums are constantly being assaulted with all sorts of sounds? The answer lies in our ability to concentrate. Isaiah wrote, "Thou wilt keep him in perfect peace, whose mind is stayed on Thee" (Isa. 26:3). Screening out unwanted sounds is a matter of concentrating on good sounds . . . God's sounds.

Luke quotes our Lord as saying, "Take heed how ye hear" (Luke 8:18). Our text indicates that listening should involve a thoughtful process of considering the idea before speaking about it. We should listen with understanding (v. 2), without argument (v. 6), without gossip (v. 8), with genuine trust in God (v. 10), and with loving friendliness (v. 24).

Small thought here
You don't always have to speak up about a matter. Prayerful, loving listening may do more good than a dozen sermons.

THE SECRET OF A SATISFIED LIFE

Scripture, Proverbs 19:1-29
The fear of the Lord tendeth to life: and he that hath it shall abide satisfied; he shall not be visited with evil.
(Prov. 19:23)

Life is never static. Everything changes, and so do you and I. The challenge is to find which way your life is moving, and either to change its course and its ultimate destination, or to flow with the tide.

Three things are mentioned in Proverbs which affect life: work, done by a righteous person (10:16); righteousness, that is, a godly character in action (11:19); and the fear of the Lord (19:23). Put these together and you have a powerful force for good. Solomon says that the person whose life is characterized by the fear of God will abide satisfied and be safe from evil. What a promise! What is the personal application of this truth? In what way will you be satisfied?

• *Satisfied because you know your labor is not in vain in the Lord.* When you and I are "laborers together with God," there is no such danger. Indeed, "Who can hinder Him?" (Job 9:12)

• *Satisfied because you know you are becoming what God wants you to be.* The "godly character in action" comes as the Holy Spirit conforms your character to the image of Christ (2 Cor. 3:18).

• *Satisfied, because there is a right relationship between you and your Heavenly Father*—what the Bible calls "the fear of the Lord." This is a combination of reverential awe, love, and trust. When your relationship with God is right, nothing else is needed to satisfy that God-shaped hunger in your heart.

Small thought here

Does "He shall not be visited with evil" mean you will never have troubles? No. Troubles come to us all. "Evil" stands for the work and power of Satan, as he harasses and attacks the believer. Since Calvary, Satan has no legal ground on which to stand, and the child of God is safe and secure. As the hymn goes, "That soul though all hell should endeavor to shake, I'll never, no never, no never forsake!"

NO DEFENSE, NO ATTACK

Scripture, Proverbs 20:1-30
Say not thou, I will recompense evil; but wait on the Lord, and He shall save thee. (Prov. 20:22)

Some things are God's job, and you and I do poorly when we try to do them for Him. He will not share His glory nor His "secret things" (Deut. 29:29). Interpretations belong to God (Gen. 40:8); so do righteousness, power, and mercy. The work of setting people straight and dispensing justice is God's work. We had best keep our hands off.

Wait on the Lord is the command given in today's text. How hard to wait when everything within and around us is screaming for action! "Don't just stand there. . . . Do something!" is a phrase familiar to us all. And yet God gently says, "Wait . . . I'll save you." The fact of the matter is that we rarely understand all that is involved in a given situation. We may think we understand it, but around and underneath are circumstances, experiences, and emotions of which we may have little knowledge. "Man's goings are of the Lord; how can a man then understand his own way?" (Prov. 20:24) So we are beset by two difficulties whenever we attempt to straighten out someone else. First, there is the amazing complexity of the average situation; and second, there is the fact that God may have something special in mind for the individual with whom we are dealing. Our heavy-handed procedure may well hinder His divine plan. "Wait . . . wait," God says.

Small thought here
Nothing is so satisfying as to realize that God has indeed "saved" the situation. The reward for waiting on God is, "He shall save thee." There is no bitter aftertaste lingering in someone's heart when God has set things right. We say of Him as they did of our Lord, "He hath done all things well!"

ARE YOU CARELESS OR DILIGENT?

Scripture, Proverbs 21:1-31
The thoughts of the diligent tend only to plenteousness; but of everyone that is hasty only to want.
(Prov. 21:5)

A Midwest judge asked me to visit a young man whom he had recently sentencd to a prison term. It seems that he and some of his buddies had stolen a car, gone for a joy ride, gotten drunk, got into a fight, and someone was killed. Now he was in jail. There was the inevitable suspicion and hostility when he was brought into the visiting area where I awaited him. After a while, we became friends, and he opened his heart to me. I shall always remember the sadness in his voice as he said to me, "Doc, I never thought it would end like this. I never thought . . . " and his voice trailed away.

To be diligent means to give steady attention and effort until the task is finished. Diligence is associated with concentration. The Bible says this combination leads to plenteousness . . . having more than enough! On the other hand, behavior that the Bible calls "hasty" leads to poverty. In the rush to "get somewhere" in life, hasty *actions* may cost a person his chance for success and get him out of fellowship with God! (Prov. 19:2) Our text also speaks of hasty *thoughts* and hasty *words*. How often we have wished that we could un-say something that has been thoughtlessly uttered! But you cannot unscramble an egg. Think . . . and pray . . . before you speak. How much better it is, Paul says, to bring "into captivity every thought to the obedience of Christ" (2 Cor. 10:5).

Small thought here
Remember: it is the thoughts of the diligent that provide the key to success. Program the computer of your mind with thoughts that honor your Lord and you will have started the process that leads to what the Bible calls "plenteousness."

CHILDHOOD TRAINING AND ADULT STABILITY

Scripture, Proverbs 22:1-12
Train up a child in the way he should go: and when he is old, he will not depart from it.
(Prov. 22:6)

For the Christian, childhood training includes more than "Come when I call" and "Do what I tell you." It puts the young life in contact with God and His Word and models the truths of that Word in everyday living. I believe in prayer today because before I was born, my sainted mother and two of her friends prayed for me each morning at ten o'clock. I believe in prayer today because during my childhood and teenage years I would often awaken to hear the sound of my father's voice, softly pleading with God, "Bless my motherless boy today. Keep him from sin and help him grow up to be a man of God."

Training in godliness includes a number of subjects which the young mind must grasp and understand: *Your reputation and the love of friends who trust you is more precious than gold* (v. 1). Guard your reputation. Once lost, it can never be bought back again. *Learn to depend upon God* (v. 2). He is running things. *It is no sin to plan ahead* (v. 3). Lay out your plans, submit them to God, and then work them out for blessing and success. *The way up is down* (v. 4). Humility and the fear of the Lord come before riches and success. *Wounds and entrapments await the person who stubbornly insists on going his own way* (v. 5). *Stay out of debt* (v. 7). Installment buying or paying on a mortgage is one thing, but getting in over your head is another. *Know the way of eternal life* (v. 6).

Small thought here
Each of us has influence on young folk around us. Your own family may be grown, but you still can model the Christian life for other young hearts and minds.

THOUGHTS AND THE REAL PERSON

Scripture, Proverbs 23:1-7
For as he thinketh in his heart, so is he.
(Prov. 23:7)

This Scripture is set against the background of a state dinner, where you are an invited guest. Indeed, everything seems to be cordial and you feel like relaxing and enjoying the occasion. For one thing, you are hungry and the table is loaded with good things. Perhaps, you also feel that if you are able to establish a friendly relationship with this ruler, you will benefit financially and may ultimately become rich. Underlying these thoughts is your conviction that you have thought the situation through and it is bound to work out. But none of these considerations is dependable as a basis for action. Verses 2 and 3 remind us that a hospitable atmosphere and good food are no proof of sincerity. The very opposite may be true!

There was company coming for dinner at a certain home. The guests were seated and all was in readiness. Mother looked at the five-year-old daughter and said, "Dearie, you may say grace for us tonight." "But Mommy, I don't know what to say!" she said. "Oh, just pray what you've heard Mommy say," the mother replied. Out of those childish lips, then, came this prayer: "O Lord, why do we have to have these people for dinner tonight?"

The second warning deals with allowing the desire for riches to become the basis for dealing with others. Riches: you don't have them, and you can't keep them, so why let the desire for them influence your relationships?

Small thought here
The *real* you is the person in your thoughts. "As he thinketh in his heart, so is he." All the more reason, then, to give God your body (Rom. 12:1), your mind (2 Cor. 10:5), and your work (Prov. 16:3). Your body, a living sacrifice; a mind that is obedient to Christ; and your works committed to your Lord, so He can establish your thoughts.

DOWN, BUT NOT OUT!

Scripture, Proverbs 24:15-34
A just man falleth seven times, and riseth up again: but the wicked shall fall into mischief.
(Prov. 24:16)

"**Y**ou can't keep a good man down!" Never is that saying more true than when applied to a child of God. There is a resiliency, not to say bounce, inherent in the believer—a quality that enables him to come back after seven defeats . . . and win! The Psalmist David believed this truth, for he wrote, "The steps of a good man are ordered by the Lord: and he delighteth in His way. Though he fall, he shall not be utterly cast down: for the Lord upholdeth him with His hand. . . . None of his steps shall slide" (Ps. 37:23-24, 31).

There are some reasons for the blessed "bounce" inherent in the believer's life. Obviously, the first and most important is that Christ indwells the believer in the Person of the Holy Spirit. Paul assured the Ephesian Christians that God "is able to do exceeding abundantly above all that we ask or think, according to the power that worketh in us" (Eph. 3:20).

There are also some commonsense reasons to follow for strength and resiliency mentioned in today's text: *Let God handle problem people* (vv. 17-20). It is not for you and me to fuss about them, nor to gloat when they get their comeuppance. *Be steady in your commitments to God and to your country* (vv. 21-22). Don't make friends with the unstable and flighty. *Tell the truth to people and about them as well* (vv. 23-26). *Take care of your work first, then relax* (v. 27). *Let God smooth out situations* (vv. 28-29). You are not His policeman. *There is no substitute for work* (vv. 30-34). The weeds are growing while you sleep.

Small thought here
Dr. V. Raymond Edman used to say, "It is always too soon to quit." Pick yourself up, dust yourself off, and go on—but always go on with God!

CLOSE FRIENDSHIPS AND OTHER HAZARDS

Scripture, Proverbs 25:1-28
Withdraw thy foot from thy neighbor's house; lest he be weary of thee, and so hate thee.
(Prov. 25:17)

My acquaintance with this verse goes back to my student days at Moody Bible Institute when one of my friends who lived down the hall posted these words on his door. Others opened their rooms for lively discussions with a dozen neophyte theologians, but not he! How friendly is *too* friendly and how thick is *too* thick? Solomon said, "A man that hath friends must show himself friendly" (Prov. 18:24). It seems that Christian friendliness depends on accepting another human being as a person (with all his virtues and faults) without intruding upon his privacy by your continual presence.

Our text mentions several ways to promote good friendships: *Don't jump to conclusions* (v. 8). Take time to get the facts straight before you give your neighbor a piece of your mind. If you take time to think, you may be spared embarrassment caused by the "open mouth, insert foot" syndrome. *Let your neighbor save face by speaking privately — and exclusively — with him in cases where the two of you disagree* (v. 9). Why should he hear from someone down the street that you have been criticizing him? *Patience and a soft answer break down most barriers* (v. 15). *Avoid gossip like the plague!* (v. 18) Rather be quiet and say nothing than to speak a word that will remain like an unhealed ulcer in another's heart for years to come.

Small thought here

The key to being appreciated is to be available and helpful when there is a need and to gracefully withdraw after the need has been met.

THE THERAPY OF CONFESSION

Scripture, Proverbs 28:1-28
*He that covereth his sins shall not prosper:
but whoso confesseth and forsaketh them
shall have mercy.
(Prov. 28:13)*

Cover-ups, from Adam and Eve to Watergate, have been the bane of the human race. Not that we don't know better; far from it. Both Scripture and our own experience tell us that the attempt to hide sin is inevitably futile, embarrassing, and ruinous. Billy Graham tells of the small boy who stole a watermelon, enjoyed it, then buried the rind and seeds in the dead leaves by the creek bed. Weeks later, the boy's father, looking for a cow that had strayed, noticed some green shootlets coming up from beneath a pile of dead leaves. He moved the leaves aside and discovered the hidden evidence of guilt. "Be sure your sin will find you out!" (Num. 32:23)

There is a therapeutic value in repentance and confession, just as there is a harmful effect resulting from "covered" sin. James wrote, "Confess your faults one to another, and pray one for another, that ye may be healed" (James 5:16).

Nowhere does the Bible advocate a chauvinist, tell-it-all approach to confession. Rather, a restrained and sensible (though always honest) approach is indicated. For instance, if you've offended a fellow believer, our Lord recommended that you go only to the sinned-against brother and settle things between you. Indeed, there is always a decent, humble way to say anything that needs to be confessed. And it ought to go without saying that some things need to be confessed to God alone, placed by faith under the shed blood of Christ and *left* there.

Small thought here
Two things need to happen before you can experience God's mercy: confession and forsaking the sin. Admit your wrongdoing, turn your back on it by faith, and watch the Lord restore you to Himself with open arms.

CONQUERING TIMIDITY

Scripture, Proverbs 29:1-27
*The fear of man bringeth a snare:
but whoso putteth his trust
in the Lord shall be safe.
(Prov. 29:25)*

Mark it down: whenever you embark on a course of action simply to gratify or get around another person, you are in for trouble. First of all, the other person can sense that your attitude is not wholehearted and sincere. Second, you have no guarantee that your action will produce the results for which you hoped. And third, your action turns out to be a trap from which you cannot escape. You can never undo those past decisions and actions.

How do you get around "the fear of man"? The answer is found in the second half of today's text: "Whoso putteth his trust in the Lord shall be safe."

• Learn to see others as they are: human beings like yourself, with burdens and needs, hurts and hopes like your own.

• Always make a conscious attempt to think with, and into, the other person's feelings. This is known as empathy. One of the nicest compliments I ever received came in the course of a hospital visit, when a young man looked up from his pillow and said, "Gee, Doc, you do know how I feel, don't you?"

• Always commit any interpersonal relationship to the Lord. He dwells within you by His Holy Spirit, and He knows your needs as well as those of the other person.

Small thought here

If you are ever afraid of people, just remember that many of those around you feel just as timid as you do! Reach out a friendly hand, get interested in another human being's problems and needs, and forget your fears.

A VALUABLE VOICE OF AUTHORITY

Scripture, Proverbs 30:1-33
Every word of God is pure: He is a shield unto them that put their trust in Him. (Prov. 30:5)

With all due respect to commentators, the Bible turns out to be its own best commentary in many cases. Take, for example, Psalm 19:7-11, where several qualities of God's Word are mentioned:

God's Word can make a difference! It is "perfect, converting the soul" and "sure, making wise the simple." The only sure way to modify human character and behavior is by applying God's Word.

God's Word is right and pure, "rejoicing the heart and enlightening the eyes." Unless an action or decision is right and done from pure motives, you won't enjoy it. How comforting and reassuring, then, should be your daily contact with God's "right" Word!

God's Word endures forever, because it is clean, true, and righteous altogether. The value of most books changes from year to year. The Bible, however, continues to be the world's bestseller because its truths never become outdated. They are just as dependable today as they were when they were written under the Holy Spirit's inspiration.

There is infinite value and unending satisfaction in God's Word. "More to be desired than much fine gold: sweeter also than honey and the honeycomb." In life's great moments . . . decision, drama, and death, you will be satisfied only with God's Word. Nothing else can equal its value and its comforting, satisfying impact.

Small thought here

The Bible provide warnings and rewards for the faithful and obedient reader. The warnings come from God's own heart and the reward is that God Himself becomes your shield. Reading and obeying God's Word makes it possible for Him to surround you with His presence.

THE LAW OF KINDNESS

Scripture, Proverbs 31:1-31
She openeth her mouth with wisdom; and in her tongue is the law of kindness.
(Prov. 31:26)

King Lemuel's description of the ideal wife and mother has never been surpassed. Shining like a jewel in this beautiful setting is his statement, "In her tongue is the law of kindness." But what is the law of kindness and how does it apply to our lives?

Kindness is love in action. Paul reminded believers, "Love suffereth long, and *is kind*" (1 Cor. 13:4). If you want to be kind, you must have a heart full of love. And if you want a heart full of love, you must open that heart to God's blessed Spirit. He wants to fill every room in your heart-house (Eph. 5:18).

Kindness refuses to seek revenge. Recall the story of Joseph, for example. When his brothers came to Egypt, seeking food, Joseph had an excellent opportunity to get even with them for all the suffering which they had caused him. Yet Joseph "comforted them and *spake kindly unto them*" (Gen. 50:20-21).

Kindness dispenses encouragement. When Rehoboam succeeded King Solomon on the throne, there was a sharp division of forces, and Rehoboam sought advice as to how to manage his kingdom. The older men said, "If thou be *kind* to this people . . . and speak good words to them, they will be thy servants forever" (2 Chron. 10:7). Good advice, but unfortunately it fell on deaf ears. Rehoboam adopted a threatening stance, provoked a rebellion, and ultimately lost out.

Kindness adjusts to the needs and shortcomings of others. Paul exhorted, "Be ye *kind* one to another, tenderhearted, forgiving one another, even as God for Christ's sake hath forgiven you" (Eph. 4:32).

Small thought here

Specialize in encouragement. There is always something about which you can encourage other people, if you just look for it.

Be thou an example of the believer in word,
in conversation, in charity, in spirit, in
faith, in purity.
(1 Tim. 4:12)

Be a Blessing
THROUGH
THE SPIRIT
YOU SHOW!

"Be thou an example of the believer," Paul commands, "in spirit." The real person who resides in a human body is called his spirit. This is the part of him that will never die, but which will live on throughout eternity. And it is this "spirit" which projects to others the feelings and moods of one's inner being. For most of us, our moods are often flawed, and as a result, the spirit we exhibit to others reflects our failings and shortcomings. Of course, the obvious alibi would be to say, "I'm only human." This, however, does not fix the mistake; it only shifts the blame. No, the real answer to the problem of one's spirit, and the need to bless others, is found in the indwelling Holy Spirit. When *He* is in control of *your* spirit, others will be blessed indeed!

Robert A. Cook

June

June is a traditional time to think about *graduation*. May I suggest, dear friend, that you think of it as a time to "graduate" from any of the emptiness you may be experiencing in your heart and life? To be sure, all of the "empty rooms" I'll be talking about won't apply to you. But check them out for size, will you, and ask God's blessed Spirit to make your heart tender and responsive to His promptings? Will this be painful? Perhaps. Will it bring blessing and prosperity to your soul? Yes! Also this month I'll be identifying some of the great thoughts that can change your life, plus some suggestions on how to handle some of the choices we all face as we walk today with the King.

EMPTY ROOMS IN EMPTY PEOPLE

Scripture, 1 Corinthians 15:1-2
Unless ye have believed in vain.
(1 Cor. 15:2)

The church is stacked high with them. Other Christian organizations have more of them than they know how to handle. You may even be one of them yourself. What? A vain professor of religion! An empty person with empty rooms. Hollow, echoing rooms. God has given me a strange, burning burden for a vast multitude of folk who are satisfactorily religious. They have a religious outlook on life and are nominally faithful to their church and to religious duties.

But they "have believed in vain"! They profess, but do not possess. Do any of the following pictures portray the rooms of your heart and life? If they do, ask the Lord Jesus to help you. If they don't, you'll be better prepared to help others who may be having difficulty in some of these areas.

You deal lightly with sin. You have enough religion to make you feel comfortable among the saints, but not enough to spoil your relationship with sin and sinners. You think that sin is "cute." You don't blush at an off-color remark or dirty story. You play with sin like a cat plays with a mouse. Only when you get caught are you embarrassed. You are perceptive about the faults of others, but are slow to admit your own. You've lived so long with some of your sins that they are not like fumes from hell but like old friends.

Small thought here

Beware when you become chummy with sin. When you no longer mourn over it. When you're puffed up about it. When you think you've really gotten away with something!

DO YOU LIE TO THE HOLY SPIRIT?

Scripture, Acts 5:1-11

Why hath Satan filled thine heart to lie to the Holy Spirit, and to keep back part of the price of the land?
(Acts 5:3)

Do you give half an offering and call it everything? Then the story of Ananias and Sapphira fits you to a tee. When you sing "I Surrender All," do you mean every word of it—body, soul, *and* things? If not, you're spelling "surrender" with a small "s". Isn't it strange how easy it is to forget that God knows how much money you spend on yourself, what kind of car you drive, what kind of clothes you wear, what type of food you eat?

Tell God the truth. He will work in your life when you do. But when you lie to God, He has no chance with you.

Have you ever subconsciously sung "My Jesus, I Love Thee," with these words, "For me, *some* of the follies of sin I resign." Lying to the Holy Spirit and to God is simply trying to convince others that God has complete ownership of your heart when He really doesn't. Do you feel obligated to put up your guard and to be just as holy as people think you are? Don't kid yourself. They're on to you! They know your faults. Drop your guard and tell them the truth. That's the first step in ceasing to lie to the Holy Spirit.

Small thought here

First John 1:9 may be so familiar that you've forgotten what it really says: God does the cleansing *when* you do the confessing. He does the changing when you tell Him the truth. He does the removing when you do the bringing.

ARE YOU EASILY OFFENDED?

Scripture, Matthew 26:33-41
Though all men shall be offended because of Thee, yet will I never be offended. (Matt. 26:33)

Are you the type of person who has to be "played up to" lest you take your ball and go home? Must you be thanked for *everything* or else you're on your way? If you're on a committee and your name is left off the program, is someone going to suffer? If someone says hello graciously to a person alongside you and merely shakes your hand, do you take offense? Do you carry a bitter spirit in your heart? You may never breathe a word about it, but that bitter atmosphere so eats its way through your life that *all* the perfumes at *all* the fragrance counters in *all* the world couldn't disguise it.

When the flesh is grieved, there's nothing else to stand on. It proves you have no real trust in God. What you do you don't do for God, but for yourself. You sing that solo not for God, but for yourself. The influence you have is not for the nail-pierced Christ, but for yourself. When your efforts are neglected, when your service is ignored, when your work is not praised, you're easily offended.

If you're depending on the plaudits of men, remember this. One day all the folks you depended on to buoy up your spirits will be gone. The only thing you'll have left then will be your relationship to Christ. Is it solid enough to hold you up?

Small thought here

You may walk with your head in the air. Things may be wonderful. But beware lest you catch yourself living for the applause of men, my friend. I would much rather wait and let God say, "Well done," than to live my life waiting for people to say it.

DO YOU NEGLECT THE MEANS OF GRACE?

Scripture, Hebrews 10:19-25
Not forsaking the assembling of ourselves together, as the manner of some is, but exhorting one another.
(Heb. 10:25)

Do you think that anyone who wants to pray all the time is a bit fanatical? Something wrong too with anyone who wants to read his Bible often? You, on the other hand, keep your prayers short and only drop to your knees in emergencies. When a particular jam is over you say, "OK, God, I can take over and manage things myself now."

What are some symptoms of neglecting the means of grace? You're not found among Christians. There's always some excuse for avoiding a spiritual meeting. You're more at ease talking about secular subjects. Bring a Bible thought up in your home . . . and an uncomfortable silence follows. You can tell exactly where the Sox or Cubs or Yankees or Angels are in the standings, but you stare blankly when thinking of the last missionary victory won.

I am amazed at how many Christians have nothing new from the Lord! They've dead-ended spiritually—no growth, no vitality! They can expertly assist you in cutting the throat of someone they do not like in the church or in Christian work, but cannot assist in feeding your soul—or theirs—from God's Word.

Small thought here
If you're not interested in the things of God, you are an empty house full of empty rooms. Unless you've had a real experience with God, how do you think you will ever enter the pearly gates? If you consistently neglect the means of grace, you had better examine yourself to see if you are truly saved.

DO YOU SHIFT THE BLAME?

Scripture, 2 Corinthians 10:1-13
But they, measuring themselves by themselves, and comparing themselves among themselves, are not wise.
(2 Cor. 10:12)

A re you in such bad spiritual shape because your pastor's sermons are boring? How easy it is to blame others for the low estate of your own soul. You cry, "I was stung by one of those so-called Christians. He took me for $2.89 and I'm mad about it!"

You blame your best friend because he isn't spiritual enough to bless your own soul. Dear friend, it's the other way around! Maybe the reason he isn't spiritual is because you're such a faker. A husband blames his wife because she is not spiritual. He laments, "She doesn't pray for me as she ought. She's not interested in my work." In heaven's name, can you expect her to respond to you if you're coldhearted and dead to God? Or a wife will say, rather languidly, "Well, if my husband were only a Christian we could have a Christian home." Your husband will become a Christian, dear lady, when you demonstrate that God is real in your life. Teenager, do you feel this way: "I could have a better Christian testimony if I were brought up by parents who were more saintly. But my parents live for the devil and I have a hard time being a Christian in such a home"? Maybe so, but when you get on fire for God, your parents will start to take notice of Christ in you.

Small thought here

Don't be more interested in excuses than changes. *If you avoid meeting God, don't blame other people.* Your home, your business, your efforts at school or work will be a carbon copy either of the coldness, deadness, selfishness, and dryness of your soul, or it will be the projection of the tender Spirit of God within you.

DO YOU EVER PREVAIL IN PRAYER?

Scripture, James 5:15-20
The effectual, fervent prayer of a righteous man availeth much.
(James 5:16)

Are you weary on your knees? More Christians don't attend prayer meetings than do nowadays. Prayer can be so discomforting, uncertain, and intimidating. You know that if you really prayed, you would weep or confess or cry out and agonize before God. And you don't dare lose your personal dignity!

If you don't get specific with God, you cannot expect any answers. Do you make sweet speeches to God and tell Him all about your theology? Speech making with God may be your strong point, but will you ever get down to your weaknesses and faults? Do you ever pray, "O God, save me from a bad temper"? Or, "Deliver me from alcohol, drugs, or tobacco," and other vices and shortcomings?

When was the last time you really agonized over the souls of men? It's been a long time since I've seen some people with tears in their eyes for souls. It's easier for some people to cry because they are angry than to cry for people's eternal destiny. Many people do not come to Christ because they don't sense that we Christians mean business. They think it's all sham with us so they do nothing about their own hearts. We need to prevail in prayer for the lost and let them know that we are really concerned about them—body and soul. Let's put away our fears and talk plainly about Jesus. If we've done our praying, God will bless what we say and do.

Small thought here

If you don't prevail in prayer, you won't see much happen. To do business with God, you must immerse yourself in His presence. If your prayers are only formal utterances to get the rubber stamp approval from other Christians, don't expect to accomplish great things for God.

DO YOU KNOW ABOUT SELF-DENIAL?

Scripture, Mark 8:34-38
Whosoever will come after Me, let him deny himself, and take up his cross, and follow Me.
(Mark 8:34)

Do you really know what it means to deny yourself? How many of us talk it but don't live it? We give grudgingly, and when we do we expect the church to fall all over us in thankfulness. Sometimes we give not to God, but to men in order to be seen of them.

We in America have not begun to know what real sacrifice means. Days will come when we will sacrifice, but in a different way. We will have to give up the things we enjoy and take for granted in order to survive. It has happened before and can happen again. Wars in this century have exacted much of our own country's resources—human and material.

Our opportunity to spread the Gospel may be severely limited and curtailed in the future. We should make the most of the opportunities *now*. Will we learn the meaning of sacrifice and self-denial when it is too late for the cause of the Gospel? Check up on yourself. How much of your time is given *voluntarily* to Christ? The evidence of a real born-again experience is that every waking moment is weighted in terms of devotion to Christ. We need to return to the Bible standard of Christian experience: "Yield yourselves to God as those who are alive from the dead" (Rom. 6:13).

Small thought here

Show me someone who is truly right with God and I'll show you someone who is keenly aware that his every moment belongs to God. Christendom today is composed of a great mixed multitude of people, thousands of whom have taken upon themselves the vows of Christianity without ever having met the transforming Master of their souls. Could you be one of them?

ARE YOU QUICK TO DEFEND YOURSELF?

Scripture, Romans 14:3-12
Why dost thou judge thy brother? . . . For we shall all stand before the Judgment Seat of Christ.
(Rom. 14:10)

Someone has said, "The harder you pray for a man who is preaching, the shorter his sermons will always seem." Yet how many times have we squirmed and complained when the preacher runs over a few minutes? We can't wait for the benediction. We're more interested in what we're going to say and do after the service is over . . . who we *must* talk to and who we *must* see before we get out of church. We never seem to recognize that Christ died for *our* faults and errors, while we are quick to expose the same failings in others.

A person who is prone to lash out shrugs his shoulders and says, "Oh, well, I blow my top now and then, but I get over it." Yes, but nobody else ever does! They bear the scars of those ill-natured outbursts. A covetous person says, "Well, I'm ambitious. I'm just built that way." Yes, but Jesus died to take away that selfish heart. A person with a haughty, egotistical spirit looks down on so-called lesser individuals and says, "Well, I've just got that kind of nature. I'm hard to get acquainted with." That really isn't the answer. Truthfully, such a person is proud. And pride—like all sin—is something God will not put up with (Ps. 101:5).

Small thought here

Convictions come not out of books but from meetings with God. Those who have met God can be real and don't have to prove their worth by criticizing others or by defending themselves. Like John the Baptist they can say, "He must increase, but I must decrease" (John 3:30).

ARE YOU CONCERNED FOR THE LOST?

Scripture, 2 Corinthians 5:11-21
For the love of Christ constraineth us, because we thus judge that, if one died for all, then all were dead.
(2 Cor. 5:14)

In some ways this is a pretty callous world. Even Christians live with a nonchalant attitude toward the lost. How many of us really care about missions? Oh, yes, we may shed a few crocodile tears when we hear a touching story, but it doesn't really change the way we live or give. Why? Because we have no heart for the lost. We go through the motions many times, but it is only to "deliver our souls" from those who pressured us to take part in the every-member canvass.

Maybe the reason we have nothing to say to our friends about Christ is that our own lives are so cluttered with sins that we would not feel comfortable counseling them about Jesus on a person-to-person basis. Yet, when the chance to be in the limelight comes, we are more than eager to serve. Sure, we'll get up and pray before the congregation. Yes, we'll give a sermon in the pastor's absence. Oh yes, we'll serve on this committee or that. But ask us to sit back and take a small or nonexistent part and we won't be there. If we have to do some thankless task that may cost us sorrow, tears, and perhaps some misunderstanding, *even for the sake of Christ*, it suddenly becomes inconvenient.

Small thought here

Don't let your religion be only something from which you will profit. That is a losing proposition. Be concerned for the lost. You may not gain the world, but you'll lay up treasures in heaven.

ARE YOU A CLIQUE FORMER?

Scripture, 1 Corinthians 3:1-9
For ye are yet carnal . . . there is among you envying, and strife, and divisions.
(1 Cor. 3:3)

The vain professor of religion, the empty person with empty rooms, will often be the one who forms cliques in the church. If this is true of you, you'll want to note carefully what our brother, Paul, wrote in 1 Corinthians 3. Some in Corinth followed Paul, some Peter, and others *Christ* (said with a holy inflection). Oh, the cliques in the church of our blessed Lord! The people who want their own way. If you're like that, it's no tribute that people follow you. It's only a reflection of their lack of intelligence and spiritual perception. There are enough naive folks in the world to follow almost anyone.

No, it isn't to your credit that you can split a church on the basis of something you want. It is only testimony to the fact that in all probability you've never met the Lord Jesus and been transformed by Him.

Our differences, dear friend, come not from the Holy Spirit but from the flesh. Vain professors and empty-room people are the ones who split churches, Christian organizations, and families. Have you been guilty of getting people to follow you in opposition to someone God has placed in a position of responsibility? My heart bleeds over the conflicts across the world generated by nothing but fleshly hearts of persons who need the touch of God.

Small thought here

If you're guilty of forming cliques, God may deal with you as He did with those who perished in the wilderness. He gave them the desires of their hearts, but sent leanness into their souls.

DO YOU SHOW THE FRUIT OF THE SPIRIT?

Scripture, Galatians 5:19-26
If we live in the Spirit, let us also walk in the Spirit.
(Gal. 5:25)

The empty-room person does not manifest the sweet fruit of God's Holy Spirit, only the works of the flesh (Gal. 5:19-21). A good deal of activity in the Christian world today stems only from the energies and the creative forces of the flesh. It is not marked by love, joy, peace, long-suffering, gentleness, goodness, faith, meekness, and temperance. Activity? Yes. Busyness? Yes. But no Calvary-love in it.

It would be helpful for you to occasionally miss a meeting and to have an hour, or two, or three, with your lovely Lord. You are not obligated to make the wheels go around in every situation, dear friend. But you *are* obligated *to meet Jesus!* If you busy yourself in your church or your youth group or whatever and come home physically and spiritually spent time after time, what good have you done if you've not met your Lord? Perhaps you are good at playing an instrument, or at singing, or at leading others, or at reading the Bible aloud, or at meeting and greeting people. Do others think of you for your ability's sake or because you have moved their hearts through the Holy Spirit's fruit manifesting itself in what you are and do?

Small thought here

Closely related to the fruit of God's Spirit is the important matter of taming your tongue. Have you ever said to yourself: "If only I could keep my mouth shut"? You'll never gain control over your tongue, your temper, or your thoughts until the sweet fruit of His Spirit is working in your life.

WHAT ABOUT ROUTINE?

Scripture, Colossians 3:12-17
Whatsoever ye do in word or deed, do all in the name of the Lord Jesus, giving thanks to God and the Father by Him.
(Col. 3:17)

If you're a vain professor of religion, you're probably more interested in routine than in glorifying God. You'll be all bent out of shape, as they say, if something goes a bit awry with your plans. While president of Youth for Christ International, I saw situations where youth leaders insisted that *everything* had to go *exactly* as they had planned. It's amazing that the young people didn't just up and walk out! So be flexible. Don't be so set on your own routine that God gets crowded out of things. You don't always *have* to have your way, do you? If you do, it's an indication that your will hasn't been broken before our blessed Lord.

Empty people are also often eager-beaver proselytizers, unusually anxious to get other people to join their church or group. Do you desire a big crowd at your meetings, but care nothing about God's presence or blessing? Do you start your meetings with "a word of prayer," which is often a highbrow way of saying, "We don't have time to pray, but let's go through the routine anyway"? Getting people to follow your group or program is a selfish goal and it grieves God. What's really important is that you point others to the Saviour!

Small thought here
What should you do? Specialize in doing the will and work of your blessed Lord. Have your heart overhauled by His dear Holy Spirit. You'll discover what a difference *that* makes.

WHAT ABOUT INWARD SIN?

Scripture, Hebrew 12:1-4
Let us lay aside every weight, and the sin which doth so easily beset us.
(Heb. 12:1)

Some who fall into the category of vain professors of religion are guilty of *inward sinning*. Our blessed Lord spoke of Pharisees who were like whitewashed graves. They looked fine outside, but inside they were full of rottenness and dead bones (Matt. 23:27). If this description fits you, you probably think nobody has caught on to your secret. But you know, God knows; and the devil, the angels, and others who aren't blind know it too!

The writer to the Hebrews reminds Christians that we have a great cloud of witnesses looking at our lives, so we are to lay aside every weight and the sin that besets us. That passage applied means as long as you're harboring sin, you will make no spiritual contribution to your generation. If you're a professor of vain religion, you're just a passing shadow, littering other lives with your refuse. When you're an inward sinner, your *spirituality* is a sham, an evil cover-up for gaining your personal desires. You are outwardly cordial to religion, but inwardly you despise it as a dull duty or nonessential. When someone seeks to engage you in genuinely spiritual conversation, you are uncomfortable and change the subject as quickly as you can—without appearing "unspiritual," of course. There's no real love for the things of God.

Small thought here
Don't be a vain professor who has become involved in the feebleness of besetting, inward sin. Get right with God, dear friend. Make your way to the Cross of our blessed Lord. Stand by faith at the empty tomb and see there the sweet evidence that Christ died and rose again for you. Let the power of Jesus' resurrection flood and fill the empty rooms of your life with His peace, joy, and victory!

FORM VERSUS REALITY

Scripture, 2 Timothy 3:1-10
Having a form of godliness, but denying the power thereof.
(2 Tim. 3:5)

Great thoughts can change your life. What is the greatest thought you've ever had? If you've never asked yourself that question, try it. You may be amazed, challenged, even inspired. Obviously, our "great thoughts," if they could all be set down, would show how different we are from one another. But from the long list that would emerge, at least seven tremendous concepts would stand out. These will be the focus of our meditations for the next week.

First, let's talk about *form versus reality*. The difference between them is no idle subject; indeed, it is as important to each of us as a jugular vein. The Bible says that if we have the Son of God, we have life. *That* is *reality*. Without it, everything else is meaningless form. It is dreadfully possible to be sitting in church, looking alive, but to actually be a spiritual corpse.

Do you really know the Lord Jesus? Does He bless you, walk with you, and guide you? Are you assured by the Holy Spirit's presence within that you are God's child? This is what matters. Not dead orthodoxy but living truth. Not busyness but the miracle of God's power working in you. One of the things I impressed upon our young people at The King's College was that to be a genuine Christian means to let the Lord Jesus into the total life, even nonreligious affairs. The Lord Jesus has to be real when you have a flat tire on the way to a wedding or when you forget to add the baking powder to the cake and it turns out to be a lovely flop just when Mrs. Gadabout is coming for tea—and she'll tell the whole neighborhood what a poor cook you are.

Small thought here

Christ has to be real on Main Street in your life, where you live and where you hurt. If He is real there, nothing else matters.

A REDIRECTED FOCUS

Scripture, 2 Corinthians 4:15-18
*We look not at the things which are seen
. . . which are temporal: but [at] the things
which are not seen [which] are eternal.
(2 Cor. 4:18)*

Whose face do you look for in a group picture? Your own? Of course, don't we all! We are all self-centered. A lot, in fact, like the disciples to whom Jesus said, "Lift up your eyes and look on the fields" (John 4:35). He said that to men who were interested in lunch. It was as though they had canvassed all the delicatessens and had finally found one that sold delicious corned beef and all the other kosher delicacies. They came back and spread out this sumptuous feast before the Lord and said, "Master, eat." But He told them that He had food to eat that they didn't know anything about. How did they react? They resented it. In effect, they said, "Isn't that a lot of nerve! Here we've been walking our feet off, trying to find a store open at noon when respectable people are taking their siesta. We finally found some great food and brought it here and *now* He says He isn't hungry!" So the Lord Jesus told them, in effect: "Fellas, you've got your eyes on the wrong thing. You're looking for groceries instead of souls. Lift up your eyes and see how many spiritually needy people there are here." Just at that moment a sizable group of men approached from the town, whose spiritual appetites had been whetted by the recently-converted Samaritan woman's missionary zeal. And Jesus said to the disciples, "There's the harvest, boys!"

Small thought here
You can, by the grace of God, change the focus of your life. When you do, He will bless you and others through you.

ACTIVIST FOR CHRIST?

Scripture, Judges 7:15-23
And the three hundred blew the trumpets, and the Lord set every man's sword against his fellow.
(Jud. 7:22)

Some time ago, somebody sent me a beautiful motto which reads, "Do something: lead, follow, or get out of the way!" It is surprising what a small amount of doing can solve. *It is possible, my friend, to become a Christian activist.* The radicals of our day have stolen the word and smeared it. But *activist* is a good word, meaning "to do something wholesome and constructive about a situation."

There is always *something* you can do. Let me illustrate: In Judges 7:21, we find Gideon with just 300 men in his army. Thirty thousand had been sent home: twenty thousand were scared and the other ten thousand were careless. Nonetheless, the Bible says of those who remained, "They stood every man in his place round about the camp: and all the [enemy] host ran, and cried, and fled." Yes, there's no substitute for personal responsibility. Each of us has his job to perform. And we can perform it best if we have learned the secret of trusting God *actively* throughout the day.

Greet your Lord in the morning. Pray before you have breakfast. Pray before you tackle you first task of the day—whether in the home, office, or schoolroom. Pray before you open a letter or answer the phone: it may be good news or it may be a bitter message from someone bent on doing you harm.

Small thought here

Yes, dear friend: do something! Pray. Become a Christian activist by praying first and then following through on what our blessed Lord says to you. Such a lifestyle allows God to work through you to accomplish glorious things for Him!

THE PRICE OF LEAD- ERSHIP

Scripture, 2 Corinthians 4:7-18
*Always bearing about in the body
the dying of the Lord Jesus, that
the life also of Jesus might be made
manifest in our body.
(2 Cor. 4:10)*

Another great thought that can change your life is that *leadership is possible though costly*. Paul said to Timothy, "The things that thou hast heard of me among many witnesses, the same commit thou to faithful men, who shall be able to teach others also" (2 Tim. 2:2). Are you faithful? "It is required in stewards, that a man be found *faithful*" (1 Cor. 4:2). If you are consistently late for Sunday School or worship services, or are not there on a regular basis, you are sending a signal to watching eyes that Sunday School and church aren't priorities in your life. If as a teacher you are unprepared and simply drone through the lesson, you are saying loud and clear that God's Word doesn't really matter much to you. Do you give up when the going is hard and the responsibility galling? The writer to the Hebrews said, "Consider Him that endured such contradiction of sinners against Himself, lest ye be wearied and faint in your minds" (Heb. 12:3). When you feel like tossing in the towel, dear friend, review again the price of leadership Paul paid (2 Cor. 4:6-7, 9). Earlier he spoke of being "pressed out of measure, above strength, insomuch that we despaired even of life" (2 Cor. 1:8). And yet the note of victory, "For our light affliction, which is but for a moment, worketh for us a far more exceeding weight of glory" (2 Cor. 4:17). Hallelujah for that!

Small thought here
Faithfulness is the price of leadership. It is a great thought that *God can make you faithful if you want Him to.*

THE CON-TEMPORARY AND THE WORLDLY

Scripture, 1 John 2:15-17
If any man love the world, the love of the Father is not in him.
(1 John 2:15)

There is a difference between contemporaneity and worldliness. I told our young people at The King's College that the Lord wants us to be sharp. I can't imagine any good purpose served by looking frumpy, freakish, or old-fashioned. Some people are really hung up on the concept that you have to be weird to be spiritually with it.

When we say "world" we don't mean the beautiful, God-made world of trees, flowers, mountains, and lakes. We are talking about the world system that bypasses God—the Garden of Eden philosophy updated: "Cheat a little; it's good for you." "Nice guys finish last." "Give yourself a break; you only go around once, so grab all the gusto you can." Worldliness cannot be defined as simply a list of "don'ts" ordinarily associated with fundamentalism. Mind you, I am a fundamentalist. I hold to the fundamentals of the Christian faith. I believe the whole Word of God and I'm going to continue to stand on it and preach it. But by the same token, I know that worldliness has gotten into the heart of many a person whose doctrine is impeccable and whose conduct seems exemplary. Worldliness can even worm its way into my heart or yours. It is the love of money or ease or position or any of a score of subtle values that sneak in and take over the leadership of one's life.

Small thought here
James said, "Whosoever therefore will be a friend of the world is the enemy of God" (James 4:4). Those are strong words. What a great and sobering thought it is that there is a difference between the contemporary and the worldly.

INFOR-MALITY AND CARELESS-NESS

Scripture, Ephesians 5:14-21
See then that ye walk circumspectly, not as fools, but as wise.
(Eph. 5:15)

Just as there is a difference between contemporaneity and worldliness, there also is *a difference between informality and carelessness.* In our day we don't stand on ceremony as we used to, and I'm glad. But there is a thin line between informality and Christian courtesy. Someone has said that courtesy is *love in work clothes.* I like that! There is such a thing as good taste and the watchful observance of the rights of others. Don't you agree? Brashness will turn off a person; friendliness will win him.

We need to guard against carelessness in dress, speech, business relationships, and at home. John G. Paton, the great missionary to the New Hebrides, tells in his autobiography of his early years in Scotland. The whole family lived in a cottage made up of a large kitchen-workshop, a small closetlike room, and a bedroom that accommodated the entire family. Paton recalls that his father would work in the kitchen-workshop and then, three times a day after meals, go into the little closet. The rest of the family knew that when the closet door was closed, Father was kneeling down and praying for them. There were eleven children and at the Judgment Seat every one of them will stand at the mention of their parents and call them blessed. That's what I'm getting at. It wasn't a formal household. You can't be very formal with thirteen people in two rooms! But it was a God-fearing, God-honoring, prayer-filled, courtesy-extending home. Don't put down your spouse in public—even under the guise of a joke. Don't be rude to a clerk or a waitress. Don't drive like you own the road.

Small thought here

Remember that as a Christian you are always on duty for your Lord. There is never a time when what you do doesn't matter.

THE LORDSHIP OF JESUS

Scripture, Romans 14:7-12
For to this end Christ both died, and rose . . . that He might be Lord both of the dead and living.
(Rom. 14:9)

This is our final meditation on great thoughts that can change your life. And here it is: *there is no substitute for the lordship of Jesus Christ.* Your whole lifestyle will be gloriously altered if you make Him Lord. Anything less than His complete control leads only to hypocrisy. He must be Lord of the mind (2 Cor. 10:5). He must be Lord of the body (Rom. 12:1-2). He must be Lord of every activity. Paul said, "And whatsoever ye do in word or deed, do all in the name of the *Lord* Jesus" (Col. 3:17). At The King's College we lost a professor by drowning, when he was caught in a sudden squall while sailing on the Hudson River. At our memorial service, the president of the college choir was among many who gave a word of tribute. He said, "The thing I remember about Dr. Arlton is that he was completely dedicated to Jesus Christ as *Lord.* To him the Christian life was really very simple: either you obey the Lord or you don't."

To make Jesus Lord means to turn over to Him every contested territory and to welcome Him into the totality of your life. The amazing thing is that when you thus invite Him, He *will* and *does* come into your heart and life to continually fellowship and sustain (Rev. 3:20). Hallelujah for that!

Small thought here
We have considered seven great thoughts that can change your life. Add your own to the list, will you? Ponder them well and invite the dear Holy Spirit to use them, and God's Word from which they are derived, to change you and make you a blessing as you walk *today with the King!*

GUIDELINES FOR HONESTY

Scripture, Romans 12:17—13:7
Provide things honest in the sight of all men.
(Rom. 12:17)

Honesty seems to be a vanishing virtue in today's culture. At a recent trial of a city official, a judge bemoaned that there seemed to be no one in the group of prosecution witnesses who could tell the truth! To a man, they all contradicted testimony previously given to the grand jury. I notice that even among believers there seems to be little concern for the truth. A Christian young person, caught in an embarrassing situation, told a "whopper" of a lie, as did her three friends. When confronted with contrary evidence, and asked why they lied, they replied, "Well, we thought that if we all told the same story, it might help."

The Bible is plain about honesty. Moses quoted God, "Ye shall not steal, neither deal falsely, neither lie one to another" (Lev. 19:11). Paul wrote that we are to manifest "the truth in love" (Eph. 4:15). Indeed, there is a loving way to tell the truth about almost anything.

What about Uncle Sam? Must we report income we know did not go into the IRS computer? The answer is yes. According to Scripture, we are to "provide things honest in the sight of *all* men" (Rom. 12:17), and be careful always to maintain "a conscience void of offense toward God, *and* toward men" (Acts 24:16). See how directly the Word of God speaks to the question of honesty!

Small thought here
The Bible is equally clear on dozens of other questions that arise. Instead of wasting time and effort mulling over all the choices in a questionable matter, go straight to God's Word and base your action on "thus saith the Lord!"

DEVELOP A CHRISTLIKE OUTLOOK

Scripture, Philippians 2:5-11
As ye have, therefore, received Christ Jesus the Lord, so walk ye in Him.
(Col. 2:6)

Do you see the world, and your mission in it, as Christ sees it? Your reaction to many questions and temptations will be settled if you ask, "How will this affect my ability to win others to Christ?" Say, for instance, that a fellow employee sees you cheating a bit on your job, loafing, or perhaps just "borrowing" some tools or materials that will never be missed. How will your coworker react if you talk with him about the Lord? Inevitably, his knowledge of your conduct will destroy any effective witness you might have. Or suppose a young man has a girlfriend he wants to win for Christ, but she remembers occasions when he was overly friendly—not to say aggressive. How will she respond to his words about trusting Jesus?

Jesus is Lord. When you and I agree with that statement and translate its truth into our lives, something wonderful happens: the process of daily living turns out to be a divine miracle, and we begin to know the meaning of "Christ in you, the hope of glory" (Col. 1:27). Christ is to be Lord of our feelings, our relationships, our minds, our motives, our entire lifestyle. When Jesus is in control, life's tough decisions become manageable and our witness, clear and effective.

Small thought here
The only reason for being different from the crowd is not to prove that you are superspiritual but to prove that God is right. You prove by your life that God's will is good, acceptable, and perfect.

MAKE BETTER DECISIONS

Scripture, Romans 8:9-17
*For as many as are led by the Spirit of God,
they are the sons of God.
(Rom. 8:14)*

A teenage girl was being reproved by her mother because she went on a high-school field trip without letting Mom know she was going. "Why didn't you tell me?" her mother asked. "What would have happened if we had to get in touch with you due to an emergency?" "Well," the daughter replied, "I was afraid if I asked, you'd say no." How like children we all are! Believer, you can trust God to give you the best. Jesus said so! (Matt. 7:7-11)

Give yourself time to mull over a decision and to seek God about it. All my mistakes have been made in a hurry. "Wait on the Lord," the psalmist urged. Your mind needs time to let an idea "ripen." What seems very attractive today may not be so alluring tomorrow after you have prayed and thought about it. Be sure of this: anything that is definitely God's will for you will grow more intense, more demanding, more attractive as you think and pray about it. "I thought on my ways," said the psalmist, "and turned my feet unto Thy testimonies" (Ps. 119:59).

You will do well to turn to God's Word each time you wonder what to do. The Bible speaks plainly to those who listen. The Holy Spirit always answers.

Small thought here

Ask yourself how a proposed decision squares up with the standard and commitments you have made previously. God will rarely, if ever, ask you to violate commitments you have made to Him and to His will as you understand it.

DEPEND ON THE HOLY SPIRIT

Scripture, Romans 8:9-17
"But the Comforter, which is the Holy Spirit ... shall teach you all things and bring all things to your remembrance."
(John 14:26)

I have a friend who says he was scared to death of calling on people as part of his church's visitation program. He would fervently hope that no one was home when he rang the doorbell and sigh with relief when he did not have to confront a stranger with the claims of Christ. When at last he realized that he could depend on the blessed Holy Spirit to speak through him (Matt. 10:20), it became a joyous experience to share his faith in the Saviour.

Our Lord Jesus taught His disciples that the Holy Spirit's ministry in believers would be to teach and to bring to their memory those things that He had said (John 14:26). Furthermore, the Spirit would guide believers into all truth and glorify God through their lives (John 16:13-14).

Remembering these key Scripture passages, form the habit of depending on the Holy Spirit. When you are under pressure, breath a positive prayer of worship, praise, and trust: "Spirit of God, I thank You that You dwell within me and that You are guiding and controlling me this moment!" When called on to witness, whether in private conversation or in public defense of your faith, just whisper a prayer and remind the Spirit that you are depending on Him to speak through you.

Small thought here

Dependence on the Holy Spirit does not require you to be pious all day long—in fact, that is impossible. You can, however, be an effective Christian in all your relationships when you look heavenward and seek the Spirit's blessing and guidance.

COMMIT YOUR TIME TO GOD

Scripture, Ephesians 5:1-16
See then that ye walk circumspectly, not as fools, but as wise, redeeming the time because the days are evil.
(Eph. 15:15-16)

A professor friend was commenting on the apparent lack of purpose of so many college students. "Come on now, Prof," I chided, "remember when you were twenty-one. You were probably doing some shifting back and forth yourself, weren't you?" He smiled, looked me right in the eye, and said, "When I was twenty-one, I had nearly finished an accelerated program that got me through college in three years! No time to drift!"

Connect your use of time with your purpose in life. The Apostle Paul spoke of having been called by God's grace "to reveal His Son in me, that I might preach Him among the heathen" (Gal. 1:16). He wanted to preach in the regions beyond (2 Cor. 10:16). He said, "I am made all things to all men, that I might by all means save some (1 Cor. 9:22). Paul's goals were all in order: to preach to the nations, to pioneer the Gospel, to know the power of the risen Christ in his life, and to be perfectly adaptable in his methods so that he could reach as many as possible.

Learn to conserve your time. Establish priorities and complete them in the order of importance. Cluster your phone calls; do your correspondence at one sitting. Learn to say no—kindly! Refuse requests that only dissipate your time and strength. Before a day ends, you may have not exhausted what you wanted to do, but you will have finished the important things and you'll feel great about it.

Small thought here

Learn the difference between spending time and investing it. Once you have determined your life goal, make every moment count in some way toward its attainment. Don't be a specialist in trivia. "This one thing I do," said Paul (Phil. 3:13). Far better that you do fewer things, join fewer clubs, attend fewer meetings, look at fewer TV programs *if* it will enable you to focus on your God-given purpose.

WHAT TO DO ABOUT PEER PRESSURE

Scripture, 2 Corinthians 10:12-17
*And be not conformed to this world:
but be ye transformed by the renewing
of your mind.
(Rom. 12:2)*

The desire to be admired and accepted by others is one of the strongest motivating forces we know. To avoid rejection we often modify our standards, our attitudes, and our conduct. This is peer pressure—the influence exerted on us by people of equal age or social status.

Peer pressure often conspires with our own natural cravings to defeat us. God-given desires, good and beautiful in their place, can be distorted and misused. The desire for love, security, approval, success, and just plain fun can be misdirected, often with disastrous results. It's extremely hard to be philosophical when your whole being is crying out for the gratification of some very human need.

The enticements to compromise with our peers often are couched in these sentiments: "Everybody's doing it." "Don't be an oddball." "What's wrong with having fun?" "Don't be chicken."

Following the crowd is not always right; in fact, it may be a big mistake. If you had been standing on the edge of the crowd in Jerusalem and heard the cry, "Crucify Him," you might have asked, "Who is He?" The answer from the worked-up mob may well have been, "Jesus of Nazareth, and He deserves to die" (Matt. 27:20-22). Think how tragically you would have erred had you taken up the same chant.

Small thought here

Be wary of any decision about which you are pressured by the crowd. Anything that has to be done *right now* merits a second look. "I didn't stop to think" is the excuse given by many whose lives have been ruined by hasty decisions. Take time to think through and pray about your decisions. Things have a way of looking different after you have prayed over them and slept on them.

CONTROL-LING YOUR BODY

Scripture, Romans 14:13-23
For ye are bought with a price; therefore, glorify God in your body.
(1 Cor. 6:20)

The Bible does not speak directly about such things as smoking marijuana or downing dry martinis. However, many of the things which we do today affect our bodies, and in turn bear directly on our spirituality and fellowship with other believers. Therefore, we need a guiding principle to help us steer a straight course through the many decisions that confront us every day.

Let's emphasize the positive rather than the negative. The question isn't, "How much can I do and still be a Christian?" but rather, "How much and how clearly can I glorify my Lord?" Paul said that whatever we do is to be done as for Him and not for ourselves (Col. 3:17, 23). The Christian life is a commitment of love between you and the Saviour. If your heart is truly His, you will want Him to control all of your life—not just what is easy to give Him.

Remember that you express your faith in Christ through your body. Some people will learn of Jesus only through what they observe in you. So it is important to ask, "What will my actions do to my effectiveness as a caring Christian? How will they affect my friends who are watching to see whether Christ lives in me?" Long ago, the wise church father Jerome said, "Do not let your deeds belie your words, lest when you speak in church someone may say to himself, 'Why do you not practice what you preach?' "

Small thought here

Paul said, "Ye are not your own" (1 Cor. 6:19), an idea contrary to all our natural instincts. The bodies in which we live are exclusively our own, some way, and what we do with them is our own business. Not so for believers. Our bodies belong to Jesus Christ and what we do with them is *His* business.

FAMILY DECISIONS

Scripture, Ephesians 6:1-4
For I know him, that he will command his children and his household after him, and they shall keep the way of the Lord, to do righteousness and justice.
(Gen. 18:19)

A young woman became concerned about the spiritual condition of her parents and her brother. They were all good, church-going people, but seemed to have no spiritual vitality. She began to pray about the matter and became convinced that, for her at least, having a daily quiet time would be the key to spiritual growth. The young lady asked to use the family alarm clock. In return for the privilege, she promised to waken the rest of the family on time each morning. Then she arose half an hour before the others to meet quietly with her Lord. Before long, the rest of the family began to show interest in spiritual things. They began to pray and have their own devotions. The family became more and more spiritually minded and both children are now active in Christian service.

You may be your family's only source of spiritual teaching. This is true not only in the case of one believer in the midst of an unsaved family; it is also true in families where all profess faith in Christ. By this I mean that you may be the one person who can show by your example that a certain scriptural truth is both real and important.

Make family decisions, then, realizing that you are God's instrument in your home. Family members will define what you really are by observing what you do.

Small thought here

Your family is something uniquely yours. These are the people with whom God has placed you and to whom you belong. And it is a responsibility which cannot be evaded. Your family may be your number one mission field. Your conduct and choices may affect their relationship to Christ.

CREDIBILITY AND BUSINESS CHOICES

Scripture, Romans 12:9-21
Not slothful in business; fervent in spirit; serving the Lord.
(Rom. 12:11)

I had a friend who foreclosed on a man who owed close to a quarter of a million dollars on his opulent home because he was six months behind in his payments. Just to tease the lender a little, I said, "How could you foreclose on a Christian?" He looked at me for a moment, then said earnestly, "This man went against the advice of his friends when he took on something far too steep for him, and he has been spending money on other things instead of meeting his obligations. His Christianity is in need of repair."

Whether or not you agree with this man's action, you surely can see that you must draw the line somewhere—and that line will probably be drawn at the point where someone asks for extra consideration because he or she professes faith in Christ. Ask God to give you compassion; then use it. But Christian compassion and softheadedness are never synonymous. You will be a better witness if people know you will always try to be honest and fair than if you are swayed by sentimental considerations.

Jesus also taught that there is a connection between a believer's good works, shining like a light in a dark place, and the observer's response, to glorify the Father in heaven (Matt. 5:16).

Small thought here

If you make a promise, keep it. If you make a commitment, honor it—even at cost to yourself or the company. True, the world is full of businessmen who operate unscrupulously and get away with it. But, as a child of the King of kings, why lower yourself to the standards of those who will spend eternity separated from our blessed Lord?

REACTION-ARY DECISIONS

Scripture, Philippians 4:4-9
Be anxious for nothing, but in everything, by prayer and supplication with thanksgiving, let your requests be made known unto God.
(Phil. 4:6)

Someone has pointed out that people are either like thermometers or thermostats. A thermometer can only react to the temperature; a thermostat controls it. With that analogy in mind, it is wise to make your plans and decisions on the basis of God's revealed will and of what you wish to accomplish within those parameters. Constructive, forward-looking decisions are more likely to be correct than choices based on reactions to past experiences.

I asked Dr. John F. Walvoord, president of Dallas Theological Seminary, his secret of administration. He said, "Whenever there is a disagreement among our top management people, I always send them back for more facts. Every problem will yield to more facts." Good idea, wouldn't you say? Most church and family fights stem from a lack of knowledge or understanding of the facts. The first law of organization is to answer the question, "*What* is to be done?" Many of us get off track and argue about the *how* and the *who* before we have a clear idea of the *what*.

Feelings may vary with conditions and temperament. If you want your decisions to be correct, stick close to the God's Word. Even when the Bible is not specific, it gives principles that will guide your thoughts and decisions.

Small thought here
Feelings are almost never a good basis for making an important decision. But you'll never go wrong when praying, "Jesus, help me now."

July

A thriving industry has developed in recent times built around books, tapes, films, and seminars on *how to be successful*—in management, sports, love and marriage, indeed almost every area of human endeavor. Our meditations this month in Joshua begin with God's surefire formula for success. And the link between meditation on God's Word and the promise of prosperity in our lives is an important backdrop for us as we move into the Book of Judges, where "every man did what was right in his own eyes," a sure sign of a life that is uninformed by the Word of God! Later in Ruth and 1—2 Samuel, we'll contrast examples of faith with disobedience to God's will and Word.

FORMULA FOR SUCCESS

Scripture, Joshua 1:1-18
Thou shalt make thy way prosperous, and . . . shalt have good success.
(Josh. 1:8)

Leadership isn't something into which you plunge all of a sudden. If you're going to be a good leader, you must learn to be a good follower. If you want to be number one, learn to do a great job as number two or number twenty-two.

Look with me, will you, at Joshua 1:8. "This book of the Law shall not depart out of thy mouth; but thou shalt meditate therein day and night, that thou mayest observe to do according to all that is written therein: for then thou shalt make thy way prosperous, and then thou shalt have good success." As this verse teaches, a real success formula for leaders begins with memorizing the Word of God. If you're talking about Scripture constantly that means you've memorized it. What's more, meditate on it day and night. That means think it over or, more in keeping with the symbolism here, chew it up. Think about God's Word in the little empty spaces each day when you are in charge of your thoughts. Last but not least, obey the Bible's truths. Make a project of obeying something from the Word of God every day. It will make a difference in your life and in its impact on others.

Small thought here

You have to be willing to be a number-two man before you can be a very good number-one man. Many a person would rather start at the top if he had his druthers, as they say, but it doesn't work that way.

YOU'VE GOT TO BE KIDDING!

Scripture, Joshua 2:1-24
*And Joshua . . . sent . . . two men to spy secretly, saying, "Go view the land, even Jericho." And they went, and came into an harlot's house, named Rahab, and lodged there.
(Josh. 2:1)*

God picks some unlikely people through whom to do His work. Rahab is a case in point. You never would have picked a person of dubious virtue who lived in a dubious place to be part of the family line involved in God's eternal plan, would you? But God did. Or had you been picking the Apostles, would you have chosen Simon Peter? Brash, always opening his mouth and putting both feet in, boasting of what he was going to do and then not carrying through. Impetuous, a shallow thinker, materialistic. "We have left all and followed Thee, what shall we have therefore?" was his question of our blessed Lord one day. Would you have picked James and John, the "sons of thunder," these men with short fuses who were also ambitious for heavenly thrones? No. You see, we wouldn't have chosen the people whom God has chosen.

Paul said that God chooses the weak things of the world and the things that are despised to bring glory to Himself (1 Cor. 1:27-28). God delights to use people who don't have anything to commend them except their faith in His almighty power. That gives me hope.

Small thought here

How much do you believe God can do? That's your only limitation. Rahab believed and she is forever enshrined in the hall of the heroes and heroines of faith. Don't emulate her weakness. Emulate her sublime faith.

YOU HAVE TO GET YOUR FEET WET

Scripture, Joshua 3:1-17
*As soon as the soles of the feet of the priests . . . shall rest in the waters of Jordan . . . the waters of Jordan shall be cut off.
(Josh. 3:13)*

How long did Joshua delay action after he'd received the spies' report? According to Scripture, Joshua rose up early the next morning and set his plan into motion. Three days later he and the other leaders went through the camp and explained to the people the procedure they were to follow in crossing the Jordan. No delay! How different, wasn't it, from the experience forty years earlier at Kadesh where ten spies came back from Canaan and reported, "We can't take the land." Only two, Caleb and Joshua, said, "Yes, we can" (Num. 13:30-33). These people had finally learned their lesson and were prepared to believe God.

Notice that the miracle of crossing the flooded river on dry ground didn't begin until somebody's feet got wet. Think of the times and situations in your own life when God's power did not really become evident until you made a commitment. Faith is not static. It's not a point of view. It's not something about which you engage in dialogue. Faith is the willingness to risk a situation on God.

Small thought here

What's the point of getting your feet wet? Just this . . . only by totally depending on God in situations beyond your expertise or control, can you become a vessel fit to display His mighty power.

LET GOD DO IT HIS WAY

Scripture, Joshua 6:1-27
Joshua said unto the people, "Shout; for the Lord hath given you the city."
(Josh. 6:16)

We come now to the story of Jericho. I wonder how I would have felt had I been one of the congregation of Israel in those days as they were ordered to march around the city in total silence. That must have been difficult. But they did it—one circuit each day for six straight days, without a word. Then on the seventh day, just as they were commanded, the people marched around Jericho seven times and, at the sound of the trumpet, shouted. In accord with God's promise and to their delight, the city walls collapsed and the Israelites utterly conquered the inhabitants. What a strange formula for victory! But it simply says to my heart, "Let God do it differently if He wants to."

We tend to routinize our lives, including our Christianity, often to our detriment. Twenty-five years ago the basis of criticism leveled by middle-aged Christians against younger believers was that they were doing things differently. And I was one of those who were doing things a little differently. Today, after the passing of the years, I find it very easy, I assure you, to look at someone who is a quarter of a century younger than I, or even younger, and say, "Oh, he's doing it differently. It can't possibly be right." But wait a minute. Maybe it is. Maybe God will use it. Look, friend, you and I don't have to be God's policemen. All we have to do is obey.

Small thought here
The secret of obedience depends on the position Jesus Christ occupies in your heart. Can you honestly say to your blessed Lord, "What wilt Thou have me to do?" And, having heard His command, will you—like the Israelites at the siege of Jericho—obey no matter what He asks?

SIN IN
THE CAMP

Scripture, Joshua 7:1-26
*And Joshua said unto Achan, "My son, give
. . . glory to the Lord God of Israel, and
make confession unto Him."*
(Josh. 7:19)

One sin can weaken your life to the point where you lose a great spiritual battle. Indeed, God says you won't be able to stand before your enemies (Satan and the world system) until you clear up the problem in the camp (your inner being). Of course we're all human, and we fail continually. Every day has its quota of blunders, failures, and sins that identify us as faulty and imperfect. How in the world can a person stand before a perfect God? By having a heart that's perfectly loving and open toward Him. As you open your life to the Lord and as you become willing to dig down under the floor of the tent, so to speak, revealing the shameful and embarrassing things you've hidden there, you'll at last have the victory that brings inner satisfaction. That's a pretty rough truth, isn't it? But friend, there isn't any other way to know God's power in your life. You may be able to slide along in a kind of never-never land of shame and pretense but you'll never mature in the faith and walk in true fellowship without "making confession unto Him."

Small thought here
Consciously identify the thing or things that you have hidden from God. Bring them to Him, verbalize them to Him, put them in His control. Let the blood of Jesus cleanse and the power of the Holy Spirit sanctify that area or areas and see for yourself the power available in a cleansed life.

ASK GOD ABOUT IT

Scripture, Joshua 9:1-27
And the men . . . asked not counsel at the mouth of the Lord.
(Josh. 9:14)

Did you ever make a big mistake because you didn't seek the mind of the Lord? That's what happened to Joshua and the Israelites in today's text. So spiritually elated were they after the victory at Ai and the building of the altar at Mount Ebal, that they failed to ask God's counsel and temporarily made a peace treaty with the deceptive Gibeonites. Fortunately, the blunder did not prove fatal.

Pray your way through the day. Pray when you wake up so you won't greet the family with a snarl. Pray on your way to school or to work. Pray before you tackle the first job of the day, whatever it may be. Pray before you answer the phone. You don't know who's on the other end of the wire. Why not be poised and ready when you say hello? Pray before you open a letter. You don't know if it's a check or a bill. There is a difference! Pray before you make a decision. Pray before you hire a person and before you fire one, if you have to. Pray before you enter into a business deal. God knows whether or not the other person has good credit or whether he's going to cheat you out of thousands of dollars. *Pray your way through the day.*

Small thought here

My mistakes have always been made in a hurry without the benefit of prayer. I can't remember anything about which I really prayed where I was misled or made a blunder. Can you? Trust God's judgment in every life decision, in every situation. Pray!

WIN A TOTAL VICTORY

Scripture, Joshua 10—11
And stay ye not, but pursue after your enemies, and smite the hindmost of them. (Josh. 10:19)

If you're going to conquer, conquer thoroughly. Every time the Israelites failed to conquer their enemies thoroughly, those enemies remained to plague them. You and I have our own Canaan to possess. Figuratively speaking, God brings us by faith across the Jordan into the land of His promise to us. But oh, the giants that need to be destroyed, the fortified cities that need to be conquered, and the territory that needs to be settled. Of course, you and I don't have to do the fighting and win the battles; God does that. But as Paul Rader used to say, the human heart is reluctant to let go and let God.

Have you thought about this truth in connection to your own life? God says to you in the face of your many difficulties, "Be not afraid because of them; for tomorrow about this time will I deliver them up all slain before Israel: thou shalt hock their horses, and burn their chariots with fire" (Josh. 11:6). Don't be afraid; you'll get the victory. So why, then, do you and I hesitate to turn things over to the Lord? Be sure of this, for every sin you leave standing in your life, you will face future embarrassment and defeat. So why not thoroughly conquer the land now, weaknesses, hangups, and all?

Small thought here

If you need to be reconciled with a person, be reconciled. Don't let the handle of the hatchet remain unburied. If you need to break a habit, break it. Don't leave the whiskey bottle around contending it's purely for medicinal purposes.

STAKE YOUR CLAIM

Scripture, Joshua 13—14
*There remaineth yet very much land
to be possessed.*
(Josh. 13:1)

What do you do when you realize you're getting old? If you're like Joshua, first of all, you still hear from heaven. "Joshua was old and was stricken in years; and the Lord said unto him" (13:1). Yes, make a practice of hearing from heaven as the days go by and getting older will be an adventure, not a calamity. Second, if you're getting older, continue to allow God to make the future dynamic. What did God say to Joshua? Verse 1 continues, "Thou art old and stricken in years and there remaineth yet very much land to be possessed." As long as you draw breath and your heart is beating, there will be land to be possessed. There will be areas of your heart house to clean. There will be spiritual territories to conquer. There will be places that have been sources of defeat and discouragement which now can become places of victory. God can do it.

Caleb is a perfect illustration of this. At age eighty-five, he was able to confidently say, "I'm as strong today as I was when I spied on the land many years ago. Now, Joshua, give me this mountain. It's full of giants and lots of difficulties, but I'll do my best. And if God gives me the victory, I'll have the victory." Imagine, eighty-five and still daring to believe God for a miracle.

Small thought here
Time is passing. You're getting a little older. Make a practice of hearing from heaven. Let God make your future dynamic and believe Him for a miracle. Hold your head a little higher and say with Caleb, "Give me that mountain," and have at it, friend. Have at it.

BE WILLING TO TAKE A STAND

Scripture, Joshua 23—24
But as for me and my house, we will serve the Lord.
(Josh. 24:15)

As Joshua came to the end of his life, he took time to remind the Israelites the way which the Lord had led them. Joshua especially emphasized the importance of the people's heart attitude: "Take good heed . . . that you love the Lord your God" (23:11). "Because," he continued, "if you go back and cleave to the remnant of those nations that remain among you and make marriages with them and they to you, and so on, know for certain that the Lord won't drive them out any more."

Victory is a heart matter, really, not an effort, not a program, not a doctrine. It's a heart given over to God. It is interesting to note that Joshua, at the very end of his life, was still taking his stand. He said, in essence, "If you don't want to serve God, choose whomever you will serve. Do you want to serve some of these gods that Jehovah has defeated in battle? All right, serve them. But as for me and my house, we will serve the Lord" (24:15). And when Joshua took a stand, the whole congregation of Israel did too. Joshua's conviction had moved a nation. The truth here is this: you motivate people on the basis of what has changed your own life, on the basis of commitments you have made in your own heart, on the basis of that for which you are willing to risk something.

Small thought here

Remember that the purpose of looking back is to look forward more clearly. Look regularly at your own life: see how the Lord has led in the past and your future steps will be on solid ground.

EXPERIENCE GOD FOR YOURSELF

Scripture, Judges 2:1-23
And there arose another generation . . . which knew not the Lord, nor yet the works which He had done for Israel.
(Jud. 2:10)

Joshua was a trusted resource used by God to bring the Israelites into the Promised Land. He stood squarely for the power, blessing, and presence of God, and so did the elders around him. But there came a day after Joshua and the elders had died when the last one who had shared in these great experiences under God's mighty hand died also. And when that time came, people began to forget what God had done and been to Israel.

You, my friend, may be God's anchor in a given situation. So be your best for Him, will you? You can keep a whole family, a whole community, a whole church, a whole organization in line for God— simply by the force of your own dedication to your Lord! It is sad, but true, that unless people experience God's power for themselves, everything else becomes merely a performance. We see this as we watch the children of great Christian leaders, children who are bored by their fathers' spiritual efforts because their own hearts have never been ignited and fueled with faith in the Lord. And so it was with the generation after Joshua . . . and, oh, the spiritual darkness that followed.

Small thought here

Be sure that you experience God firsthand in your heart and life. Otherwise religion and spiritual things will become sentimental traditions at best and tedious chores at worst. People who first become bored then become cynical, then critical, and finally bitter and despairing. Don't give Satan a foothold. Live as God's resource person all the time.

YOU CAN COUNT FOR GOD

Scripture, Judges 4—5
Deborah, a prophetess . . . judged Israel . . . and the children of Israel came up to her for judgment.
(Jud. 4:4-5)

At a time when there is increasing emphasis and concern for women's rights, these chapters will be of special interest to many. God is always willing to give you all the leadership you can stand—whether you are a man or a woman. In Christ there are no such things as men's or women's rights. The Apostle Paul wrote there is neither male nor female, bond nor free, Jew nor Greek, but that we are all one in our blessed Lord (Gal. 3:28). Now when it comes to leadership in the church, there is a place for women and a place for men. And when it comes to leadership n the home, there is a place for the husband as head and a place for the wife as the helpmeet—the one who sets the family's heartbeat. But when it comes to being an influence for God, ladies, your opportunities are unsurpassed. Your lives can count for God.

On another matter, Barak was instrumental in Israel's victory over the Canaanites, but he missed all that could have been his because of unbelief. Deborah had told him God would deliver Sisera, the enemy commander, into his hand and he would experience a great victory. But Barak told Deborah that he wouldn't go without her—he needed her for insurance, so to speak. God didn't say to Barak, "Take Deborah with you." He simply told Barak to go against Sisera.

Small thought here

Always be sure you are allowing God's direction in your life and not simply your own inclinations or desires. Barak was in on the victory, yes, but he missed out on some of the glory by not heeding the voice of the Lord. Seize the moment, follow God's directive, and enjoy the best He has for you.

GO IN HIS MIGHT

Scripture, Judges 6:1-40
The Lord is with thee, thou mighty man of valor.
(Jud. 6:12)

Do you think God can really change a person's personality? Psychologists and others who study human behavior tell us that once people reach adulthood they don't ordinarily change very much. But that view doesn't include God in the equation. Take Gideon, for example. He viewed himself as the least in his father's house and certainly didn't aspire to a leadership role. When the Angel of the Lord came to Gideon and announced that Jehovah was with him and called him a "mighty man of valor," Gideon answered in effect, "You've got to be kidding! There's been some mistake here." But the Lord replied, "Go in this thy might, and thou shalt save Israel from the hand of the Midianites: have not I sent thee?" (6:14) Gideon still wasn't totally convinced. Even after the Spirit of the Lord had come upon him and he had blown the trumpet and sent out the messengers to call the people to battle, Gideon was still saying, *"If* You're going to save Israel by my hand, show me by putting this sign upon the fleece of wool" (6:36-37).

What's the point of all this? First, God chooses whom He chooses. If you or I were to choose leaders we wouldn't have picked those whom God has chosen in centuries past, or even today, to carry out His will and work. Second, when God gives you a job He fits you for it. God gave Gideon what he needed to carry out his assignment.

Small thought here

It doesn't do any good to pray, "Lord, make me a leader," if it will do more good to pray, "Lord, help me do Your will." When you are busy doing God's will He does whatever is necessary in your personality to make you capable of obeying His Word.

MAN PROPOSES, GOD DISPOSES

Scripture, Judges 9:1-57
And upon them came the curse of Jotham the son of Jerubbaal.
(Jud. 9:57)

P eople are often surprised and horrified at the excesses and cruelties of human nature, whether it's mass executions in some parts of the totalitarian world, or the gas chambers at Auschwitz and elsewhere. But we ought to learn from Gideon's son Abimelech that evil is the lone result of the heart set on rebellion.

Abimelech planned his campaign well. He established himself with confidence among the people. He financed his rise to power through idolatry. He hired "vain and light persons, which followed him" (9:4). And then he proceeded to exterminate his opposition—his seventy brothers—all except Jotham, that is. Fortunately, Jotham seemed to have inherited some of his father's spiritual sensitivity, for he cried out in desperation against Abimelech and the men of Shechem. He told the parable about the olive tree, the fig tree, the vine, and finally, the bramble. And Jotham said, "Let fire come out from Abimelech, and devour the men of Shechem . . . and let fire come out from the men of Shechem . . . and devour Abimelech" (9:20). It was a prophetic utterance, for only a short time later Abimelech was killed when a woman cast a millstone on his head during a battle, fracturing his skull. It says, "Thus God rendered the wickedness of Abimelech, which he did unto his father, in slaying his seventy brethren" (9:56).

Small thought here
Be under no illusion, my friend. Human nature is capable of any extreme—once you decide to pursue your own will apart from God. Stick to God's will and be willing to take responsibility when you have a chance.

MEAN WHAT YOU SAY

Scripture, Judges 11:29-40
*And Jephthah vowed a vow unto the Lord.
(Jud. 11:30)*

It seems to me that one of the great truths in this text is an emphasis on the importance of keeping one's word to God. "I have opened my mouth unto the Lord," Jephthah said, "and I cannot go back" (11:35). I don't know what possessed Jephthah to make such an ill-advised promise to God, which in essence can be translated, "If God will be with me and give me victory, I'll offer as a sacrifice the first person or thing that walks out my front door when I return home." Upon his victorious return, who should meet Jephthah but his daughter and only child. Commentators debate whether Jephthah literally sacrificed his daughter or whether he committed her to a life of celibacy and spiritual service. Whatever the case, Jephthah made a rash promise, one which God didn't dictate.

Many times we make promises to God that are not really part of His directive will. They are our own ideas. By the same token, we'd better mean what we say to God. As King Solomon wrote, "When thou vowest a vow unto God, defer not to pay it; for He hath no pleasure in fools: pay that which thou hast vowed. Better is it that thou shouldest not vow, than that thou shouldest vow and not pay. . . . Neither say thou before the angel, that it was an error" (Ecc. 5:4-6). In other words, don't say, "God, I was just kidding." You can't do it that way. God holds you responsible for what you promise Him.

Small thought here
Give some thought today to your unfinished business in this matter of promises. Ask yourself, "What have I promised to my Lord in years past that I have not yet fulfilled?" This will be a fruitful exercise and one that will enrich your life.

SAMSON, WEAK STRONG MAN

Scripture, Judges 13—16
[Samson] wist [knew] not that the Lord was departed from him.
(Jud. 16:20)

Samson is a prime example of what happens to a person who never overcomes his besetting sin. You know, of course, that different people have different weaknesses. Samson's was women. For you, it may be a towering pride and ego that will not be denied. Or it may be greed and love of money. Perhaps it is sloth and the love of easy living. Yes, each of us knows his own weaknesses and the faithful Spirit of God reminds us of them from time to time.

Samson started out on a course which reinforced his weakness for more than twenty years. After he had a date with a Philistine girl, he said to his parents, "Get her name for me, for she pleaseth me well" (14:3). The controlling philosophy of Samson's life was "I want what pleases me and I will have it at any cost." Because his weakness was sex he proceeded to find gratification for those desires wherever he could. It led him finally to the lap of Delilah, the shearing of his hair, the putting out of his eyes, and finally, the loss of his life.

Small thought here

The answer to all of this, of course, is to commit your weaknesses to God. Paul wrote, "Most gladly therefore will I rather glory in my infirmities, that the power of Christ may rest upon me" (2 Cor. 12:9). Besetting sins can be transformed into divine strengths by the grace of God.

BEWARE OF FALSE RELIGION

Scripture, Judges 17:1-13
And his mother said, "Blessed be thou of the Lord, my son."
(Jud. 17:2)

False religion *lives easily with human frailties, faults, and sins.* In Judges 17 we read that a man named Micah had stolen 1,100 shekels of silver from his own mother. When he heard her cursing the person who took it, he said, "Sorry about that, Mother dear," and brought back the silver because he didn't want to be included in his mother's curse.

Second, false religion *lives easily with parental permissiveness.* His mother said, "Blessed be thou of the Lord, my son." Is this a normal response of a mother who wants her son to be an upright person, a man of integrity? Micah was obviously beyond the age when he could have profited from a spanking, but he received no rebuke whatsoever. Indeed, his mother was indulgent, even accepting, when he returned the money.

Third, false religion *lives easily with dishonesty.* Though the mother knew the money had been stolen, she started to make excuses. "I had wholly dedicated the silver unto the Lord from my hand for my son, to make a graven image and a molten image: now therefore I will restore it unto thee. . . . And his mother took 200 shekels and gave them to the founder, who made thereof a graven image" (17:3-4). Whatever happened to the other 900 shekels?

Small thought here

Beware of actions and attitudes that reveal something less than real godliness, such things as dishonesty, moral permissiveness, and the breakdown of personal integrity. Only a real meeting with God can cure the heart overcome by false religion.

DOING YOUR OWN THING?

Scripture, Judges 19—21
Every man did that which was right in his own eyes.
(Jud. 21:25)

What is the relationship between what we call common sense and the direct guidance and sovereignty of God? Like a dirge the statement, "Every man did that which was right in his own eyes," recurs in the latter chapters of the Book of Judges. From one story of treachery to the next, the people of Israel fell deeper and deeper into sin, farther and farther from God's holy standards, more and more into lawless self-interest.

Do you think that "I want to do my own thing" is a new statement attributable only to the younger generation? My dear friend, the concept of doing what is right in one's own eyes, doing one's own thing, in other words, is as old as the human race. Satan used that idea as the basis for his initial temptation of Adam and Eve in the Garden of Eden. Here you have it in today's meditation. And what is the result? A shifting moral pattern. A de-authorization of those who ought to have responsibility and the ugliness and devastation of moral perversion that follows the loss of values. All of these things happen every time you depend *only* on what you think is right.

Small thought here
How truly the Bible says, "There is a way that seemeth right unto a man, but the end thereof are the ways of death" (Prov. 14:12). Our standards must be founded in "the Law and the testimony" (Isa. 8:20). "Let God be true," wrote Paul, even though every man is found to be a liar (Rom. 3:4). Common sense is great . . . when it is directed by God.

WHEN OPPORTU- NITY KNOCKS

Scripture, Ruth 1—2
Then said Boaz unto his servant that was set over the reapers, "Whose damsel is this?"
(Ruth 2:5)

Two thoughts occur to me as I read these two chapters. One is that what life and its sorrows do to you is generally up to you. The other is that life's opportunities are up to God, but you alone determine what to make of them. Elimelech, a man from Bethlehem-Judah, went to live temporarily in the country of Moab—he and his wife, Naomi, and two sons—because of a famine in the land. The short visit stretched into permanent residence. Long enough for Elimelech's two sons to marry girls from Moab. Long enough for Elimelech to die. And long enough for the two sons to die, leaving Naomi widowed and living with her two daughters-in-law. I'm struck with the fact that when Naomi returned to Bethlehem, she said, "Don't call me Naomi, call me Mara," which means, "I'm bitter." Her troubles had gotten the best of her. Just remind yourself, my friend, that sorrows and troubles come to us all. Whether you become sweet and mellow or hard and bitter depends in large part on your attitude. Think it over.

And what of submissive Ruth, who found herself a virtual stranger in a foreign land? She went to glean in the fields, which was the right of poor people under Jewish custom. Whatever bits of grain the reapers dropped—in their haste to reap—she could pick up. As it happened in God's providential plan, the field belonged to Boaz. He noticed Ruth, heard about her loyalty to her mother-in-law, and showed her special favors. Obedience in opportunity means God's provisions.

Small thought here

Yes, opportunity comes from the Lord, and it is up to you to obey Him by taking full advantage of His open doors. Ruth did and she became a part of a very special family tree—that of our blessed Lord.

TIME TO VENTURE, OR WAIT?

Scripture, Ruth 3—4
*Then said [Naomi], "Sit still, my daughter,
until thou know how the matter will fall."
(Ruth 3:18)*

There's a time to venture in faith and a time to wait in faith, and it is a wise person who knows which is which. Reading the final chapters of Ruth, it's not hard to tell that Naomi was setting up her daughter-in-law with a fine eligible bachelor named Boaz. Matchmakers have indeed been with us since ancient days, but there's more here than matchmaking. Ruth had espoused her mother-in-law's God. She had said, "Whither thou goest, I will go . . . thy people shall be my people, and thy God my God" (1:16). And now Ruth was engaged in actively trusting God through the divinely led promptings of Naomi. Part of that active trust was to make herself available in God's way and time. Many believers pray, "O Lord, use me. O Lord, guide me. O Lord, help me." But that's where it stops. There is no venturing in faith, no moving ahead. The best rule is first pray until God speaks to your heart; then obey, in other words, *act*. Venture in faith today.

The second rule is be willing to wait while God works. "Sit still," said Naomi to Ruth. Yes, there's a time to venture and a time to wait, but how do you know the difference? By trusting the faithful Holy Spirit to tell you when to move. And by letting the peace of God rule in your heart whatever the circumstances.

Small thought here

The Holy Spirit will give you perfect peace on any matter concerning God's will. When the Spirit urges you to move, do it. But when He tells you to wait, then wait. You will find that either way you'll have the energy or patience you need.

LET'S TALK ABOUT FAMILIES

Scripture, 1 Samuel 1—3
For this child I prayed; and the Lord hath given me my petition which I asked of Him. (1 Sam. 1:27)

How do you plot a course for your family? Note three crucial elements evident in today's text: first, prayer; second, commitment; and third, responsibility.

Hannah prayed earnestly. In agony of soul, she cried out to God. And God answered her prayer beautifully, in the arrival of a baby boy, Samuel. Prayer makes the difference between a family full of God and a family full of self. This has to be more, by the way, than a prayer now and again in formal fashion. It takes that personal intercession where mothers and dads, sons and daughters, are each seeking God.

Second, commitment. Hannah vowed that Samuel would be lent to the Lord as long as he lived (1:28). Would you be willing to give your child to God—perhaps even for overseas missions service? Would you be willing to give up your home, your financial security, your prestige? My dear friend, the willingness to give your most precious possession to God, and yourself with the gift, makes all the difference.

The third factor, of course, is responsibility. Eli knew that "his sons made themselves vile and he restrained them not" (3:13). Eli was a chief priest, and, as such, it was his responsibility to say who would serve with him in the tabernacle. He *could* have, and he *should* have, said, "Boys, if you're not going to walk with God, you're not going to work here either."

Small thought here

My father said to me on many occasions, "Boy, as long as you have your feet under my table I'm responsible to God for you." And parents, it's true!

VISUALIZE GOD'S PRESENCE

Scripture, 1 Samuel 4—7
Samuel spake unto all the house of Israel, saying, "If ye do return unto the Lord with all your hearts . . . He will deliver you out of the land of the Philistines."
(1 Sam. 7:3)

Whenever the presence of God is out of place you can expect trouble. The Israelites certainly had their share of it and so did the Philistines because the ark, the visible presence of God in those days, wasn't where it was supposed to be. The Philistines at last decided to do something about it. So they got oxen, filled a cart with golden idols as a kind of trespass offering, and sent them along with the ark up the coast to Beth-Shemesh. When the men of Beth-Shemesh saw it, they sacrificed to God and rejoiced that the ark was back. But Samuel warned the Israelites that possession of the ark was not enough. "If you really want to get right with God," he said in effect, "you have to put away your strange gods and serve Him only. Then He will deliver you from the Philistines" (7:3). And that is exactly what happened. Israel repented; a battle ensued; and the Philistines were terribly defeated. Why? Because the Lord "thundered with a great thunder on that day upon the Philistines" (7:10).

Where and how is God visible in your life? Are you, like the ark, a symbol of God's presence to a watching world? Or has your spiritual vitality been "kidnapped" by that same system, leaving you powerless and troubled?

Small thought here
What needs to be cleaned out of your life so that God can bless you? Samuel pinpointed the sin among the Israelites and laid down the alternatives—strange gods or the one true God. When the people did spiritual housecleaning and when Samuel prayed, God's blessing was restored and His victory was given.

GIVE US A KING!

Scripture, 1 Samuel 8:1-22
And the Lord said unto Samuel . . . "they have not rejected thee, but they have rejected Me."
(1 Sam. 8:7)

One of the great snares you and I must guard against is the desire to be like other people. "Make us a king . . . like all the other nations," the Israelites demanded (8:5). Indeed, what distinguishes you as a Christian is that *you're not to be like other people*, but like Jesus. This, of course, doesn't mean you should stick out like a sore thumb. Some of the most spiritual people I know are also the most human, not averse to a hearty laugh or enjoying a good joke, but full of compassion and the Holy Spirit. Yes, the Lord Jesus didn't die to make you like everybody else. He died and rose again and lives today to make you like Himself.

Here's another thought: if you want the right perspective on your relationship with God, just review what He has done for you and for others in the past. Samuel took time out to review for his people what God had done for them—all the way from Moses to the present (1 Sam. 12). He reminded them how God had been their King; had answered their prayers; and had heard them when they repented from their sinning, time and again delivering and restoring them.

Small thought here

Samuel said, "Ye said . . . 'Nay but a king shall reign over us,' when the Lord God was your King" (12:12). One of the best ways to keep your life in perspective is to think about the elements that reveal the leadership and lordship of your God.

THE PROBLEM WITH SAUL

Scripture, 1 Samuel 15:1-35
To obey is better than sacrifice, and to hearken than the fat of rams.
(1 Sam. 15:22)

Saul sounded perfectly selfless when he returned from his first victory over the Ammonites, exclaiming, "*The Lord* hath wrought salvation in Israel" (11:13). As you watch him develop, however, the element of self shows up more and more. He's too interested in himself; too interested in what people will say; too interested in making sure that his commands are obeyed. Saul's problem was not that he wasn't fit to be king, but that he never allowed God to be God in his life.

The last straw occurred when God told Saul that the wickedness of the Amalekites had surpassed divine mercy. It was time for judgment, indeed total annihilation, and the Lord commanded Saul to do the job. But Saul failed to follow orders and took the king of the Amalekites alive. After all, in those days, if you won a battle over another nation you brought back the enemy king so you could gloat a little and maybe torture him a bit before killing him. "Besides, the glory would be nice," Saul must have reasoned. Saul also spared the best of the sheep, oxen, fatlings, and lambs—also forbidden by God. When confronted with his disobedience by Samuel, Saul blamed the people for something he orchestrated (compare verses 9 and 15). What's more, he was so blinded by self-interest that he actually thought he had done right: "I have performed the commandment of the Lord" (15:10). Oh, what trouble we unleash when we don't see past ourselves to God!

Small thought here

My friend, neither an alibi, which Saul was trying to use here, nor the best of "reasons" can ever excuse disobedience. And be very sure of this: unless you put self on the cross, crucified with Christ, so that your blessed Lord is really Lord, you'll end up disobeying Him at some point when self asserts, "I want my way."

ANOINTED OF GOD

Scripture, 1 Samuel 16—19
And the Spirit of the Lord came upon David from that day forward.
(1 Sam. 16:13)

Look for God's surprises. Jesse thought that his firstborn or one of his other sons would be God's choice for Israel's next king. No one had thought of the youthful and ruddy David, out in the fields tending sheep—no one, that is, except God.

Notice also some of the results of being anointed of God. First, He enables you to be a blessing to other people. David played his harp and sang to calm Saul when the king was upset. Second, when the Spirit of God fills your life, you have courage for the impossible. Who would have thought that a young man, not grown up enough to carry a set of adult armor into battle and proficient only with a slingshot, would be used of God to vanquish the giant Goliath? And yet he was. Third, when you are divinely anointed, as David was, you can expect enmity between you and those who do not obey God. The more David behaved wisely and lived a life of blessing among people, the more King Saul resented him. Don't be surprised if ungodly and carnal people resent you if your life is Spirit-filled. Expect opposition without getting a martyr complex, but also expect God's blessing.

Small thought here

The Lord's presence also resulted in Jonathan cleaving to David in a beautiful friendship and fellowship. One of the most precious things in the world is to have a God-given friend. Thank Him for such a blessing.

LOVE GOD? LOVE OTHERS!

Scripture, 1 Samuel 21—24
Then Saul said unto his servants . . . "all of you have conspired against me."
(1 Sam. 22:7-8)

It must have been hard getting along with someone as egotistical as King Saul, let alone work for him. He blew his stack and had a pity party at the same time when he realized that David—now on his "most wanted list"—was hiding in the area and his servants had not informed him. It must have been sad indeed to hear the king of all Israel pout, "There is none of you that is sorry for me" (22:8).

Friend, beware of a growing interest in your own concerns. You'll find the closer you get to God, the more you'll be interested in the welfare of others. "Look not every man on his own things," said Paul, "but every man also on the things of others" (Phil. 2:4). Every time I've really sought the Lord and have waited before Him until my own heart was blessed and made tender, there was immediately a proportionate increase in my concern for other people. Not something that I'd tried to work up, but rather the result of God's working in my heart.

Another thought here: you can afford to let God straighten out the situation. David made one of the wisest moves of his career when he kept back from killing Saul when he had a chance there in the cave. His gesture of merely cutting off the skirt of Saul's robe was proof that there was no evil in his heart.

Small thought here

You don't have to get even with other people. " 'Vengeance is Mine. I will repay,' saith the Lord" (Rom. 12:19). Give God time with people. He knows how to take care of every situation. Just make sure your own heart is right.

HANDS OFF GOD'S ANOINTED!

Scripture, 1 Samuel 26—27
I would not stretch forth mine hand against the Lord's anointed.
(1 Sam. 26:23)

If you had been in David's place, what would you have done when you came upon Saul and all of his chief captains sound asleep? You gave him a chance once before when you found him sleeping in the cave. But he's still trying to kill you. Now what? David's exemplary attitude was this: "God is going to take care of this man. His time will come to die or he's going to perish in battle. However it happens, I'm not going to be the one to lay my hand on the Lord's anointed." It's important to realize that the Lord's anointed applies to people today whom God has chosen for Himself, not just to the kings of Israel in Bible times. Be careful before you criticize your pastor. Be careful before you gossip about another child of God. Let God take care of His servants and tend to your own heart.

There is some question in my mind as to whether the Lord really wanted David to go down to Gath for safety or whether David got discouraged and rationalized, "Saul's going to get me anyway. I'd better get out of here for good" (27:1-3). You don't have to go into the "land of the Philistines" to get away from your troubles. There is a godly way to cope with your troubles without compromise.

Small thought here
Things went from bad to worse for David. His own followers threatened to stone him, as we learn in 1 Samuel 30. Though he was in a bad way, David did not give up. He remembered his sure foundation and "encouraged himself in the Lord his God" (30:6). When you get to the end of yourself and when people get to the end of you, look to the Lord and He will see you through.

PUT YOURSELF IN GOD's HANDS

Scripture, 2 Samuel 1—5
David waxed stronger and stronger, and the house of Saul waxed weaker and weaker. (2 Sam. 3:1)

I get upset when someone opposes me, don't you? Or when someone lies about me or tries to harm me. And I think I need to be reminded, as do all of us, that if we profess to be in the Lord's hands, then we had better be in the hands of the Lord. Right up to the time of Saul's death, David maintained an attitude of respect for Saul because he was God's anointed.

Notice all of the politicking and finagling recorded in these five chapters. The Bible is so clear, factual, and impartial that it tells people's faults as well as their good points. Here's somebody trying to set up a kingdom and somebody else trying to curry favor with David, and all of the pulling and hauling that goes along with a "power play." Aren't you glad there are no politics in churches? Oh, my. "We'll do this, and he'll do that, and we'll elect the other person and then we'll get our way in such and such a program." How people scheme! Don't be upset at the tendency of other people to do a little politicking. Just keep obeying God until He sees to it that you find your proper place in leadership. David kept right on serving the Lord no matter the circumstances. He also kept the right attitude toward other people, even his critics and enemies, who conspired against him. And God established him!

Small thought here

Put yourself in God's hands and He'll keep your attitude right and protect you from every power play that could possibly be brought against you. You are unsinkable when you're in the hands of God. Hallelujah for that!

GOOD INTENTIONS AREN'T ENOUGH

Scripture, 2 Samuel 6—9
*Uzzah put forth his hand to the ark of God
... and God smote him there for his error;
and there he died.*
(2 Sam. 6:6-7)

You and I can learn from Uzzah; he had good intentions but made a fatal mistake. What cost him his life? In transferring the ark from the house of Abinadab to Jerusalem, King David ordered it brought up on a new cart; that was *his* mistake, for it was supposed to be carried by men of the priesthood. Uzzah and Ahio, Abinadab's sons, guided the cart, and Ahio walked before the ark. When they came to Nachon's threshing floor, Uzzah reached out to steady the ark because the oxen stumbled. It was a seemingly noble reason, yet God smote Uzzah there "for his error" (6:7). What error? Before the trip started, someone had to put the ark on the cart. That responsibility probably belonged to Ahio and Uzzah. Had they loaded it so carelessly that it could not stand the journey? Perhaps. But there's further reason here for Jehovah's sudden judgment on Uzzah. God's holiness doesn't need protecting. The minute we lay our hands on the glory of God, we will suffer for it. God said, "I am the Lord; that is My name; and My glory will I not give to another" (Isa. 42:8). So what we have here is a tragic example of someone whose good intentions were not properly directed.

Now let's look at a *positive* example. About two years after this tragedy, David wanted show kindness to the house of Saul "for Jonathan's sake" (9:1). So he found Jonathan's son, a lame youth named Mephibosheth. David brought him in and made him a member of his own household. He showed kindness to a descendant of a person who had hunted him and had often tried to kill him. What a blessed way to follow through on a *good intention!*

Small thought here
Give your intentions to our blessed Lord, will you? Ask Him to help you show a little kindness today to someone who has wronged you, and see what He'll do *for you* in the process!

SOWING AND REAPING

Scripture, 2 Samuel 11—12
*Wherefore hast thou despised the
commandment of the Lord, to do
evil in His sight?*
(2 Sam. 12:9)

The story of David's adultery with Bathsheba falls strangely upon our ears today, when almost every bestselling novel contains at least one bedroom scene. Psalm 51 is a record of what David felt *after* he repented. But we don't have any record of his motivation or his thoughts *before* he sinned. All of which reminds me that God holds us responsible for our actions, no matter our intentions. You and I *know* that we yield to temptation because we are inclined to by nature and because we have never decided that it is tragic, costly, and often fatal to indulge in sin. But sadly, despite knowing the facts, we sin anyway.

David discovered afterward how tragic his mistake was. First, it cost the life of an innocent man; second, according to Nathan the prophet, it gave the enemies of God a chance to blaspheme (2 Sam. 12:14). Next, it cost the life of the child that was born; and finally, it sowed the seeds of tragedy, dissension, hatred, murder, and strife in David's own family. What a horrible harvest from a few moments of folly.

Small thought here

Sin pays terrible wages—to believers and unbelievers alike. An unbeliever may yield to temptation because he doesn't care or he thinks he can get away with it. But for a believer who has faced with God the ultimate folly and tragedy of sin and has yielded his life to the lordship of Jesus Christ, sin has an entirely different look to it. Think about the harvest, dear friend, before you give in to the tempter.

HAIR WAS HIS HANG-UP

Scripture, 2 Samuel 14:25—18:33
*Absalom stole the hearts of
the men of Israel.
(2 Sam. 15:6)*

It's interesting that the very thing of which Absalom was so proud—his beautiful hair—at last became his undoing. The text says that there was no one in Israel to be so much praised as Absalom for his beauty (14:25). He was the glamour boy of his day. Not only that, Absalom knew something about press agentry and public relations. He prepared chariots and horses and fifty men to run before him and rose up early and stood beside the way of the gate. When anyone had a problem, Absalom would say, "If I were king, you'd get a better shake." Sheer politics. Absalom also knew how to conspire. The conspiracy against his father lasted twenty years and eventually succeeded. Finally when David was run out of town, ambitious Absalom proclaimed himself king. But then his chicanery backfired. The beauty of which he was so proud became his undoing, as did his politics. And God brought him down to an untimely death—hung by his hair in an oak tree, there to be finished off by General Joab.

Small thought here
The Bible is filled with stories of people who failed because they refused to correct their besetting sins. Greed was never corrected in Lot's life. Lust was never corrected in Samson's. Ambition was never mastered in Absalom's. Watch out for the besetting sin that has never been left at the Cross.

TRUE SACRIFICE WILL COST YOU

Scripture, 2 Samuel 24:1-25
Neither will I offer burnt offerings
unto the Lord my God of that which
doth cost me nothing.
(2 Sam. 24:24)

You would think that when God had established David in his kingdom that he would have no more problems with people, conspiracy, or opposition. But this just wasn't so. Expect opposition when you are doing God's work. I used to tell our Youth for Christ workers to expect things to go wrong once in a while and then when they did, to look up and pray, "Lord, this is just what I was looking for. Help me now." And He will.

David made two great mistakes in his life. One was the matter of Uriah the Hittite; the other was numbering all the people of Israel and Judah, which obviously involved some self-will and a desire for personal glory. God was angry that David conducted such a census. But David was as great a repenter as he was a sinner and psalm writer. After David repented, he wanted to make an offering to the Lord. David went to Araunah the Jebusite and said, "I need your threshing floor as a place where I can offer a sacrifice." Araunah said, as you would have if the king had talked to you, "Go ahead, take it; it's yours. You're the king." But David replied, "No, I will surely buy it of thee at a price." So he bought the threshing floor and the oxen for fifty shekels of silver and offered burnt offerings and peace offerings to the Lord (24:25).

Small thought here

The value of your service for God very frequently is directly proportional to what it costs you. David said, "I'm not going to offer a sacrifice to God that didn't cost me anything." What is your service for God really costing? Is it a sacrifice or just a pleasant hobby?

Be thou an example of the believer in word, in conversation, in charity, in spirit, in faith, in purity. (1 Tim. 4:12)

Be a Blessing
HAVE A DIRECT WIRE TO HEAVEN

"Be thou an example of the believer," Paul said, "in faith." Faith, to use my own definition, is the quality of risking a situation on God. *You can risk the situation on God when you are sure of His Word.* "Faith cometh by hearing, and hearing by the Word of God," said Paul. When asked why the church was filled an hour before prayer meeting, a Korean believer replied, "We are looking up promises that we can throw up to heaven when we pray!" *You can risk the situation on God when you are sure of His power.* He is "able to save to the uttermost," and "He knoweth how to deliver the godly out of temptation." When you thus risk the outcome of a situation on God, you are of great encouragement and blessing to those around you. They say, "God did it for him, and I can trust Him too!"

Robert A. Cook

August

Pitirim Sorokin, celebrated sociologist at Harvard University, said that we're living in a "sensate culture." That's a fancy way of saying that the world you and I live in is morally and spiritually rotten. Depravity and corruption are the order of the day. Wherever you turn—books, magazines, movies, or prime-time TV—it's there like the smell of rotting flesh! Corinth was rotten too. To be called a "Corinthian" was not intended as a compliment. The Christians at Corinth had problems too. In our meditations this month, we'll be looking at some of the things Paul wrote about in his two letters to those troubled saints in "Sin City."

THE RIGHT PLACE TO START

Scripture, 1 Corinthians 1:1-31
Christ the power of God, and the wisdom of God.
(1 Cor. 1:24)

The quality of your relationship with people is directly proportional to the quality of your relationship with the Lord Jesus Christ. Thus, the closer you are to Him, the better will be your relationships with the people around you, and vice versa. The reason the believers at Corinth were having difficulties with each other was that they had allowed their vision of the Lord Jesus to dim. And so, Paul had to remind them at the very outset of this letter, dealing with critical issues of the church, that the Lord Jesus Christ is the center of life itself. He said, "We preach Christ crucified, unto the Jews a stumbling block, and unto the Greeks foolishness; but unto them which are called, both Jews and Greeks, Christ the power of God, and the wisdom of God" (1:23-24).

To apply this truth personally, I think you and I must make sure that our hearts are fixed on the Lord Jesus. We tend to think of life in terms of jobs to be done, and indeed we all have responsibilities. Let's just remember not to leave Christ out of the picture, for He is the One who has given us the responsibilities to begin with.

Small thought here

Spend time with your Lord—worshiping and adoring Him, confessing your needs and failures to Him, and drawing nigh to Him in honesty of soul. At that point, I guarantee you that all Scripture says about Him will come alive—because your own heart has been thrilled with your Saviour. Make Christ the center of your life today, this week, and for the rest of your life.

HOW TO GROW

Scripture, 1 Corinthians 2:1-16
The natural man receiveth not the things of the Spirit of God . . . because they are spiritually discerned.
(1 Cor. 2:14)

If it's true that the secret of your relationship to people is your relationship to the Lord Jesus, it is also true that your growth in relationship to people depends entirely on your growth in the Lord Jesus. Paul speaks of the *natural man* (2:14), which is another designation for the unsaved, dead-in-trespasses-and-sins person. But there are also, as you may know, two kinds of Christians: carnal, baby Christians, still on the milk bottle, so to speak; and spiritual, grown-up, believers, feeding on solid food.

How do you grow up into Christ, as the Apostle Paul commands in Ephesians 4:15? Very simply by "desir[ing] the sincere milk of the Word, that ye may grow thereby" (1 Peter 2:2). In other words, if you want to grow, get into the Word of God—and let it get into you. Read and reread Scripture. The first reading lets you scan it for fact. The second reading lets you understand it for truth. The third, fourth, fifth, and tenth readings *let the truth get into your life.*

Small thought here

Pray Scripture back to God. Whatever He has said to you, repeat to Him until your heart is warm and tender with the truth. Also try sharing Scripture with another person as soon as you can. You'll find that you grow in the process. And so will your relationships with fellow believers.

THE TEST OF FIRE

Scripture, 1 Corinthians 3:1-23
And the fire shall try every man's work of what sort it is.
(1 Cor. 3:13)

The whole matter of building one's life in our blessed Lord is much more important than most Christians realize. Paul begins this sermon to the Corinthians with the figures of speech from agriculture: planting, watering, and harvesting. That, of course, is the way God works. The Christian life and ministry is a living thing. But when it comes to realizing that there is a divine design, a godly plan, and a sovereign set of specifications for a believer's life, Paul changes the figure to architecture and writes, "According to the grace of God, given unto me, as a wise master builder, I have laid the foundation, and another buildeth thereon. But let every man take heed how he buildeth thereupon. For other foundation can no man lay than that is laid, which is Jesus Christ" (3:11-12).

Yes, it's very important how we build our lives by our actions and attitudes because these "construction materials" will one day be tested by fire at the Judgment Seat of Christ (3:13). Let's be sure that our "house" will not crumble due to "bad bricks"!

Small thought here

How do you find and fulfill God's plan for your life? First, yield to God every day. He is the master architect and will use the Holy Spirit within you to superintend the work. Second, as you deliberately and daily obey the Lord's will, you also become a part of the building process. Together God and you are achieving an eternal design, something which will be shining and God-glorifying a million years from now. Hallelujah for that!

FAITH-FULNESS IS REQUIRED

Scripture, 1 Corinthians 4:1-21
Moreover it is required in stewards, that a man be found faithful.
(1 Cor. 4:2)

Consider the word *faithful* as it relates to the stewardship God has given to every one of us. You, my friend, are one of the most important factors in God's plan, no matter how seemingly insignificant your task. It is His desire that you willingly minister His truths to your public—the people who know, trust, and respect you. You are a minister even if you have no pulpit. You have a unique public, perhaps not a congregation, but family, coworkers, friends, the person in the hospital bed next to yours. Remember too that the ways in which you differ from other people are not accidental, but by divine design. "Who maketh thee to differ from another? And what hast thou that thou didst not receive?" (4:7) *Who you are* and *what you are* and *where you are*, and the gifts and talents you have or do not have— these are God's provisions. Don't fight them. Use them. The uniqueness of your personality can be a source of real glory to God if it's yielded to Him.

Small thought here

One of Paul's most tremendous statements is, "I beseech you, be ye followers (that's our word *imitators*) of me" (4:16). Your goal and mine has to be such a close daily walk with Christ that other people can imitate it with perfect safety. Remember, people imitate you anyway. Make sure that the "you" whom they are imitating is "Christ in you, the hope of glory" (Col. 1:27).

CLEANUP TIME AT CORINTH

Scripture, 1 Corinthians 5—6
And such were some of you, but ye are washed.
(1 Cor. 6:11)

I think we're a little naive in our approach to human nature most of the time. We keep our own failings carefully under wraps, at least in public. But when someone else displays a glaring defect of character or conduct, we raise an evangelical eyebrow and say, "Oh, I never thought that of him. He seemed to be such a good Christian." Did you ever hear that before? Did you ever say that before?

Look at these Corinthians: they suffered from moral breakdown—all different kinds of moral breakdown, as a matter of fact. They were suing one another, fellowshipping with fornicators, cheating their neighbors. And these were the Christians! Certainly Paul did not fail to point out these people's faults. But then he came to their rescue by reminding them of their position in Christ and urging them to live in light of that standing. In essence he said, "Don't you remember? Some of you were just like that! But now you are washed, sanctified, and justified in the name of the Lord Jesus and by the Spirit of our God. You need to live on the level of what God has already done for you. When you trusted the Lord Jesus Christ, He did away with all that old stuff. You don't have to live like spiritual prostitutes anymore." Don't be surprised when somebody else has faults. Help him to get closer to Jesus. And realize you aren't perfect yourself.

Small thought here

The secret of modifying conduct is obeying the Holy Spirit. As you obey the One who dwells within you, He'll make you holy and spiritual. He'll change your perspective. Yield to Him today, dear friend!

YOU DON'T HAVE TO BE HAPPY

Scripture, 1 Corinthians 7:1-40
For what knowest thou, O wife, whether thou shalt save thy husband? Or how knowest thou, O man, whether thou shalt save thy wife?
(1 Cor. 7:16)

Now and again a married couple comes to me and says, "We're not happy together." Frequently I'll reply, "Well, you're not required to be happy; you're required to be faithful, godly, and full of the Holy Spirit. Are you?" Happiness is a by-product, ladies and gentlemen. It's not something you seek. Husbands and wives can't simply decide to be happy. It just doesn't work that way. As the years pass and the children come along and the burdens of life bear down, sometimes there's too much month left over at the end of the money. Illness takes its toll. A few gray hairs sprout here and there. You find out why they call it middle age, because that's where it shows first. Combine all this and what becomes of the marriage relationship if there is not one solid, challenging, satisfying purpose that a husband and wife have set as their goal? What is the cement that holds it all together? It is ministering the things of God to your mate. That doesn't happen by sitting down and saying, "Now I'm going to minister to you." And it doesn't happen by walking around either early in the morning or late at night with a gloomy "spiritual" expression and saying, "Don't disturb me; I'm having my devotions." You minister spiritually to your life partner by living Christ before him or her every moment of every day.

Small thought here

Your biggest job is to bless your mate and thus to sanctify your relationship—physical, emotional, and spiritual. When you fulfill this God-given purpose, your home will be a haven within and a beacon without.

TWO IMPORTANT TRUTHS

Scripture, 1 Corinthians 8—9
Take heed lest by any means this liberty of yours become a stumbling block to them that are weak.
(1 Cor. 8:9)

Two points of view contained in 1 Corinthians 8 and 9, taken together, help wrap up this package of truth. The first is found in 1 Corinthians 8:13: "If meat make my brother to offend, I will eat no flesh while the world standeth, lest I make my brother to offend." The key words here are *my brother*. The second is found in 1 Corinthians 9:27: "I keep under my body (the Greek word here is a prizefighter's term meaning to beat black and blue), and bring it into subjection: lest that by any means, when I have preached to others, I myself should be a castaway." The key words here are *I myself*. What is the relationship between these verses?

Your responsibility as a follower of our blessed Lord is twofold: first, to make sure that you place no stumbling block in the way of your Christian brothers and sisters. In other words, your conduct should edify the family of God. Second, your attitude toward every matter of choice not clearly revealed in Scripture should be one that keeps your ministry to others untarnished. Beware: it's possible to be disapproved and set on a shelf, even after you have been successfully busy in God's work.

Small thought here
Put these two concepts together and God's will is certain. I am responsible *to my brother*—to encourage him rather than to discourage him, to build him up rather than to tear him down, to guide his footsteps rather than to cause him to stumble. And I am responsible *to myself*—to keep on becoming the man or woman God planned me to be.

EXAMPLES WE CAN FOLLOW

Scripture, 1 Corinthians 10:1-14
Now all these things happened . . . and they are written for our admonition.
(1 Cor. 10:11)

God's Word is so plain. That's why I think it's to our criticism and sometimes to our shame that we try to make it difficult to ascertain His will. Today's text clearly says that the wilderness journey of the Israelites still serves as an example for you and me in our journey to heaven. What can we learn from this forty-year sojourn?

First, we should not desire evil things (10:6). Don't go on wanting something you know is not really the will of God. Many years ago I remember a church member asking me rather naively, "Well, Pastor, couldn't I just divorce my husband and marry this other man and then ask God to forgive me?" No, friend, it doesn't work that way. Second, we should put nothing in God's place (10:7). You don't have to have a little tin god on the shelf to be an idolater. People make idols of money, things, pleasures, success, and other people. Putting anything or anyone in place of God is sin. Third, we should not become victims of moral breakdown (10:8). Even if the world around you is giving in, don't make the same fatal step. It cost 23,000 Israelites their lives. Fourth, we should not tempt God (10:9). Don't say, "Well, I'll see if I can get away with this." God cannot be fooled. Finally, we should not complain or murmur (10:10). Complaining is in the same league with idolatry, evil desires, and moral breakdown and its consequence is also the same.

Small thought here
Let me say it again: the history of God's ancient people is given to you and me as an example—so we won't make the same mistakes they made. But let's not stay in a spiritual vacuum. Let's replace these negative traits with a desire for what is good, a wholehearted love of God, moral purity, and contentment.

DISORDER AT HIS TABLE

Scripture, 1 Corinthians 11:17-22
When ye come together in the church, I hear that there be divisions among you. (1 Cor. 11:18)

In the early days of the New Testament church, the observance of the Lord's Supper was preceded by a common meal called the "love feast," to which each believer brought his own contribution of food and shared it with others. Its purpose was twofold: to relieve the hunger of the needy saints and to provide opportunity for those who "had" to share with the "have nots." Within the Corinthian fellowship a great disparity of economic status existed. Probably a few were quite well-to-do and could bring rich food and wines. Others were poor and had only a piece or two of coarse bread and cheese and possibly a small jug of sour wine. Instead of sharing, however, some of the wealthy gorged themselves with some of the delicacies of the "pot luck" while the poor munched their "peanut butter sandwiches."

Needless to say, the "love feast" could not have been a great success under those carnal conditions. Some were satiated or drunken, and others were bitter and jealous. Paul rebuked them sharply, reminding them that if they were interested only in eating, they could do that at home. The tension and resentment created by the Corinthian situation hindered any fruitful exchange of confidences, confessions, or counsel. Furthermore, it left believers in no frame of mind to think of the meaning of the Lord's death for them or to partake meaningfully of the emblems that represented His body and blood.

Small thought here

How sad, my dear friend, that a service that had been the means of bringing revival blessing through unity now served as an occasion of stumbling and division among believers.

UNITY
IN THE
BODY

Scripture, 1 Corinthians 12:12-31
*As the body is one and with many numbers
... so also is Christ.*
(1 Cor. 12:12)

The body of Christ is more than an organization, dear friend; it is an *organism*, united by a vital conviction. At Corinth the Christians had lost sight of their essential oneness in Christ's body. Jealousy and rivalry had developed over the possession and exercise of spiritual gifts which God had bestowed on the church, as described in verses 4-11. Each boasted about the gift that he possessed and tended to look down on those who did not have his particular endowment. Those who possessed the more obvious and spectacular gifts, such as tongues, were most boastful of all. Paul told them that the gifts were *all* the result of God's grace, by His Spirit, and that no one could claim credit for whatever powers or abilities he possessed. The church, said Paul, is the body of Christ, and each individual believer is like some part of the body. Each member is an important, integral part of the whole. Therefore, each member should honor fellow members. There must be no divisions or factions (v. 25) which would bring sickness and sap the church's vitality. A person who has the gift of administration ought not to be considered inferior by one who can teach.

Each of these abilities conferred by the Holy Spirit is to equip the church for a complete ministry. A business firm has craftsmen to make its product, salesmen to market it, and maintenance personnel to care for the plant. In a similar fashion, the blessed Holy Spirit places in the church persons with a wide variety of spiritual gifts to carry forward its ministry in the world.

Small thought here
The key to this passage, it seems to me, is *understanding* and *accepting* that God is sovereign. The pressure disappears when you remember that God the Holy Spirit equips people, individually, as *He* wills.

THE GREATEST GIFT OF ALL

Scripture, 1 Corinthians 13:1-13
And now abideth faith, hope, charity, these three; but the greatest of these is charity. (1 Cor. 13:13)

During World War II, many orphaned babies in France were cared for in overcrowded hospitals. Though adequate food and physical care were provided, the mortality rate was astonishingly high—until it was noted that the babies who died had the least personal attention. When *all* the infants were given attention, the death rate dropped dramatically. The now well-known principle of "tender loving care" was discovered. Human nature requires more than just food, shelter, medication, and exercise for survival. Love provides a cushion for the hard knocks of life and a reason for living.

First Corinthians 13 is often considered a self-standing passage—a charming poem written as a tribute to love. But it must not, my friend, be taken out of its setting and be viewed only in that light. For it is an integral part of the whole discussion of the matter of spiritual gifts (1 Cor. 12—14). Paul reminded the Corinthian believers of their great need for love—a quality far more influential than the spiritual prowess they professed to have attained by some startling manifestation of wisdom or power, and a "more excellent way" of winning and holding them together as fellow members of Christ's body.

The important qualities of the Christian life are not the powers we exercise but the motives that control all our behavior, don't you agree? *Love* is essential. *Faith* is vital, for without it no one can please God (Heb. 11:6). *Hope* is founded on faith, for belief in God's promises produces the confidence that He will keep His Word by accomplishing all He has included in salvation.

Small thought here

The promise of the Lord's return, with the accompanying victory, the abolition of sin and death, and the establishment of His kingdom, is the hope that Christian faith engenders. Faith and hope and love—they abide and will endure. But the greatest of these is love.

HE LIVES!

Scripture, 1 Corinthians 15:1-58
He rose again the third day according to the Scriptures.
(1 Cor. 15:4)

In his book, *The Passover Plot*, Dr. Hugh J. Schonfield tried to explain away the resurrection of Christ and His deity by saying that Jesus had planned His own crucifixion and contrived to be given a sleeping potion to put Him into a deathlike trance. This writer dared to call the Son of God an imposter, liar, and cheat who schemed to carry out the Old Testament messianic prophecies and win a following for Himself among the Jews. The Gospels—according to Schonfield— were a web of fabrications calculated to carry out the illusion of the Resurrection. This blasphemous book is just one in a long line of futile attempts to discredit the truth of the Resurrection. The very day our blessed Lord arose, Jewish leaders in Jerusalem began spreading the story that Jesus' disciples had stolen His body (Matt. 28:11-13) in an attempt to fulfill His resurrection predictions.

When Paul preached in Athens, the very idea of resurrection "turned off" the philosophers (Acts 17:32). Greek philosophy taught that everything physical is inherently evil. Even if a body *could* be resurrected, they reasoned, such an event would hardly be "good news." The Corinthians shared this pagan viewpoint.

Unfortunately, 1 Corinthians 15 has been read too exclusively at Easter, when many who come to church do not understand it; or at funerals, when most people are too occupied with grief to fully appreciate what is being read. It was written to correct the notion that resurrection of the dead is impossible. If Christ was the victim, not the conqueror of death, how could He give eternal life to men?

Small thought here

Our blessed Lord Jesus was the firstfruits of resurrection; the resurrection of believers will be the full harvest. Then the corruptible *will* put on incorruption; the mortal, immortality (v. 53). Hallelujah for that!

PARTAKERS IN PROBLEMS

Scripture, 2 Corinthians 1:1-24
We were pressed out of measure, above strength, insomuch that we despaired even of life.
(2 Cor. 1:8)

I am excited about 2 Corinthians because it fairly bristles with thrilling, challenging truth every place you look. My desire is to pass along some of that same enthusiasm to you throughout the remainder of this month.

The main point of today's text, to me at least, is found in the word *partakers*. Have you ever asked, "Why does all of this have to happen to me?" with the unsaid portion of that question understood to be, "especially when I'm such a nice person." Paul said, "We would not, brethren, have you ignorant of *our* trouble which came to us in Asia." (Trouble is *always* personal.) He continued, "We were pressed out of measure, above strength, insomuch that we despaired even of life." *Out of measure* means "I'm getting more than my share." *Above strength* means "I can't stand any more." *Insomuch that we despaired even of life* means "if I have to take any more, it's going to kill me." We've all felt this way at one time or another, but somehow we manage to fight off the defeat and discouragement and keep on keeping on. In fact, human nature by itself is capable of rising to magnificent heights of heroism, bravery, and endurance. But what happens when troubles become too great to humanly bear? That's when you, as a believer, become a focal point to the unbelieving world. It's especially then when non-Christians will watch to see whether the Lord Jesus Christ is going to carry you beyond the give-up point, beyond the point at which other people cave in. And when He does, they're going to say, "*That's for me.*"

Small thought here
O my friend, go through it, not just to get through it, but to bring others to the Lord Jesus Christ.

FORGIVE AND FORGET

Scripture, 2 Corinthians 2:1-17
Wherefore I beseech you that ye would confirm your love toward him.
(2 Cor. 2:8)

A splinter in your finger, though tiny, can cause an infection that will endanger the whole body. Likewise, an unforgiven sin can poison the life of the one who commits it and may be a source of bitterness and alienation in an entire church. I spent enough years in the pastorate to know that for a fact! Paul was aware of this and in his second letter to the Corinthians he dealt with the case of a man who had committed a grievous offense against the church. Apparently this person had repented of his sin and had sought forgiveness, but the church had been slow to grant it.

Paul urged that the Corinthians forgive the man, lest he be swallowed up by his sorrow and return to sinning. Converted from paganism, the man had probably fallen into one of the sins that had been a common indulgence in his unsaved days. He had already been disciplined (v. 6) by being cut off from group fellowship. Now, if he was to be made once again a useful member of the Christian community, the church must forgive him freely and completely. Indeed, he should not only be forgiven, but encouraged (v. 7). Only with the united support of his fellow brothers and sisters in the Lord could this man abandon his former evils and move forward in his new life in Christ.

Small thought here

The first element in forgiveness, my friend, is love (v. 8). Forgiveness *also* means that the forgiver *forgets*. To say, "I'll forgive but I won't forget," is tantamount to saying that you will never truly forgive at all. Think about it, will you?

IN HIS LIKENESS

Scripture, 2 Corinthians 3:1-18
Our sufficiency is of God; who also hath made us able ministers of the New Testament.
(2 Cor. 3:5-6)

Second Corinthians 3 is a glorious chapter, beginning with a thought about lives changed from the darkness of sin and ending with a thought about lives changed into the very image of our blessed Lord. What a transformation when Christ enters a human heart. But thank God that the work doesn't end there. Paul, the Corinthian Christians, and all of us who have trusted Jesus will one day reflect the glory of God Himself (3:18).

Another truth that I always marvel about when I look at 2 Corinthians 3 is the flat-out statement that we are not "sufficient of ourselves to think anything as of ourselves; but our sufficiency is of God" (v. 5). Did you know that it takes God to manage your thoughts? Dwell on that for a while, will you? Ask God to manage your thoughts so that He will make you an able minister of the New Covenant, the New Testament, the new relationship between God and man. Oh, that's a ministry of life and glory. It's a ministry of boldness and openness. It's a ministry of the heart, not simply of the head. And it's a ministry of transformation.

Small thought here

Realize that in and of yourself you can't think one thought worthy of eternity. But the Holy Spirit of God, managing your thoughts, will lead you to a ministry that shines and blesses, one that transforms other lives step by step. Hallelujah for that!

BE OPEN WITH GOD

Scripture, 2 Corinthians 4:1-18
[We] have renounced the hidden things of dishonesty.
(2 Cor. 4:2)

Has it ever occurred to you that every Christian has a ministry? You *do* have one, you know, whether you're using it or not. You have an effect on everyone you meet, for good or ill. Either you move people closer to Jesus or farther away from Him. Besides a ministry, you've also received God's mercy. He's in the process of seeing you through so that you don't collapse on the job. Indeed, God does not give you work to do without also the strength to do it.

What makes for success in the ministry? Paul claims the key is renouncing all dishonesty. If you want your ministry to be effective, pinpoint that which you have been keeping hidden from the gaze not only of other people, but also from your own conscious mind and—hopefully, you thought—from God. God won't make any discoveries about you in the next fifteen minutes; He already knows all about you—past, present, and future. So tell Him the truth. Leave it right there with Him at Calvary and it's no longer hidden; it's covered—by the blood. Oh, what a difference!

Finally, what happens when you try to minister your own way? My good friend Lloyd Cory talks about a person living according to Finagle's Law, which translated means, "He who finagles often gets finagled in return." You don't have to be crafty or try to work things out your own way. God's way, in God's power, is an unstoppable combination!

Small thought here

Don't try to get your way by guile or smartness or by some power play that leaves your opponents in the dust. Just be what you are by the grace of God. Give out His Word just as it is written; don't handle it deceitfully. Manifest the truth. Do it and see what God will do through you. What makes your ministry successful? Being open with God!

HAVE YOU THOUGHT ABOUT DYING?

Scripture, 2 Corinthians 5:1-21
We have a building of God . . . eternal in the heavens.
(2 Cor. 5:1)

A friend of mine recently asked me, "Bob, have you ever thought about dying?" Jokingly, I replied, "Yeah, I think about it all the time. But I'm planning to postpone it for another thirty years!" Seriously now, can you talk about dying without flinching? Paul could, and I think anybody who understands the truth of 2 Corinthians 5 can too. That's because our perspective is not merely on the here and now, but on eternity: "We have a building of God, an house not made with hands, eternal in the heavens."

This whole chapter holds together for one reason: Paul starts with "we know," and ends with "He hath made Him to be sin for us." How do we know anything about eternity? Because of what the Lord Jesus Christ has done for you and for me. What else do we know? We *know* there's a job to do: "we persuade men" (v. 11). We *know* there's a driving force behind our mission that derives from the very heart of God: "the love of Christ constraineth us" (v. 14). We *know* Christ's love is rooted not simply in emotion but in the solid fact of Calvary: "He died for all" (v. 14). We *know* there is a new relationship between anyone who trusts the Lord Jesus Christ as Saviour and everything else in the universe (v. 17). And we *know* that we've got a new job: we are ambassadors for Christ (v. 20).

Small thought here

What a blessed outlook for our future! No longer the morbid fear of dying. If Jesus tarries, we will, of course, experience physical death. But oh, the solid awareness that we are living, not just for the here and now, but for eternity because Jesus Christ died and rose again.

IS YOUR IMAGE GENUINE?

Scripture, 2 Corinthians 6:1-18
Giving no offense in anything, that the ministry be not blamed.
(2 Cor. 6:3)

As a Christian, you are always on stage. People are constantly forming judgments about you. Vastly more important, they are evaluating Jesus Christ as they see Him in you.

As the Lord's representative, His "minister," Paul says you are to make certain "that the ministry be not blamed." Ask yourself: "Am I careless with the truth?" "Am I prone to break promises—not show up for engagements, play fast and loose with commitments?" "Am I more eager to talk about Christ than to live for Him—especially when it costs or hurts?" If you are living what you profess to believe, if Jesus Christ is filling your life with His presence and power, you will not only honor your blessed Lord but also gain the kind of respect that is eminently worth having. Not that you'll always be warmly accepted or willingly agreed with! Just the same, remember that Christians who are ridiculed and given a wary glance are usually those whose lifestyles do not quite measure up to what they say.

Which brings us to the question, "What identifies a Christian?" There are many answers, of course. It would appear that Paul sweeps through the whole long list and comes to the bottom line: "in much patience." Patience is an indisputable mark of the Christian. To be patient means, literally, "to stay down—to be willing to wait on God." In other words, don't blow up ... and don't give up either. More on patience tomorrow.

Small thought here
Consistent, day in and day out patience is humanly impossible to achieve. It requires the person of the Lord Jesus Christ, with you and in you.

PATIENCE IN DISTRESS

Scripture, 2 Corinthians 6:1-18
*In all things approving ourselves as the
ministers of God in much patience.
(2 Cor. 6:4)*

Distress is the normal human reaction to trouble and sorrow. Paul felt distress. On one occasion he was "pressed out of measure, above strength," so much so that he "despaired even of life." When you became a child of God, the Father did not make you less of a human being than you were before. You still cry when you are hurt, bleed when you are cut. What God does do, my friend, is to make you a victor in your situation, to make you Exhibit "A" to a watching world, revealing what *He* can do.

I recently heard of a young woman who several years earlier received news that her fiancé had been killed. As she boarded the airplane to attend his funeral, her heart was filled with sorrow and anger. "Why did God do this . . . wreck my whole life and our plans?" She wondered. But on that sad flight, she at last turned to her loving Heavenly Father. "God," she prayed, "please give me something from Your Word that will see me through this." And the Word came to her immediately and sweetly, "Call upon Me in the day of trouble: I will deliver thee and thou shalt glorify Me" (Ps. 50:15). Her rage, despair, and complaining began to melt away and peace filled her heart. Not that following days were without tears. Some time later, this woman returned to her fiancé's hometown, where a building was being dedicated in his honor. As she saw the beautiful structure engraved with her beloved's name, a flood of memories swept over her and she prayed, "O God, help me again, help me *now!*" At once there came to her the blessed reassurance, "I am the Lord, I change not," and again her heart was filled with peace.

Small thought here
Beloved, let God handle your distresses. Whatever they are, turn them over to Him. He knows. He cares. And He *will* deliver.

TRUST GOD AND SING PRAISES!

Scripture, 2 Corinthians 6:1-18
As the ministers of God . . . in stripes, in imprisonments.
(2 Cor. 6:4-5)

T he classic example of how one can live to the glory of God, even in prison, is found in Acts 16, beginning at verse 23. "When they [the accusers] had laid many stripes upon them, they cast them [Paul and Silas] into prison, charging the jailor to keep them safely. Having received such a charge, [the jailer] thrust them into the inner prison and made their feet fast in the stocks." What a terrible, discouraging predicament, yet "at midnight Paul and Silas prayed, and sang praises to God" (v. 25). They said, in effect, "Lord, we are Your servants. We have sought to be obedient to Your commands. So we are going to trust You to see us victoriously through this experience. And *that's* something to sing about!" You know what happened. The prisoners heard their joyful testimony. The foundations of the prison were shaken by a great earthquake and the doors were flung open. The prisoners were free! No wonder the jailer was ready to take his own life, knowing the blame that would fall on him if his charges escaped. "But Paul cried with a loud voice, saying, 'Do thyself no harm, for we are all here.' Then he [the jailer] called for a light, and sprang in . . . and fell down before Paul and Silas, and brought them out, and said, 'Sirs, what must I do to be saved?' " (vv. 28-30)

In all probability, nobody is about to throw you behind bars. But you may be a captive of your circumstances. Perhaps you are hurting from wounds that others have inflicted. For you, this is the hour of darkest midnight. What ought you do? Trust God and sing praises! In so doing, you commend yourself as His servant.

Small thought here
If you want a believable Christian testimony, you must face the fact that there *will* be some terribly hurtful and unwarranted treatment accorded you. How you stand up to it will be a visual demonstration of God's wonderful keeping power.

PURITY OF CHARACTER

Scripture, 2 Corinthians 6:1-18
Approving ourselves as the ministers of God . . . by pureness.
(2 Cor. 6:4, 6)

Paul begins his line of reasoning regarding credibility in the Christian life with a subject that is not popular in our day—pureness. Let us say you purchase a carton of milk. You bend back the top and the contents smell sweet. But you look inside and there, to your horror, you see a dead fly afloat in the white sea. Though the milk itself is suitable for drinking, you'll certainly return the entire carton to the grocery store and demand a new one because of that nasty fly! *Similarly, one little bit of defilement can spoil the effectiveness of your testimony.*

If you ask, "How do I get my testimony to mean something?" Paul would answer, "Make sure your life is pure. Let there be not the slightest unconfessed sin." The reason for desiring purity in heart and life is not that you might gloat over your superior attainments, but so that your words about Jesus are believable. But is pureness really possible? Yes. First John 1:7 indicates *it is possible* to "walk in the light." As the Holy Spirit brings to your awareness anything that is out of line with God's will, confess it, forsake it, and let Jesus make you clean. Whenever I find myself straying from God's will—by a flash of temper, a touch of greed, a show of pride, or whatever it may be—it is such a delight and relief to say, "God my Father, I know Jesus died for this sin of mine. Handle it, please. Cleanse and forgive me and make me what You want me to be." In that moment, one can sense the calm, peace, and purity that God gives His child.

Small thought here

Do you desire to live a holy life? Trust Christ. He is made unto us "wisdom, and righteousness, and sanctification, and redemption" (1 Cor. 1:30). It is blessedly possible to appropriate these qualities on a daily basis.

THE FORCE OF TRUTH

Scripture, 2 Corinthians 6:1-18
*Approving ourselves as the ministers of God
. . . by the word of truth.
(2 Cor. 6:4, 7)*

By the word of truth" (v. 7) we are enabled to give a believable testimony. Truth, like pureness, is part of God's leverage to move people to Himself. Certain clear requirements are necessary:

• First, we must *know* the truth. This is much more than intellectual perception or truth-telling. The only way to *know* the truth is through a personal, intimate relationship with the Person who is the embodiment of truth, the Lord Jesus Christ. "Ye shall know the truth and the truth shall make you free. . . . If the Son therefore shall make you free, ye shall be free indeed" (John 8:32, 36).

• Second, we must *obey* the truth. God's Word is a transmission, so to speak, from our Commanding Officer. God is the one who directs the "troops." He does this through His Word administered by the Holy Spirit. Every time we disobey those orders we harm the relationship between ourselves and the Lord. We do not lose salvation, but we break the slender thread of fellowship that binds us to Him.

• Third, we must *speak* the truth in love (Eph. 4:15). There is always a loving way to tell the truth. If, for example, you say to your girlfriend, "When I look at you I lose all sense of time," she'll be impressed. But if you say, "Your face would stop a clock," there is no telling what she will do to you! Love should so permeate truth that the end product is powerful in its ability to convince.

• Fourth, we must *live* the truth. Paul said: "By the manifestation of the truth [we are to be] commending ourselves to every man's conscience in the sight of God" (2 Cor. 4:2). The word *manifestation* means, roughly, "wrapped up in a human package"—a visible demonstration of God's truth.

Small thought here

When you obey God, your life becomes a sermon that speaks directly to people's consciences. Often we are unaware of how effective the language of the life can be!

IS YOUR REACTION CONVINC- ING?

Scripture, 2 Corinthians 6:1-18
As deceivers, and yet true.
(2 Cor. 6:8)

The word *deceivers* (v. 8) has the overtone of seduction; it pictures a person who leads someone astray. Inevitably, if your life is counting for the Lord Jesus, other people who don't know Him will object to its impact on them. Let me illustrate: I once held a series of meetings at a naval base in the Caribbean. At a special meeting for youth on Sunday afternoon, a young lady was among those who responded to a straightforward Gospel message. That evening I noticed a man enter the auditorium and slump into a rear seat, obviously very angry. Later this officer of high rank came up to me and said, with a volley of profanity, "What have you done to my daughter?"

"Sir," I said, "I'm afraid I don't know what you mean."

"Oh, yes, you do," he countered. "She came home and said she had been 'saved' or something like that. And I demand to know what you have done to her." I had been told about this man, including the fact that he was a heavy drinker.

"You are an Episcopalian, aren't you?" I asked. Startled, he replied, "Why yes, but what has that got to do with it?" "Just this ... if you had read your prayer book recently you would have known that everything I said to your daughter about Christ, sin, and salvation is all there. The theology is sound. It's beautiful and scriptural. These are the truths you subscribe to every time you go to your church. And these are the truths your daughter has chosen to embrace." At that, his attitude and countenance softened. He even attended some of the meetings and seemed to enjoy them.

Small thought here
When that father first approached me, he saw me as an imposter, or "deceiver," misleading his precious daughter. But I wasn't misleading her or anyone. I was telling the truth as it is in Christ. It is vital that we respond or react convincingly ... empowered by His Spirit.

FIGHTING THE WRONG THING

Scripture, 2 Corinthians 6:14–18
"Come out from among them, and be ye separate," saith the Lord.
(2 Cor. 6:17)

People are hemmed in or hindered, not by circumstances, but by their own selves. Several years ago, a student at The King's College came to me, deeply concerned, and said, "You know, Dr. Cook, these rules at the college are terrible. I think we should do away with them because they're hindering my Christian growth and testimony." I answered, "Well, my dear friend, I'm not in a position to do away with these rules. Let's talk to the Lord about them instead." And we did. Some time later, the same young fellow confessed in a chapel service, "Though outwardly I've been fighting the rules and the administration, inwardly I realize that I've been fighting against God. I got right with God and things have been different."

One of the greatest lessons you and I will ever learn is that Christian separation is not primarily from things or by things; not from people or by people. Christian separation has to do with your own heart and mine. Isn't that right?

Small thought here
My friend, you are not limited by anything except your relationship with God. Cut clean from the world and sin and let the Lord have His way. And when He does, He will dwell in you, walk with you, and be God and Father to you (vv. 16, 18). What a difference! Where does it all start? When you realize the heart of the problem is inside, not outside.

TRUE REPENTANCE

Scripture, 2 Corinthians 7:1-16
Ye sorrowed after a godly sort.
(2 Cor. 7:11)

Some people show their sorrow for sin and their repentance by going forward at a meeting or by raising their hands in response to an invitation. The Corinthians showed their godly sorrow and their sincere repentance in several ways—mentioned in verse 11:

• First there was *carefulness*. This translates in more current English usage to *earnestness* or *diligence*. They got down to business about the sin in their lives and in their church.

• Then there was a *clearing* of themselves. Today, we'd call it *vindication*. This didn't mean self-justification. No, the church was identified with the sin of its members as long as the congregation ignored the wrongdoing. But when the church disclaimed the sin and excommunicated the guilty member, the repentant Christians had "cleared" themselves.

• Also we find here *indignation*. There was holy anger against sin— we could use more of it today—and fear of God's wrath and of wickedness.

• Next we find that there was *vehement desire, zeal, and revenge*. That translates into a deep spiritual longing for renewed fellowship with God, enthusiasm for spiritual matters, and the firm correction of an evil condition (not "revenge").

Among the Corinthians, repentance had resulted, then, in new spiritual pursuits and priorities. Gone were their indifference and apathy, their feeling that holiness was an optional matter, and their willingness to tolerate or condone sin in their midst.

Small thought here

Holiness, my friend, involves constant surrender to the will of God, constant recognition of His standards, and unflagging interest in His blessed work in the world.

YOU AND YOUR MONEY

Scripture, 2 Corinthians 8:1-15
As there was a readiness to will, so there may be a performance also out of that which ye have.
(2 Cor. 8:11)

Have you noticed that people get very quiet when you talk about money? A person's use of his money is one of the most accurate measurements of his relationship to God. The rich young ruler, whose account is recorded in Mark 10:17-23, is the classic example. Eagerly running up to Jesus, he inquired, "What must I do to inherit eternal life?" He was certainly asking the right question of the right person. But when the Lord Jesus in essence put His hand on the man's wallet, he went away sad because he had great possessions.

Where does mastery of money start? It starts with giving yourself to God. "This they did, not as we hoped, but first gave their own selves to the Lord, and unto us by the will of God" (2 Cor. 8:5). A friend of mine gathers his family together once a year to discuss their missionary pledge. They put down how much Father makes, and they put down how much Mother makes from an occasional secretarial job. They put down how much the son makes, and how much the daughter makes by baby-sitting. Then they add up their fixed expenses—the house, car, doctor bills, dentist, insurance, tuition, clothes, and so on, including their 10 percent tithe. Then they go a step further and say, "Now, Lord, how much can we give to You?" And each year that I've known them, they've been giving a little more as a family because they give themselves to the Lord that way.

Small thought here

Assess your financial potential, whatever it is. Then bring it all before the Lord, dear friend, and say, "Lord, how can I use my money for You because I want to give myself totally to you?"

A SPRING THAT KEEPS FLOWING

Scripture, 2 Corinthians 9:1-15
And God is able to make all things abound toward you.
(2 Cor. 9:8)

The word *abound* conjures up an image of an artesian well, a spring of water that just keeps flowing and flowing and flowing. It reminds me of when I was a boy, and my aunt and uncle used to take me to Green Springs, Ohio. Those springs had a high sulfur content and a faint aroma of ancient eggs, but because their water was supposed to be "good for you," occasionally we'd go and have a drink from them. I used to think to myself, "this water just keeps on coming," and it did. Thousands of gallons of it every hour, pouring out of the earth, crystal clear, icy cold, with that blessed sulfuric content that used to turn my nose!

Spiritual vitality can be just as abundant as spring water. It comes when you take God at His word in this matter of giving yourself away. Paul wrote, "He which soweth bountifully shall reap also bountifully" (9:6). That means giving your time without grudging; that means giving your strength without withholding; that means investing your money without miserliness.

Small thought here

Give yourself away and God will make you like an artesian well, just producing and producing and producing, capable of doing everything that you ought to do for Him. Want to abound in every good work? Want to be able to carry the load God wants you to carry at home, or at church, or wherever? Try giving yourself away and then watch God keep His part of the bargain.

HOW TO WIN THE WAR

Scripture, 2 Corinthians 10:1-5
The weapons of our warfare are not carnal, but mighty through God to the pulling down of strongholds.
(2 Cor. 10:4)

Did you once think the Christian lite was a quiet and beautiful journey to heaven? If so, it probably didn't take you long to realize you were looking through rose-colored glasses. You're in a war, my friend. And your adversary, the devil, is like a roaring lion seeking to devour you. How do you win the war? Paul says the weapons of spiritual warfare aren't *carnal* but are *mighty through God.* Then he goes on to explain how to use these weapons to live victoriously. First, make the Lord Jesus Christ master of your thoughts. Cast down every thought that isn't pure. Cast down every motive that wants its own way instead of God's.

How do you think about the things you ought to think about? And what do you do about thoughts that come unbidden to your mind? Every psychologist knows and will quickly tell you that if you try to repress or bury a thought, you will only drive it into your unconscious mind, there to remain until it pops out under some other guise to embarrass you again. So if repressing sinful thoughts isn't the answer, what is? Give them to Jesus. Confess them to Him and substitute for them His blessed Word. Two things. Pray about your thoughts and give them to Jesus.

Small thought here

Fill your mind with Scripture and you won't have room for garbage. "I thought on my ways," the psalmist said, "and turned my feet unto Thy testimonies." Bring every thought into obedience to Christ and you'll win the war.

HOW TO HANDLE CRITICISM

Scripture, 2 Corinthians 11:1-33
*Seeing that many glory after the flesh,
I will glory also.
(2 Cor. 11:18)*

Think with me a moment about criticism. First, expect it. Not everyone knows that you are as nice as you really are. Or as smart, charming, or generous! Herbert Hoover, when asked how he remained unembittered by so much criticism, replied, "Well, I can think of two possible answers. In the first place, I'm an engineer, trained to anticipate problems. I knew that sooner or later every one of my predecessors had to face a barrage of criticism. . . . The other (answer) is that I'm a Quaker." The latter statement referred to the God-given quietness Quakers have traditionally sought.

Any successful person faces criticism, either because of opposition to the principles he stands for or because of personal jealousy. Paul was opposed not only by hostile Jewish or pagan leaders who argued with him openly, but by those who tried to undermine his work and character and lead his churches astray. Pretending to be apostles of Christ, these imitators were really creating schism in the church.

Paul was driven to defend himself by the pressure of the personal attacks and by the misunderstandings which they had created. Apparently the problem was acute in Corinth, where a wealthy church of impressionable and untaught people made his work especially vulnerable, and where the possibility of annexing a large following would be especially tempting to his rivals. Therefore, Paul set the record straight for all involved, reminding them: "For the Lord's sake I've been beaten, stoned, shipwrecked, and robbed. Then add to that my weariness, pain, and caring for all the churches!" (11:25-28)

Small thought here

When criticism comes, state your case accurately and in a loving spirit—then get on with what you're doing for God's glory. You'll detour around a lot of criticism that way.

HIS STRENGTH FOR MY WEAKNESS

Scripture, 2 Corinthians 12:1-10
My grace is sufficient for thee: for My strength is made perfect in weakness. (2 Cor. 12:9)

It's natural to try to improve your strengths; it's also natural to try to strengthen your weaknesses. Most of us attempt this at the human level: for example, if you're a salesman, you try to be a better salesman—to learn a better approach to the client, to close the deal better, and to follow it up more efficiently. And if you're weak in some area, you try to guard against that weakness. But the biblical approach is far more glorious. Paul said, "Most gladly therefore will I rather glory in my infirmities" (v. 9). Oh, this is the blessed secret of divine grace: that when you give your life to our blessed Lord, He endeavors to make His strength perfect in the places where you are weakest.

Let me tell you how my father taught me to ride a bicycle. One day he came home from work with a used bicycle. I think it was second cousin to a Sherman tank; it weighed a ton! He said, "Boy, I'm going to show you how to ride this bicycle. Get on." Well, I climbed on the thing somehow or other and he put that big hand of his on my hand, and with an iron grip on the handlebars, he said, "Now peddle and I'll steer." And the two of us cyclists, father and son, rode down Cedar Road in Cleveland, Ohio with his hand on mine.

Small thought here

As long as you're depending on yourself in an area where you are strong, God can't teach you very much. His strength can only be made perfect in your weakness, dear friend. Let Him do it today in your life by His grace, will you?

TIME TO TAKE INVENTORY

Scripture, 2 Corinthians 13:1-14
Examine yourselves, whether ye be in the faith; prove your own selves.
(2 Cor. 13:5)

Let's take inventory, shall we? Think about the establishment of the truth in the mouth of two or three witnesses (13:1); the proof of real Christianity (v. 3); the power of Christ in a life that is weak (v. 4); *the necessity of examining oneself* (v. 5); and the thrill of genuine faith, not bogus religion (v. 8). Paul reminds us, "We can do nothing against the truth, but for the truth."

We've all heard the expression, "The truth will out," and, of course, it will. In Southern California many years ago, a contractor built a number of schools. Some time later an earthquake damaged several buildings in that area, mostly schools built by that one particular contractor. An investigation showed that he had cheated in the construction of those buildings. It didn't show on the outside, but when the earthquake came, the structural shodiness became readily apparent. Mercifully, the children were not in school at the time.

Yes, my dear friend, *the truth will out!* What you do in the name of the blessed Lord Jesus is going to be proved true, because *He is the truth.*

Small thought here

You have nothing to prove or promote but Jesus. Live for God and His glorious truth will shine through your face *and* your life. Hallelujah for that!

Be thou an example of the believer in word, in conversation, in charity, in spirit, in faith, in purity.
(1 Tim. 4:12)

Be a Blessing
IN PURITY

"Be thou an example of the believer," commanded Paul, "in purity." Holiness may well be something like the weather: everyone talks about it, but no one does anything about it! There is something about a pure and holy life that at once challenges and encourages others. Daniel, we read, "purposed in his heart that he would not defile himself with the portion of the king's meat." The reason was obvious: the food that came from the king's table had first been dedicated to the idols; and Daniel would have no part of idolatry! His decision resulted in others around him taking the same stand (it was "Daniel and his companions") and a spiritual leadership was born which lasted through three dynasties! Keep your life clean and you will encourage others to live for your Lord!

Robert A. Cook

September

A father and son banquet was a big occasion when I was a boy. It was a special time of wholesome entertainment and a table laden with more than enough food to satisfy the hunger pangs of dads and lads. What a delightful and delicious time of fellowship! This month I want you to join me in looking in on a father and son fellowship feast enjoyed by Paul and his son in the faith, Timothy. Also this month I want to share with you some concepts found in the Epistle to the Hebrews, a Bible book rich in practical principles that both *warn us* and *warm us* as we seek to walk more closely to our blessed Lord!

WHAT'S YOUR SPIRITUAL I.Q.?

Scripture, 1 Timothy 1:1-20
Paul, an apostle of Jesus Christ . . . unto Timothy, my own son in the faith.
(1 Tim. 1:1-2)

Certain issues profoundly affect Christian life and work. How "up" on them are you? For example, what do you know about:
• How the Gospel works?
• How prayer works?
• The price of leadership?
• Being a proper model for others?
• Priority values?

These are just a few of the issues that Paul took up in his first letter to Timothy, which I'd like to use as a broad framework for our meditations in the next several weeks. In between these anchor thoughts, I'll be talking about other related matters that will help illustrate or expand on some of these topics. As we do this together, we will be assessing how much we really know about the practical application of God's Word to our lives.

We all need to realize that it is not enough just to have an acquaintance with the data or a superficial knowledge of our evangelical position. The fact that you have trusted Christ Jesus as your Saviour and believe yourself to be a child of God through faith in Him is significant only as you realize that this commitment means something for all the rest of your life. You can never again be your own person, operating independently of your sovereign Lord and Saviour.

Small thought here
In another of his letters, Paul pinpointed this glorious truth: "Ye are bought with a price: therefore glorify God in your body and in your spirit, which are God's" (1 Cor. 6:20). When you make that your priority, dear friend, your spiritual I.Q. will be right on target.

LOVE AND UNFEIGNED FAITH

Scripture, 1 Timothy 1:1-20
Now the end of the commandment is charity out of a pure heart, and of a good conscience, and of faith unfeigned. (1 Tim. 1:5)

Some of us remember the hippie generation, when people sang about love, sweet love (which they pronounced and spelled "luv"). Well, I had the experience of meeting some of those "luvly" folk and I found them decidedly disagreeable and vindictive. The kind of love that Paul speaks of here is not man-generated at all. You and I have to have it, but we don't come by it naturally.

The One who cleansed our sinful hearts initially, and who keeps on cleansing us daily by "the washing of water by the Word," is the One who has entrusted us with "the glorious Gospel of the blessed God" (v. 11). *He* has done it. Praise God!

One of the great heartaches for the world traveler lies in seeing so many people who have a God-shaped vacuum in their hearts yet have never found Him. So they go on reaching and groping to satisfy their constant hunger, not knowing that only the Gospel satisfies. A missionary friend of mine told of meeting a man in India whose right hand was stretched high above his head. It had been in that position for fifteen years. The joints of his shoulder had calcified; the arm was useless. "Why did you do this?" my friend asked the man. "Years ago," the man replied, "I made a vow that I wouldn't lower my right hand until I had found forgiveness for my sin and cleansing for my heart." My friend asked, "Well, Sir, have you found forgiveness?" The poor seeker looked away with sadness and said, "No, Sahib. Not yet . . . not yet."

Small thought here

The problem with the human race is that there is only one way to a holy God. Spurning the way, all our best efforts are simply a "feigned" approach—something not genuine, something put on.

THE GOSPEL IS A PROBING TOOL

Scripture, 1 Timothy 1:1-20
And the grace of our Lord was exceeding abundant with faith and love which is in Christ Jesus.
(1 Tim. 1:14)

I meet people everywhere who have an acquaintance with the facts of the Gospel, but who have not allowed the Gospel to probe deeply into their hearts. My wife's mother, Grandmother Nilsen, lived in our home for some twenty years. We called her *Bestemor*, which is Norwegian for "Grandmother." Our kids couldn't pronounce the name, so they shortened it to *Bemore*—and that is what she was to us. She slipped away to Glory on the eve of her ninetieth birthday. During most of the months that preceded her homegoing, she was able to get about and always did the family washing on Monday morning.

During one of those busy days I happened to be at home and I said, "Bemore, tell me something. What does Jesus mean to you now, after so many years have passed?"

She looked me full in the eye and said, "The older I get, the more I need a great Saviour." The Gospel was a probing tool to her decade after decade. Do you want the Gospel to accomplish something real in your life? Follow nineteenth-century evangelist Charles Grandison Finney's advice and make a list of your failings. See what Jesus died for *in your case*. For your inherent sinfulness, of course, but what else? How long has it been since you wept over your own sins? You can't lie to yourself and to God when you're alone with Him. If, when you're praying—just you and your Lord—your eyes are dry *then*, if your heart is cold *then*, if you manipulate and rationalize *then*, my dear friend, you need what the old-time holiness people used to call "a new touch."

Small thought here

This has been my experience: every time I have sought my Lord with tears and waited on Him until my heart was touched—cleansed and broken, melted and made tender—at that very juncture I was enabled to believe God for the next step of obedience.

THE GOSPEL GENERATES DIVINE LOVE

Scripture, 1 Timothy 1:1-20
This is a faithful saying, and worthy of all acceptation, that Christ Jesus came into the world to save sinners; of whom I am chief. (1 Tim. 1:15)

Do you think the Apostle Paul was the worst sinner in the world at the time he wrote? Probably not. Then why would he use such an expression? Either he was employing what is called *hyperbole* or he was mistaken about himself. I refuse to believe Paul was mistaken. And I refuse to accept the idea that he was tinkering with language, trying to manipulate his hearers. What then? Let me share a simple illustration that may shed some light on the subject. I imagine myself preaching in an auditorium. I'm holding my Bible in front of my face, about eighteen inches away. So doing, I can see most of the audience before me. I bring the Book a little closer, about six inches from my eyes. When I do, it shuts out the center section of the auditorium, though my peripheral vision still allows me to see people seated near the walls. But then I bring the Book so close that it touches my nose. It shuts out completely all that I had been looking at before.

It seems to me that what Paul was saying was that when you achieve that kind of closeness to the Lord Jesus—when you have honestly faced and admitted your failings, when you have pleaded the precious blood of Jesus for cleansing, when God has made your heart tender and yielding—your awareness of other people's faults is shut out, and you know that, had you been the only person in the universe, Jesus would have died for you.

Small thought here

When you experience this blessed reality, you'll speak to and about others in a different tone and with spiritual effectiveness. The love of God that the Gospel speaks about will dominate your life. Hallelujah for that!

WHAT MAKES THE DIFFERENCE?

Scripture, 1 Timothy 1:16-20
For this cause I obtained mercy, that in me first Jesus Christ might show forth all long-suffering . . . to them which should hereafter believe on Him to life everlasting.
(1 Tim. 1:16)

One of the greatest things that God does, as the Gospel works in your life and mine, is to make us strong at the point where we were weak. Let me tell you a story about my father, Charley Cook, that illustrates this truth. One day I said to him, "Pop, I've noticed that you are often very shy when you are with people. But when you are talking about the Lord Jesus, you're as bold as a lion. Why the difference?"

"Boy, I'll tell you," he answered. "When I was a youngster I was so shy that when anybody came to our farm I would run away. My stepmother decided she would break me of this trait. So one day she dressed me in nothing but a bed sheet and tied me to a tree in our front yard so that everybody who went by would see this miserable little guy tied to a tree.

"Well," he continued, "all that did for me was to make me decide to run away for good. So I did. I found work, later joined the army for the Spanish-American War, and came back and married your beautiful mother.

"We settled down in Rossford, Ohio. About that time an evangelistic campaign was held in our area. We heard that there was a need for personal workers to be trained. Your mother and I went to that class and there we learned for the first time the sheer joy of telling somebody about Jesus."

Pop looked at me intently. "That experience changed our lives. We were never quite the same after that. So if I'm not embarrassed on some occasions, it's because God makes me strong where once I was weak."

Small thought here
What God did for Charley Cook He can do for every one of us, if we let the Gospel of our blessed Lord Jesus work in us.

WHAT PRAYER IS NOT

Scripture, 1 Timothy 2:1-8
I exhort therefore, that, first of all, supplications, prayers, intercessions, and giving of thanks be made for all men. (1 Tim. 2:1)

When I was a boy, my father arranged for me to have two lessons a week on the violin. I practiced two hours a day—not voluntarily, I can assure you. When I was about seven years old, some thoughtful person in the church handed me a piece of sheet music.

"Here, Robert," she said, "this might interest you. Perhaps you can learn to play it." I thanked the lady very much, went home to put the music in the bottom drawer of a clothes chest that was my private domain, and promptly forgot about it.

One day several months later the lady said to me, "Have you finished learning that music yet?"

"Well," I said, "I'm not quite through."

"Perhaps you should return it to me," she replied.

I went home and opened the bottom drawer. Sure enough, the music was there. But mice had been there too and one whole corner of the sheet was chewed up. I was absolutely aghast, for I had been brought up to treat others' property with care and respect.

So I said to myself (age seven, mind you), "I'll pray about it." Holding that gnawed piece of paper in my hands, I closed my eyes tightly and said earnestly, "O Lord, fix this!"

When I cautiously opened my eyes and saw that nothing had changed, I knew I was reduced to the embarrassing expedient of returning the lady's property and explaining both my carelessness and lack of truth.

Small thought here
I learned a great lesson that day: prayer is no substitute for honest repentance and change.

PRAYER IS SUPPLICA-TION AND WORSHIP

Scripture, 1 Timothy 2:1-8
Supplications, prayers.
(1 Tim. 2:1)

A supplicant is one who has nothing to offer, whose only hope is in the goodness of the one to whom he appeals. That great writer on prayer, Dr. O. Hallesby, makes the point that it isn't our prayer, or our worthiness, or even our need that moves the heart of God. It is our utter *helplessness.* Supplication makes us face the question, "How much do we really need God?" The essence of humility is to have God's empowering every moment of our lives. It is interesting that Paul puts "prayer" second in verse 1, and yet that is logical for unless our hearts are open and broken before God as supplicants, we cannot genuinely worship Him.

The importance of waiting silently before God was a lesson I learned many years ago when my sister Mildred took me to visit a friend of hers who was known as a great woman of prayer.

I said, "We've come to pray with you because I understand you have a great ministry of prayer." She said, "Well, the Lord has given me some effectiveness in prayer. Would you like to pray now, young man?" So I launched into a vigorous Bob Cook prayer, touching all the bases. When I had finished, I said "Amen"—and there was absolute silence. Now sixty seconds can seem like an eternity when you're in a room and nothing's going on but the rent. In fact, I feared this dear, elderly lady might have fallen asleep. So I peeked—but she was not asleep. She sat erect in her chair, her hands folded in her lap. I waited . . . and *finally* she spoke. When she said "Our Father," I knew this woman was plugged into the switchboard of heaven.

Small thought here
Afterward, I told this lady that I had gotten a little nervous waiting for her to start praying. To which she so wisely replied, "You wait until your soul is in a right attitude to pray in the Spirit. You don't rush into the presence of Almighty God." Good lesson!

PRAYER IS INTERCES- SION

Scripture, 1 Timothy 2:1-8
Supplications, prayers, intercessions.
(1 Tim. 2:1)

The index of your life's overall effectiveness will be the amount of praying you do for other people. As Christians, we are to pray for people in many walks of life: for the unsaved; for our critics and enemies; for blessing on the many who cannot possibly make us any more successful or secure.

Dawson Trotman was founder of The Navigators. He was a great man of God—often very direct in his insights, perceptions, and demands. He went right to the point of any issue, whether he was announcing the weather or some fault in your personality. He was a beloved brother, full of God's Word and of the Spirit of his Lord.

I dropped into his office one day and found, not surprisingly, that he had some things written on the palm of his hand. Using pen and ink, he would write on one hand a reminder of the Scripture verse he was meditating on that day. On the other hand he would write the initials of one of his staff members for whom he was praying. Aware of this practice, I asked, "What are you meditating on today?"

He showed me. It was 2 Timothy 1:7: "God hath not given us the spirit of fear; but of power, and of love, and of a sound mind."

Then I said, "What's on the other hand?"

He showed me the initials O.W.

"I don't know any of your staff with those initials," I said. "Oh," he replied, "they stand for 'Other Work'—people serving in different parts of the Lord's vineyard from ours. As a matter of fact, I just got through praying for you."

Small thought here

Outreach to others in prayer is the secret of effective Christian living. Put that to work on Main Street where you live, will you?

PRAYER REACHES OUT

Scripture, 1 Timothy 2:1-8
Supplications, prayers, intercessions, and giving of thanks . . . for all men.
(1 Tim. 2:1)

Praise opens the door to miracles. One of the best illustrations of this truth is found in the Old Testament. As King Jehoshaphat was being pursued by a mighty army, he prayed, "O our God . . . we have no might against this great company that cometh against us; neither know we what to do; but our eyes are upon Thee" (2 Chron. 20:12). Then Jehoshaphat took immediate action: "He appointed singers unto the Lord, and that should praise the beauty of holiness, as they went out before the army. . . . And when they began to sing and praise, the Lord set ambushments against those . . . which were come against Judah; and they were smitten" (vv. 21-22). It is always so. If you are not getting answers to your prayers, *stop asking and start praising.* Praise always makes a difference.

Effective prayer reaches beyond one's own bailiwick, your own community, to the very highest levels of government. I doubt that we really do very much concerted praying for our leaders. If we did, it would surely make a difference. God says so. Listen to this great promise: "If My people, which are called by My name, shall humble themselves, and pray, and seek My face, and turn from their wicked ways; then I will hear from heaven, and will forgive their sin, and will heal their land"(2 Chron. 7:14). Effective prayer reaches out to individuals too. What a thrill it is to pray for an unsaved relative or friend and see God answer, even though it may not always come immediately. George Muller prayed for forty years for two individuals he wanted to see brought to Christ—and they were!

Small thought here

How about your prayers, dear friend? Are they focused only on your own little world—"Me, my son, us four, and no more"—or do they reach out to those needy folks next door to you, then on to a whole world that needs your blessed Saviour?

DESIRE AND REPUTATION REQUIRED

Scripture, 1 Timothy 3:1-16
If a man desire the office of a bishop, he desireth a good work. A bishop then must be blameless.
(1 Tim. 3:1-2)

Paul spells out in crystal-clear language the qualifications of certain church leaders: a *bishop* (pastor) and *deacon* (Christian worker). As we look at this list, we need to remember that each of us believers is a leader in his own area of activity, small as it may be; thus the counsel given here applies to us all.

To be effective as Christ's servant, you first must *want* to be used by Him. Ask yourself: "What do I really want in life?" Make a list of the things for which you would be willing to be shot tomorrow morning at sunrise. It will be a significant list—and probably very short! If there isn't any drive, any "mustness" or urge such as dominated the Apostle Paul when he said, "Woe is me if I preach not the Gospel," you need more time with your blessed Lord to sharpen your concept of dependence on Him and your relation to a dying world.

Perhaps you've noticed that your peers are able to (and will) evaluate your reputation with uncanny accuracy. Of course, there may be times when your words are misunderstood and your motives misinterpreted. But in the main, what people say and feel about you is often close to the mark. If you are fair and compassionate, that shows up. If you are perceptive and generous, people know it. By the same token, if you are careless in you relations with others, that carelessness follows you. If you are a deadbeat or immoral, these traits will nullify or destroy your testimony.

Small thought here
Are your desires for serving God pure and holy? How sound is your reputation? Examine yourself. Your spiritual effectiveness is at stake.

THE PRICE OF LEADERSHIP

Scripture, 1 Timothy 3:2-12
*A bishop then must be blameless . . .
vigilant, sober . . . not given to wine.
(1 Tim. 3:2-3)*

To be a leader, you must be vigilant. All too often we elders do not exert ourselves to be current with what is happening in our world. To be *vigilant* means to "stay on the job mentally." Don't let your mind go out to lunch. *Sober* is a compound word that means "saved mind." It does me good every now and then to back off from a particular situation that concerns me and say, "Lord, give me Your perspective on this. I want to think with a saved mind." *Not given to wine* suggests matters related to the appetite—self-indulgence. The late Dr. William Culbertson said in my hearing, "You ought to say no to yourself on something every day, just to keep in practice." Fight the tendency to give in to those bodily desires that can rob you of your spiritual growth and victory. If you lose your temper or become resentful, your testimony is forfeited.

When you don't measure up in the bishop's list, look up and say, "Jesus, I am Yours; help me now!" Only as you surrender the problem area to Him can you begin to experience His cleansing and victory through His resurrection power. To have an effective ministry for God, you must also have a clean conscience that enables you to personally demonstrate the "mystery of the faith" (v. 9) and "the mystery of godliness" (v. 16). And that mystery is the showing forth of Jesus Christ—God manifested in the flesh—the living, dying, risen, ascended Lord who is coming again.

Small thought here
The price of leadership is a life so clean, so pure, so committed to God, that when people meet you they will realize that Jesus is truly alive in your heart.

BE A MODEL OF GODLINESS

Scripture, 1 Timothy 4:1-16
Exercise thyself . . . unto godliness.
(1 Tim. 4:7)

W e have already looked at the importance of demonstrating Christ in daily life. The verses that follow in this passage continue that emphasis: "Be thou an example of the believers, in word, in conversation, in charity, in spirit, in faith, in purity" (4:12).

To oversimplify the word, *godliness* means that God is walking in our shoes and manifesting Himself in "the ordinaries of life." It means we will be like God when we're washing the dishes, cleaning out the garage, putting up the storm windows, or taking care of the baby. It means we will be like God when we drive the car or when we talk with fellow family members. (We seem to reserve the right to be impertinent to the most precious and important people in our lives— our family. We often treat them with much less courtesy than we treat total strangers. Shame on us!)

"Godliness is profitable unto all things, having promise of the life that now is, and of that which is to come" (4:8). Your life and mine will be meaningful in direct proportion to the amount of eternity we build into them. Many of us have a little motto on our wall that says: "Only one life, 'twill soon be past; only what's done for Christ will last." We know this truth in an intellectual sense; we need to put it into practice by a conscious daily commitment of all that we are and have to our blessed Lord.

Small thought here
The measure of whether or not you are a model of godliness will be reflected more by what you are on Main Street of your life than by how you stack up in your round of religious duties.

BE A WORKING MODEL

Scripture, 1 Timothy 4:1-16
We labor and suffer reproach ourselves because we trust in the living God.
(1 Tim. 4:10)

Make up your mind that it is abundantly worthwhile to be associated with the Lord Jesus Christ. But when you so choose, expect two things: hard work and identification.

The Apostle Paul says, "We labor." That's roll-up-your-sleeves kind of work. It is my convicton that most of us never get tired enough in the work of the Lord. We save our best energies for those things that we regard as important and that bring us personal pleasure. Dare to get tired for the Lord Jesus, my friend.

Paul also says, "We suffer reproach." It is impossible to avoid being tagged as a believer if you really are one. If you have committed yourself to the Saviour, that fact ought to be as apparent as chicken pox or the measles. Yes, you will be tagged, and at that point two courses of action are open to you: you can be embarrassed, hide your head, try to become anonymous and get lost in the crowd. Or you can stand tall and say clearly with conviction and delight: "Of course I belong to the Lord Jesus."

The time has come when men, women, and young people all across the land need to stand up and be counted for our blessed Lord. And it need not be apologetically or defensively. A sweet spirit, dearly beloved, works wonders.

Small thought here
You can be radiantly happy because you belong to Jesus and you can let that joy shine wherever you are. You'll attract more people with "honey" than with "vinegar."

BE A LIVE MODEL

Scripture, 1 Timothy 4:1-16
Be thou an example. . . . Meditate upon these things. . . . Take heed unto thyself, and unto the doctrine; continue in them. (1 Tim. 4:12-16)

I had been asked to preach in Altoona, Pennsylvania back in the days when we traveled mostly by train. Two young men met me at the station in an ancient Buick. As we traveled over ice-slick streets that wintry night, I asked one of them, "Do you know the Lord Jesus Christ as your Saviour?"

"Yes, indeed," he responded. And he proceeded to tell me about his experience with the Lord. When he finished, I asked the other boy, "How about you?"

"Oh," he said, pointing to his buddy, "there's the fellow who led me to Christ—in a railroad shop.

"I was an alcoholic," he continued. "My wife couldn't live with me. She took our baby and went back to her mother. At night, after working in the shop, I'd go home, grab my guitar, and head straight for the nearest bar. I'd play and sing for free drinks until either the place closed or I passed out.

"All the time, right next to me at work was this guy, and he seemed so happy. He'd whistle snatches of hymns, though I didn't recognize them at the time. At noon he'd pull out a little New Testament and prop it up against his lunch pail to read it. He never preached to me. But one day, just at quitting time, I went to him and said, 'Jim, you've got to tell me what it is you've got that makes you so happy all the time because I want it.' And he led me to Jesus."

Small thought here

To be an example, a *model*, in the sense that Paul used the term, doesn't require great spiritual insight or powers of persuasion. What *is* needed is a person wholly committed to the Lord Jesus, from whose life flows the love of God.

PEOPLE ARE IMPORTANT

Scripture, 1 Timothy 5:1-25
Rebuke not an elder, but intreat him as a father; and the younger men as brethren; the elder women as mothers; the younger as sisters, with all purity. Honor widows. (1 Tim. 5:1-3)

Paul speaks of various groups of people here; together they compose a *family*. The inference and application is to treat one another as family. You know how it is in our own homes. We tend to stick up for one who is under attack. Likewise, we ought to lovingly defend one another in the family of the redeemed.

Your pastor is important. Look at him, not in terms of his being a fallible, often quite human individual (as we all are), but as one whom God has specially touched and commissioned to a very important piece of work—the shepherding of His earthly flock. Honor your pastor. Esteem him highly in love. Pray for him regularly. Not all of us preachers are easy to live with. You remember the old jingle: "To live above with the saints we love, oh, that will be glory; to live below with saints we know is quite a different story!" Nonetheless, you and your pastor are family. Is he perfect? No. Does he make mistakes? Yes. Does he struggle with sin and failure? Yes. Should you pretend his faults don't exist? No. Should you forgive him and encourage him? Yes!

Small thought here

Your value system determines your reaction in any given situation. Early on in your life and ministry you must decide what is of vital importance to you and get on with it. Put God first and other people before yourself.

SATISFAC-TION IS IMPORTANT

Scripture, 1 Timothy 6:1-21
Let as many servants as are under the yoke count their own masters worthy of all honor, that the name of God and His doctrine be not blasphemed.
(1 Tim. 6:1)

Your employer is important. You ought to do a dollar's worth of work for every dollar you receive in pay. And just because you are a Christian does not mean you should be shown any special favors on the job. Do a good job with the work that is assigned to you, will you? It will have three happy results: first, it will have a positive effect on you personally; second, it will build a good reputation for you; and third, perhaps indirectly, it will speak to others for you of your Lord and Saviour.

Each of us must decide what it is that really pays off for us in life. There are certain activities which, under God, satisfy the needs and desires of your particular personality. There is a sense, whether you are in business, or medicine, or law, or full-time career service for the Lord, that everything you do must be a *ministry*.

What is it that satisfies the drive, the appetite, the longings of your soul? According to our text, it is *godliness*: "Godliness with contentment is great gain" (6:6). The scope of godliness is limitless within God's overall parameters. You can be godly when you are playing basketball, or adding up your bills, or in any of the other "ordinaries" of life. What a delightful thought that through all eternity you may be meeting people who have been blessed to some degree by godliness they discovered in your life.

Small thought here

If you feel trapped in some situation you cannot possible enjoy, if you are in a job for which you feel over-qualified and under-appreciated, look up into the face of your lovely Lord and ask Him to satisfy you *with Himself.* And He will!

ATTITUDE TOWARD MONEY IS IMPORTANT

Scripture, 1 Timothy 6:1-21
They that will be rich fall into temptation and a snare.
(1 Tim. 6:9)

The ability to amass money is no indication of godliness. When once I dealt with an individual on a spiritual matter, he snapped back with a statement that went something like this: "Well, I certainly must be doing all right because I'm making more money than I ever did before." Then he added, as a low blow, "You preachers don't seem to mind cashing my checks."

The size of your bank account proves nothing, of course, except your ability to make money. When Andrew Mellon, the great financial genius, died, the question arose, "How much did he leave?" And the accurate answer was, "He left it all."

We need to develop simple rather than extravagant tastes. "Having food and raiment," Paul told Timothy, "let us be therefore content" (6:8). The fact is, some of the most miserable people in the world are those with worries about how to manage their money.

I know a man who decided he had to become president of his corporation in order to feel successful. But after he became president, he told me, "Bob, I'm president of the company, but in the process I've lost my children; they won't speak to me. My wife has left me. I've lost my health. There's nothing left to live for." Would you say that this poor soul had gotten his money's worth?

Paul says, "Trust . . . in the living God, who giveth us richly all things to enjoy" (6:17). What do you know about the enjoyment of investing your money, small or large amounts, for eternity? It's a real thrill, I can assure you.

Small thought here

Most of us don't have vast sums of money to manage or worry about. But the *desire for money*, the I-want-more attitude, is hazardous to your spiritual health and may be the first step toward personal spiritual decline or disaster.

DECIDE WHAT IS IMPORTANT

Scripture, 1 Timothy 6:1-21
O Timothy, keep that which is committed to thy trust.
(1 Tim. 6:20)

Prior to the Korean War, Dr. Bob Pierce went to Seoul to conduct an evangelistic campaign. A sponsoring committee of Korean laymen had planned the campaign thoroughly and many unbelievers came to know the Lord. When the war started, thousands of refugees poured into South Korea. Bob Pierce raised funds to buy tons of rice and went to Korea to oversee its distribution. While feeding a group of refugees, Bob noticed a man with his feet wrapped in dirty cloth strips, huddled on the ground. "Aren't you Mr. Kim?" Bob asked. "Yes," the man replied. "But when I saw you in Seoul, you had a thriving business," Bob recalled. "What happened to you?"

"It is a painful story," Kim said. "Before you came to Seoul for the campaign, my fellow Christians asked me to serve on the sponsoring committee. But I told them I must not neglect my business. I said I had to build my new wife a nice house, so they should please count me out." So they counted Kim out. The meetings were held and thousands were blessed. Soon after that the Communists occupied Seoul, and Kim and his bride had to flee to the mountains for their lives. "One week later," Kim continued, "my wife died in my arms of pneumonia. I made my way south, hiding by day and traveling by night, living on roots and berries until I arrived here." Then Kim laid his head on Bob's shoulder and cried his heart out. When he could speak again, he said, "If only I had done *what* I could *when* I could!"

Small thought here
Yes, dear friend, we are to be true to our trust, the Gospel. We are to scorn the trivial and embrace the eternal. Decide today, will you, what is really important *in your life?*

THE ONE WHO FULFILLS US

Scripture, Hebrews 1:1-14
Who being the brightness of His glory, and the express image of His person, and upholding all things by . . . His power, when He had . . . purged our sins, sat down at the right hand of the Majesty on high.
(Heb. 1:3)

The Lord Jesus Christ speaks to our deepest needs. Nowhere is this better brought out than in today's text. "The brightness of His glory." The first visible effect of sin in the human race was when the glory of God (which I believe was Adam and Eve's original covering) was lost. Our Lord Jesus restores that lost glory. The shine of life is gone till He comes in. Our Lord Jesus is also "the express image of [God's] person." We ought not be content with a religious viewpoint, though some have given their lives for that. The only thing that will satisfy our hearts, fulfill us, and take away sin's loneliness is the person of the Lord Jesus Christ. He "upholds all things by the word of His power." He restores our lost capabilities. The bankruptcy of the human race since the Fall is obvious to any observer. All we can bring to the business of living is the capacity to fail. But our blessed Lord solves the sin problem: "when He had by Himself purged our sins, He sat down at the right hand of the Majesty on high."

Small thought here

You need a person, not just an idea, to deal with your sins, to take away the lonesomeness in your soul, to fulfill you with the fellowship of God Himself, and to put His shine on you. Your blessed Lord Jesus fills all those needs. Hallelujah for that!

THE UNPARDON-ABLE SIN

Scripture, Hebrews 2:1-18
How shall we escape if we neglect so great salvation?
(Heb. 2:3)

Neglect is an incurable illness, an unpardonable sin. God can offer salvation, and He does. God can convict by His Holy Spirit, and He does. God can surround us with loving and solicitous people whose lives and words are constant sermons in shoe leather, reminding us of Christ's claims. And He does. But God gives a sober warning: "We ought to give the more earnest heed to the things which we have heard, lest at any time we should let them slip" (2:1).

One who ignores God's salvation is ignoring the Word, which the Lord has given. He is ignoring those who walked with and heard Jesus. He is ignoring the testimony of the signs, wonders, and miracles, the extraordinary things God does when He breaks into earthly affairs. He is ignoring the blessed Holy Spirit and His wonderful gifts, and he is ignoring God's will. This is the essential rebellion of sin. Sin says, "I want to be God instead of God." Satan said it (Isa. 14:14). The serpent's original temptation offered the same enticement (Gen 3:5). Similarly, neglect is a way of rebelling against God and saying, "I'll not listen now because I want my own way." Serious? Very. Fatal? Yes.

Small thought here
How shall we escape? Oh, let us be sure that we do not slip into the error of neglecting the Lord Jesus and His truth!

FAITH PLUS OBEDIENCE EQUALS REST

Scripture, Hebrews 3:1—4:13
Let us labor, therefore, to enter into that [God's] rest, lest any man fall after the same example of unbelief.
(Heb. 4:11)

Anyone who thinks there's no effort in the Christian life has, as my father used to say, another think coming. There *is* effort. True, we're saved by grace through faith, which is the gift of God, not of works. But most people stop after they quote Ephesians 2:8-9. They don't go on to verse 10, which says we're created to do good works. So there *is* something to do—not to be saved but because we're saved.

A distinct effort is involved in giving oneself to God. Have you ever tried to get to sleep but you couldn't because the day's problems were racing in your mind and your body was tense? You might opt for a sleeping pill but you might also try to relax your body and mind without medication. To make this effort to relax, your will is involved. Likewise, there's an effort involved in giving yourself to the Lord Jesus: the rest of faith, ceasing from your own works, letting God's sharp Word penetrate your heart's motives. Indeed, the effort you must put forth to make faith dynamic is simple obedience. By an effort of your will, yield your life's circumstances to Christ. Then after you've turned them over by faith, obey His precious Holy Spirit as you read the Word and pray.

Small thought here
Remember, resting is not simply lying there, tossing and turning and wishing things were different. Resting in Christ is actively turning your life over to Him. Faith plus obedience and commitment equal rest.

BOLD
BUT NOT
BRASSY

Scripture, Hebrews 4:14—5:10
Let us therefore come boldy unto the throne of grace, that we may obtain mercy and find grace to help in time of need. (Heb. 4:16)

Holy boldness is not brassiness. I deplore the approach many take toward God today, where He is a "Big Buddy" in the sky to approached with less courtesy than you'd show an alderman. We take Almighty God for granted far too much. He is not only the Judge of all the earth who always does right, but if our faith is in the Lord Jesus Christ, He is also our Heavenly Father.

A great lady from Pakistan told how our Lord had brought her to Himself out of an entirely different faith. She had been reading the Koran; then she read the Bible. She began to pray to Almighty God for guidance. She found her heart opening to the truth of Jesus Christ as Lord and Saviour. But what led to her complete commitment to Jesus was realizing that she could pray to God as her Father. On her knees she said, "O God, I want You to be my Father, and I want Christ to be my Saviour."

Yes, God becomes our Heavenly Father through faith in the Lord Jesus. No longer children of sin and Satan, we're translated into the kingdom of His dear Son. We can walk into His very presence with a holy boldness, not impudence or the brassy familiarity of a yokel on the street of life. And we get what we really need. What do we need? First, "mercy," because we're sinners. Second, "grace to help," because we're helpless.

Small thought here

G. Campbell Morgan said, "Grace to help in the time of need really means grace to help in the nick of time." Just when you need Him most, Jesus is near, to comfort and cheer. Be confident—your Father hears.

USE IT OR LOSE IT

Scripture, Hebrews 5:11—6:20
Strong meat belongeth to them that are of full age [mature, grown up], even those who by reason of use have their senses exercised to discern both good and evil. (Heb. 5:14)

Strong meat means solid food. We give a newborn liquid—mother's or cow's milk or a synthetic product. It's not solid because we wouldn't give beefsteak to a baby. Similarly, Paul told the Corinthians: "I've not fed you meat; I've given you milk because you're still babies in Christ." He told the Ephesians: "Grow up into Christ; become mature."

What makes us grow? According to Hebrews 5:14, it's spiritual exercise—walking with and obeying the Lord. Just sitting around and "singing ourselves into sanctified senility," as Vance Havner says, won't make us grow. The idea that Christianity is just something to enjoy is a vapid concept which doesn't get down to where we live. The truth is that by exercising our faith we can have joy in the Lord Jesus even when tears are falling and the skies are dark.

My father used to say, "Use it or lose it, Boy." After you pray a little, pray a little more and God will become nearer. Can you think a little? Think some more; God will become clearer to you. "Discern both good and evil" with God as your absolute, His Word at your side. You'll learn up from down in a way people of our sensate culture never can.

Small thought here

How do you grow? Walk with God; use the faith He's given you; exercise your spiritual senses to sharpen them; let God show you His perfect will and obey it. Want strong meat? God will feed it to you as you grow up in Christ.

CEILING UNLIMITED

Scripture, Hebrews 7:1-28
Wherefore He is able also to save them to the uttermost that come unto God by Him, seeing He ever liveth to make intercession for them.
(Heb. 7:25)

Here's the fact: Christ can save to the uttermost. The method: come unto God by Him. The reason: He ever lives to make intercession for us. I think it was Hubert Mitchell who asked me years ago, "Did you know that the main job of our Lord Jesus Christ right now is to talk about Christians—you and me—to God the Father?" Well, I hadn't quite thought of it that way. I knew that Jesus is seated at God the Father's right hand. I knew redemption's work is done and that Jesus has ascended into God's presence and that He'll come again in power and glory. But until that moment I had never fully contemplated Christ's work on our behalf today.

What does the word *uttermost* mean to you? It can mean the most difficult problem in your life, something you've agonized over . . . in vain. Can the Lord Jesus handle that? Yes. Can the Lord Jesus handle an unbroken habit, a chain of slavery bound around your personality? Yes. Can He remove the stain of an old guilt? Yes. Can He repair a broken relationship? Yes. Can He give a sense of usefulness to a life that has largely been wasted? Yes. Can He send you into a situation that you fear and make you a victor, not a victim? Yes.

Small thought here

Uttermost means "boundless"—ceiling unlimited. Spread your wings, believer, and fly. There's no limit to what God can do if you belong to His Son.

A BETTER COVENANT

Scripture, Hebrews 8:1—9:10
Now hath He [Christ] obtained a more excellent ministry, by how much also He is the Mediator of a better covenant, which was established upon better promises. (Heb. 8:6)

What is God's "better covenant"? "This is the covenant that I will make with the house of Israel. . . . I will put My laws into their mind and write them in their hearts, and I will be unto them a God, and they shall be to Me a people" (Heb. 8:10). It's "a better covenant" because it provides a relationship that changes a person. This is one of the most thrilling of all Christian truths: when we come into this better agreement, written in precious shed blood at Calvary, and stand in the shining shadow of Jesus our Mediator, High Priest, Saviour, and All in All, we are not only given a perfect relationship with God, but are being changed by it. As Paul wrote, this covenant is not written on "tables of stone, but in the fleshy tables of the heart" (2 Cor. 3:3).

Someone once defined education as that which modifies behavior. Carrying this concept to the extreme is brainwashing which says, "We'll starve you, isolate you, keep you from sleeping, and interrogate you till you cave in and your conduct and attitudes change." But God says, "Stand with the Saviour, in His shining shadow. Trust in His precious blood. Give yourself absolutely to Him and become a different person." "If anyone be in Christ," exclaimed Paul, "he is a new creation. Old things are passed away. All things are become new" (2 Cor. 5:17).

Small thought here

It's the relationship that makes a different person. Make sure your relationship with the Lord is right and you will find your conduct, your behavior, being modified heavenward.

DON'T ENDURE— ENJOY!

Scripture, Hebrews 9:11—10:18
How much more shall the blood of Christ, who through the eternal Spirit offered Himself without spot to God, purge your conscience from dead works to serve the living God?
(Heb. 9:14)

Before Calvary, acts of faith in obedience to God's commands about animal sacrifices produced cleansed lives. The Old Testament describes many sacrifices of lambs, bullocks, and goats. Their shed blood pictured Christ's upcoming sacrifice on Calvary. For many Jews, these sacrifices were acts of obedience and commitment to the God who said, "Without shedding of blood is no remission" (Heb. 9:22). Since that was true before Calvary, how much more so now that the Person who fulfilled these types has shed His precious blood for us. "How much more . . . the blood of Christ" (9:14).

Notice all the richness of this precious verse: "the blood of Christ . . . the eternal Spirit . . . God" the Father, a purged conscience, and acceptable service. What a blessed combination! When you start at Calvary, friend, you're going far beyond all you could ever imagine. Beyond all of the pre-Calvary ordinances, surely. But also beyond all of the human preconceptions that we bring to our dealings with God. The world is full of people who are trying to be worthy enough to be saved. But we can't come to God that way. We must start with the blood of Christ. By trusting in Him and His sacrifice, the blessed Spirit of God mediates salvation to us. And God the Father accepts us in Christ's precious blood, cleansed from dead works. The things we tried in order to impress God are dropped, and we have a new commission. What is it? To serve the living God. No more dead works, but now a life of serving the living Lord. Hallelujah!

Small thought here
Salvation is not something to be endured; it's something to be enjoyed.

LET'S DRAW NEAR

Scripture, Hebrews 10:19-39
Let us draw near with a true heart in full assurance of faith, having our hearts sprinkled from an evil conscience, and our bodies washed with pure water. (Heb. 10:22)

Faith never feels sure till it lets God cleanse the conscience and control the behavior. Notice that this passage speaks of His work for us, His work *in* us, and His work *through* us; then it speaks of our attitude and basis for faith. Having boldness through the blood of Christ and "having an high priest over the house of God"; that's His work *for* us (Heb. 10:19, 21). "Having our hearts sprinkled from an evil conscience and our bodies washed with pure water" (10:22); that's His work *in* us. Finally comes this exhortation: "Let us consider one another to provoke unto love and to good works" (10:24); that's His work *through* us. What's our attitude to be in all of this? We ought to "draw near with a true heart, in full assurance of faith" (10:22). What is a true heart? It's absolute honesty with God in all that you think, do, and say. Then you must be willing to meet the requirements for faith's assurance. It's not enough to kid yourself into saying, "I believe everything's all right." Real faith meets God's requirements, brings a guilty heart, and says, "Lord, cleanse it." Real faith brings a body that needs to start living for God and says, "Lord, control it." After doing these two things, you can look up and say, "Lord, I believe You because You are now in charge." It's easy then to meet the challenge of verse 23: "Let us hold fast the profession of our faith without wavering, for He is faithful that promised."

Small thought here

There's no question about God. There won't be any question about you either, my friend, if you follow this route.

GET YOUR FAITH LIFTED

Scriture, Hebrews 11:1-40
Now faith is the substance of things hoped for, the evidence of things not seen. (Heb. 11:1)

W hat is faith? It's risking all that you know about yourself on what you know about God. Here's an Old Testament illustration (2 Kings 6:32—7:2, 17-20): One day the king of Israel sent his executioner to remove the head of God's prophet because a siege was on and there was nothing to eat. This prophet, Elisha, said to his guests, "See how this murderer is sending someone to cut off my head? When the hit man comes, don't let him in. The king is also coming; let's wait for him." When the king arrived, Elisha told him, "Thus says the Lord: tomorrow about this time a measure of fine flour will be sold for a shekel, and two measures of barley for a shekel in the gate of Samaria." An officer of the king answered, "Behold, if the Lord would make windows in heaven, this might happen." Elisha replied, "You will see it with your eyes, but you will not eat any of it." As you know, Elisha's predictions came true. But he didn't call a prayer meeting; he didn't wait for advice; he simply stepped out and said what God would do.

Now, of course, we ought to use our minds and be sensible about things. But the fact remains that most times we are afraid to trust God with a difficult situation. We try to finagle our way through, like Jacob, thinking, "If I do this, He'll do that, and then it'll work out and we can praise the Lord." But faith risks the situation on God.

Small thought here
Think about something you ought to risk on God. Take that risk in faith and you'll find it most fruitful, I promise.

HORIZON-TAL PEACE, VERTICAL HOLINESS

Scripture, Hebrews 12:1-29
Follow peace with all men, and holiness, without which no man shall see the Lord. (Heb. 12:14)

As you know, we are declared holy when we are saved. Paul said of the Corinthian Christians, who surely needed some spiritual house-cleaning, "Such were some of you, but ye are washed, but ye are sanctified" (1 Cor. 6:11); that means made holy. When you trust the Lord Jesus Christ you receive by faith His righteousness and holiness. But the fact remains that God expects you to grow still more, so Paul says, "I beseech you therefore, brethren ... that ye present your bodies a living sacrifice, holy, acceptable unto God, which is your reasonable service" (Rom. 12:1). How do you do this? "Be not con-formed to this world" (12:2). Don't let the world jam you into its mold, its matrix. You don't have to be like everybody else. Just be like Jesus. Be transformed by the renewing of your mind that you may prove what is good, acceptable, and perfect—namely God's will. And how do you "stay" holy and remain in God's will? "By taking heed thereto according to Thy Word" (Ps. 119:9). Our Lord Jesus said, "Now are ye clean through the word which I have spoken unto you" (John 15:3). So the Bible takes effect as you put it into your heart and mind, and your behavior is modified as a result. "Follow peace with all men" (Heb. 12:14). That's godliness in a horizontal relationship; holiness is godliness in a vertical relationship. Make godliness the pursuit of your life.

Small thought here
God declares you holy, but He also expects you to work at it.

FULLY EQUIPPED

Scripture, Hebrews 13:1-25
Now the God of peace ... make you perfect [equip you] in every good work to do His will, working in you that which is well-pleasing in His sight, through Jesus Christ; to whom be glory forever and ever. (Heb. 13:20-21)

How beautifully our Lord equips believers for service! When we come to the Lord Jesus we come spiritually bankrupt, absolutely incapable of anything except failing. But our Lord takes us in, saves us by His grace, and makes us His own children. Then He equips us. Think of that the next time you get discouraged and say "I can't do this. If I were more gifted, or if I had a different background, or if circumstances were otherwise—but they aren't, so what's the use?" All of us get discouraged sometimes. The next time you do, remember that Almighty God is supremely interested in you.

What does God do for you? The word translated *perfect* doesn't mean "without flaw," but "mature, grown up." Don't fight against the experiences of life. Realize that God is using them to shape you. Imagine Him saying just to you, "Don't resent what I'm doing for you. Maybe it hurts; maybe you don't enjoy it; maybe you would have chosen differently; but I'm doing something in your life because you're worth it. I'm growing you up." You know, friend, I want the Lord Jesus to be able to look down on us Christians from His Father's right hand and say, "Calvary was worth it all. Look at them."

Small thought here
Let the Lord grow you up. Remember that His shining covenant and everlasting promises are yours. Remember that He wants to do something in your life that's going to glorify God for all eternity. Hallelujah for that!

October

It is true that the Christian life is *more* than do's and don'ts. It's also a fact that God gave directly to Moses ten *very specific* "thou shalt" and "thou shalt not" commandments to govern man's relationship with God and with the rest of humankind. Today, as in ancient times, many choose to view God's *commandments* merely as *commendments*—to be observed when convenient but ignored when bothersome. This month we'll be "observing" (looking into) the Ten Commandments with a view to "observing" (obeying) them in our lives. Also this month we'll consider the "fruit" that the Spirit of God produces in obedient believers, plus some practical concepts from the "blessed" Beatitudes.

NO OTHER GODS

Scripture, Exodus 20:1-26
Thou shalt have no other gods before Me.
(Ex. 20:3)

When Moses first read the Ten Commandments to God's chosen people, one can well imagine someone saying to his neighbor, "Now there is a command that anyone can understand and obey!" The mind plays strange tricks, however; and to a consideration of this first commandment one must add the memory of the late-lamented golden calf and the judgment that ensued when Moses came down from Mount Sinai. Mingled with these memories would be recollections of Egypt's many deities and the ceremonies and celebrations associated with their worship.

The question of "no other gods" has plagued human nature ever since our first parents walked in the Garden of Eden. Satan's ploy is rarely "no god at all." Rather, he speaks of God *and* something else. In the Garden it was God *and* the forbidden fruit, with a promised benefit that would make them independent of their Creator. Yet our Lord Jesus Christ said clearly, "No man can serve two masters: for either he will hate the one, and love the other; or else he will hold to the one, and despise the other. Ye cannot serve God and mammon" (Matt. 6:24). The glorious truth is that Jesus Christ enables the believer to obey this first commandment. "Christ liveth in me," said Paul, and "it is God which worketh in you both to will and to do of His good pleasure." Yes, for the committed and obedient believer, God takes care of the "want to" as well as the performance.

Small thought here

All too frequently, God is far down the list of important things and people. A man once said to me, "I know I should pay more attention to God, but He isn't bothering me as much as some other people!" Is there any doubt about who is first in your life?

NO GRAVEN IMAGE

Scripture, Exodus 20:1-26
Thou shalt not make unto thee any graven image.
(Ex. 20:4)

The continuing tragedy of the human race is that things and people tend to become more important to us than Almighty God. The *logic* of the second commandment is plain: to worship something created is to elevate a created thing or person to the level of Deity—something which God will not permit. Jehovah declares, "I am the Lord: that is My name; and My glory will I not give to another, neither My praise to graven images" (Isa. 42:8). The *dynamics* of the commandment are also inescapably clear: God cares how you feel about Him, and His control of events reflects that deep desire for your love. "If you hate Me," He says, "you will reap the results of that hatred in your own family, generation after generation. If you show that you love Me by keeping My commandments, I will show you mercy." In other words, mercy depends on sincere worship and love!

Why tie God's loving, jealous heart to this commandment about graven images? Because your attitude toward things shows where your love really is. Indeed, "where your treasure is, there will your heart be also" (Matt. 6:21).

Small thought here

Notice the progression of thought in verses 5 and 6: *Make* . . . any graven image; *bow down* thyself to them; *serve* them. Sin starts with a concept, becomes respectable, and ends with slavery. Put God first and enjoy His love and mercy instead!

WHAT IS PROFANITY?

Scripture, Exodus 20:1-26
Thou shalt not take the name of the Lord thy God in vain.
(Ex. 20:7)

What does "taking the Lord's name in vain" really mean? Ordinarily we think only of profanity, which the dictionary defines as "the act of violating or treating with irreverence or contempt something regarded as sacred." Certainly this is included but much more is involved than we might realize. So let's consider the third commandment in light of a more extended application.

What about words like "gee" or "gosh" or "darn" or "heck"? Most people agree that "gee" and "jeez" are short for Jesus, and "gosh" is slang for God. Does our Lord care about such usage? What about a testimony that is given ostensibly to praising the Lord but which has no real sincerity or conviction? And what about the hymns we sing without giving thought to what we are saying to God? Can you remember what you really meant when you last sang, "All to Jesus I surrender, all to Him I freely give"? As a matter of fact, maybe we ought to consider the way we use God's name as "fillers" in our prayers while forming the next sentence. You don't need to get under bondage in this matter, but just once notice the number of times you use "Lord" and "Father" and other names for Deity simply in a repetitious, nonthinking way. It's something to think about within the context of "using His name in vain."

Small thought here

Careful, intelligent, and prayerful use of the names of God makes for better communication of the Word of Life. See the connection for yourself in Philippians 2:9-16. Verse 11—"Jesus Christ is Lord." Verse 12—"Work out your own salvation (which has been in-worked by the Holy Spirit) with fear and trembling." Verse 13—"God worketh in you." Verses 15 and 16—"Ye shine as lights in the world, holding forth the Word of Life."

HOW DO YOU OBSERVE GOD'S DAY?

Scripture, Exodus 20:1-26
Remember the Sabbath Day, to keep it holy.
(Ex. 20:8)

Based on New Testament practice, the first day of the week is now observed by most believers as the Lord's Day. The risen Christ appeared to Mary and to other disciples on the first day of the week. Paul preached at Troas on the first day of the week, which was the regularly appointed meeting time. Church offerings were also to be collected then. The Apostle John received the beginnings of his Book of Revelation when, as he said, he was "in the Spirit on the Lord's Day."

The underlying truth, and one that is yet significant, is that one day in seven belongs to God. We are not to be in bondage "in respect of an holy day" (Col. 2:16). On the other hand, one of the marks of the end of the age is that "men shall be . . . lovers of pleasure more than lovers of God." The increasing secularization of the Lord's Day must indeed grieve our Lord. As He reminded Isaiah (Isa. 58:13-14), God's day is to be kept holy. Secular duties and concerns are to be set aside, replaced by eternal matters. Miners' mules and manufacturers' machines break down if used continuously. So it is with your soul and body. You need a break from the work-a-day pressures. God's day was to reflect His own procedures in Creation: six days of work and a seventh day of rest.

Small thought here
Sunday should be a day of joy, not of prohibitions; a day of worship, not of selfish preoccupation; a day of blessing, service, and renewal for spirit, soul, and body. Pray about these things, and adjust your Sunday program accordingly. "Remember," God says, "keep it holy!"

GOD AND THE FAMILY

Scripture, Exodus 20:1-26
Honor thy father and thy mother: that thy days may be long upon the land which the Lord thy God giveth thee.
(Ex. 20:12)

In this verse we have these essential ingredients: an attitude, a relationship, a life to invest, a place to live, and a God on whose sovereignty it all depends. The word *honor* means "respect, reverence, esteem, and obedience." All of these concepts are found in Scripture. Paul tells children to "obey your parents in the Lord; for this is right. Honor thy father and mother" (Eph. 6:1-2). Under Mosaic Law, the son or daughter who mocked, scorned, or cursed his or her parents was in danger of being put to death.

One of the marks of a decaying nation is the de-authorization of men and women who previously were held in high esteem . . . governmental and community leaders, teachers, the clergy, and parents. Totalitarian countries have always deliberately trained their youth to give their first allegiance to the state, not to their parents. And it is the present trend in the free world, where the family is breaking up and children deliberately scorn and disobey their parents, which deeply concerns thoughtful people, Christians and non-Christians alike. Praying families, reinforced by wholesome discipline and obedience, are the backbone of a strong nation. But strong nation or not, children who respect their parents is God's design and standard.

Small thought here

To my younger readers: certainly, your parents are not always right; surely, they have their faults. But remember: they are still your parents and God says that you are to respect and honor them. He will keep His end of the promise if you keep yours.

WHEN DOES KILL REALLY MEAN KILL?

Scripture, Exodus 20:1-26
Thou shalt not kill.
(Ex. 20:13)

Murder is the *unlawful* killing of another human being. Nowhere does Scripture imply that it is *always* wrong to take a human life. Executing a criminal and taking up arms in defense of one's homeland are clearly sanctioned in Holy Writ. The just punishment of evildoers is cited by Paul with the words, "If thou do that which is evil, be afraid; for he beareth not the sword in vain" (Rom. 13:4).

The tendency of fallen human nature is to want to remove anything or anyone who gets in its way. A recent report on international gangsterism remarks that these people know only one ultimate procedure: "Get rid of him!" Murder—like every other outward evil action—originates in the heart. And in its heart-form, it is called hatred. "Whoso hateth his brother," John wrote, "is a murderer: and ye know that no murderer hath eternal life abiding in him" (1 John 3:15). What better biblical illustration than Cain, the first murderer.

We come now to the ultimate application of this sixth commandment. Our blessed Saviour said, "Ye have heard that it was said by them of old time, 'Thou shalt not kill.' . . . But I say unto you, that whosoever is angry with his brother without a cause shall be in danger of the judgment: and whosoever shall say to his brother, 'Raca,' shall be in danger of the council: but whosoever shall say, 'Thou fool,' shall be in danger of hell fire" (Matt. 5:21-22). The waters that spawn murder, therefore, turn out to contain such quasi-respectable sins as envy, hatred, anger, and abusive and contemptuous speech! A far cry from what we may have thought when first reading this commandment!

Small thought here

Pray this prayer: "O Lord, save me from the murderous feelings that spring up in my heart . . . envy, resentment, hatred, anger. Fill me with the love of God, shed abroad in my heart by the Holy Spirit. Amen."

THE SCARLET SIN: ITS CAUSE AND CURE

Scripture, Exodus 20:1-26
Thou shalt not commit adultery.
(Ex. 20:14)

Leviticus 20 pronounced the death penalty not only on adulterers but also on practitioners of other forms of immorality, including homosexuality. There was no uncertainty about God's command in that day nor should there be any vagueness about it today. You and I, believers in the Lord Jesus Christ, are God's vessels, and are therefore to keep ourselves clean (1 Cor. 16:19-20).

Our Lord Jesus boiled down the problem of adultery to a wayward look: "Whosoever looketh on a woman to lust after her hath committed adultery with her already in his heart" (Matt. 5:27-28). And Simon Peter, having learned his lessons from the Master, spoke of those "having eyes full of adultery, and that cannot cease from sin" (2 Peter 2:14). Human beings *do* have physical temptations. But what do we do about them? Are we forever to be condemned by God's command or can we hide behind the fact that "I'm only human, after all"? Though there is no hiding place or excuse for the person who cannot or will not face God's truth, there is a resource available to anyone who will take it: the Lord Jesus Christ Himself. It is *His* life, taken by faith, and exchanged for our poor, failing human natures, that will give victory over adultery. When our blessed Lord looks through our eyes, it will be a clean look. When He speaks, the words will be wholesome, helpful words; and when He touches another, the touch will be healing and helping, not hindering and defiling.

Small thought here

Never try to fight temptation alone. The moment you are tempted, either to do wrong or not to do right, yield yourself to your living Lord. "I can," said Paul, "do all things through Christ, which strengtheneth me" (Phil. 4:13).

"BORROWING" AND OTHER FORMS OF STEALING

Scripture, Exodus 20:1-26
Thou shalt not steal.
(Ex. 20:15)

There is a little larceny—sometimes a lot—in every human heart. The sinfulness of the human race is demonstrated early in life, when before he learns to toddle, Daddy's pride and joy is not above grabbing for himself something that belongs to another. As the years pass, of course, humans learn to steal in more subtle ways. The tendency is there, however. Why else did the most spiritual church in New Testament times need Paul's admonition, "Let him that stole steal no more; but rather let him labor with his hands the thing which is good, that he may have to give to him that needeth"? (Eph. 4:28)

When we think about God's commandment against stealing, we generally think in terms of *things* or money. But there are many other areas of life to which this commandment applies as well. Gossip, with its double-edged sword, steals something more valuable than money. Shakespeare said: "Who steals my purse steals trash; 'tis something, nothing. . . . But he that filches from me my good name robs me of that which not enriches him, and makes me poor indeed." And what about stealing time? Each time you are late for an appointment or stretch a ten-minute coffee break into a half-hour siesta, you are stealing time.

The cure for stealing lies not in its prohibition but rather in a changed attitude. Look again at Ephesians 4:28. "Rather," Paul says, "let him labor, working with his hands . . . *that he may have to give to him that needeth.*" The reason for working productively is that we may be in positions to help others! Give, not get, is the essence of the change God wants to make in a dishonest heart.

Small thought here

Once you know the joy of *giving*, you will disdain forever the practice of *grabbing.*

OCTOBER 9 *TODAY with the King*

"PEOPLE WILL TALK!"

Scripture, Exodus 20:1-26
Thou shalt not bear false witness against thy neighbor.
(Ex. 20:16)

This commandment, quoted both by our Lord Jesus Christ and by the Apostle Paul, has particular significance for us today. With the rapid advance of high technology, we are well into the shift from an industrial society to what John Naisbitt, in *Megatrends*, calls an "information society." Today, more people know more about more things, and they know it sooner and in more detail! The result is that information about people—some of it very damaging—can be spread far and wide before the subject is even aware of it! Some years ago a Christian leader called me from the West Coast to check on something that I had allegedly said about him. In a matter of hours, the misinformation had traveled across the North American continent!

Here are some of the things the Bible says about false witnesses:
• When you speak an untruth about another, you are joining hands with wicked people (Ex. 23:1).
• To display righteousness, stick to the truth. False witness only demonstrates deceitfulness! (Prov. 12:17)
• Think seriously about *why* you must speak any critical word. Many a criticism and false statement comes from thoughtlessness about this matter of "cause" (Prov. 24:28).
• A person who bears false witness, says Solomon, is like a maul (makes bruises), a sword (wounds deeply), and a sharp arrow (pierces deeply, and kills something that cannot be revived: friendship).

Small thought here
The Christian cure for false witness is "speaking the truth in love" (Eph. 4:15). Indeed, Paul's admonition to the Ephesian believers points out that Christian growth and the lordship of Christ are tied to this simple but dynamic habit: the truth always ... in love always.

318

COVETOUS-NESS, THE CLOAK OF IDOLATRY

Scripture, Exodus 20:1-26
Thou shalt not covet . . . anything that is thy neighbor's.
(Ex. 20:17)

Is it sinful to want something—say, new drapes for the living room or a car to replace the one that is about to expire? Are we in danger of backsliding if we want a better computer or a college degree? Quite the contrary! God wants to give us what we want, if we are first bent on worshiping and serving Him (Ps. 37:4). The trouble with longing for something is that it tends to become paramount in one's life; and when that happens, then according to Paul, covetousness has become idolatry—it has taken God's place in the heart! Our Saviour pointed out that to be really *living*, one does not depend on "the abundance of the things which he possesseth." Things can never satisfy. God said to the greedy farmer, "Thou fool, this night thy soul shall be required of thee" (Luke 12:20).

If you would be a leader in God's work, Paul says, you must be one who is "not covetous." There is a built-in antipathy between true consecration to God and His work on one hand, and love of things and money, on the other. If people discover that you are in God's service for what you can get out of it, they will refuse to follow you. The cure for covetousness is contentment; and the source of contentment is to know God Himself is all you ever need! "Let your conversatin be without covetousness; and be content with such things as ye have: for He hath said, 'I will never leave thee, nor forsake thee'" (Heb. 13:5).

Small thought here
This is the logic of contentment: when you delight in your Lord, you want what He wants; and when you want what He wants, He is glad to give you "the desires of your heart." No need for coveting, then, for you have what you wanted all along!

SPIRITUAL POVERTY AND WHAT TO DO ABOUT IT

Scripture, Matthew 5:1-16
Blessed are the poor in spirit: for theirs is the kingdom of heaven.
(Matt. 5:3)

Apart from God, the spirit of a man—however courageous—is not sufficient. Sooner or later, one comes to the end of himself and is forced to admit that he has run out of human resources. There is nothing left with which to confront life's storms. What then? One of the best things that can happen to a person is to be faced with his spiritual bankruptcy. As long as the alcoholic keeps saying, "Give me one more chance . . . I'll lick this thing!" he is doomed to repeat his mistakes. As long as the prodigal says, "I'll get by some way . . . let me go to work for this farmer," he will remain unsatisfied, rejected, and lonely. Only when, like the prodigal, we come to the end of ourselves and turn to God do we find the help we need.

What our Lord was saying here was this: "When you come to the end of yourself and are ready to make Me your Lord and to put Me on the throne of your heart, *then* you will be truly "satisfied." The Greek work translated *blessed* is one which denotes the condition of being happy, blithesome, joyous, and prosperous. The way to this kind of experience is to give up depending on yourself, to become truly poor in spirit, and to enter into a relationship with God where He truly is King of your life. That's what the word *kingdom* really means, doesn't it?

Small thought here
Write on a piece of paper the areas in your life where you have been depending on yourself. Now bring them, one by one, to your Lord, and ask Him as your King to direct you in each of them. You'll be blessed—Jesus said so!

SAD HEART, GLAD HEART

Scripture, Matthew 5:1-16
Blessed are they that mourn: for they shall be comforted.
(Matt. 5:4)

Humanly speaking, the one who can best comfort us when our hearts are breaking is another human being whose heart also has broken with sorrow and grief (2 Cor. 1:3-4). Sorrow and mourning are experiences we try to avoid. We do not so much as think about the subject if we can help it. We are embarrassed and stiffly correct in the presence of another who is going through it. We are the victims of the unspoken question, "Why?"

Sorrow was not part of the original Creation. Sorrow, bereavement, grief, and heartbreak are the result of sin (Gen. 3:16-17). But part of the glory of God's redemptive plan is that the Holy Spirit, who indwells every believer, is our "Comforter." The Lord Jesus called Him that, and the early church found Him so for Luke wrote that the churches, "walking in the fear of the Lord, and in the comfort of the Holy Ghost, were multiplied" (Acts 9:31). Where sin (and sorrow) abounded, grace did much more abound!

How does God comfort? By His presence: "Thou, Lord, hast . . . comforted me" (Ps. 86:17). By His Word: "Mine eyes fail for Thy word, saying, 'When wilt Thou comfort me?' " (Ps. 119:82) By other believers: "Nevertheless God, that comforteth those that are cast down, comforted us by the coming of Titus" (2 Cor. 7:6).

Small thought here

Are you going through sorrow? Don't fight your tears and thus waste them. Paul exhorted believers to "weep with them that weep" (Rom. 12:15). God comforts you so you can comfort someone else and lead him or her to Jesus.

DOES MEEK MEAN WEAK?

Scripture, Matthew 5:1-16
Blessed are the meek: for they shall inherit the earth.
(Matt. 5:5)

Our Saviour, the Lord Jesus Christ, is the embodiment of this truth. He said of Himself, "I am meek and lowly." His triumphal entry into Jerusalem was a fulfillment of Old Testament prophecies, one of which said, "Behold thy King cometh unto thee, meek." Our Lord was actually quoting Psalm 37:11 when He uttered these words in the Beatitudes.

The believer is not only exhorted to be meek, but is enabled to achieve this attribute by the indwelling Holy Spirit. "The fruit of the Spirit is . . . meekness" (Gal. 5:23). Meekness beautifies the life. Peter spoke of "the ornament of a meek and quiet spirit, which is in the sight of God of great price" (1 Peter 3:4). Meekness enables one to deal gently and helpfully with the weakness and failures of others: "Ye which are spiritual restore such an one in the spirit of meekness" (Gal. 6:1). Meekness is one of the qualities after which we are commanded to strive: "Follow after righteousness, godliness, faith, love, patience, meekness" (2 Tim. 6:11).

Now back to our original question: Does *meek* mean "weak"? Definitely not. Two examples will suffice: Moses, we read in Numbers 12:3, was "very meek, above all the men which were upon the face of the earth." Read the life of the "Great Lawgiver" and tell me whether you think he was weak! The greatest example of all, of course, is our Lord Jesus Christ. He is "the lion of the tribe of Judah, King of kings and Lord of lords," but He said of Himself, "I am meek."

Small thought here

Meekness is the human side of humility, a godward virtue. If you are truly humble before God, you will be mild, gentle, and meek with your fellow man.

HUNGRY FOR GOD!

Scripture, Matthew 5:1-16
Blessed are they which do hunger and thirst after righteousness: for they shall be filled. (Matt. 5:6)

Some people seem hungry for God from childhood on; others seem to lack this trait entirely—a strange and baffling fact. Capacity for spiritual things often *seems* to be inherited, much as color of hair and eyes. *Seems*, I say, because every so often the facts of the Christian life knock out this theory. The truth of the matter is that when Jesus Christ becomes Lord of your life and Saviour of your soul, He implants within you a new nature—a nature which is always hungry for God! "As newborn babes," Peter said, "desire the sincere milk of the Word, that ye may grow thereby" (1 Peter 2:2). Jeremiah exclaimed, "Thy words were found and I did eat them, and Thy word was unto me the joy and rejoicing of my heart" (Jer. 15:16). Jesus told His disciples, "These things have I spoken unto you, that My joy might remain in you, and that your joy might be full" (John 16:24).

"Hunger," said our Lord, "*and* thirst." This brings us to the thought that the God-thirst of our hearts is satisfied only by the indwelling Holy Spirit. Our Lord said, " 'If any man thirst, let him come unto Me, and drink.' . . . This spake He of the Spirit, which they that believe on Him should receive" (John 7:37-39). Here, then, is the answer to the hunger and thirst of that new nature that God has given us: our hunger is satisfied by the Word of God and our thirst is assuaged by the Holy Spirit as He fills every room in our "heart-house."

Small thought here

If you are hungry for God, you will not be disappointed. "Draw nigh to God," said James, "and He will draw nigh to you" (James 4:8).

MERCY IN ACTION

Scripture, Matthew 5:1-16
Blessed are the merciful: for they shall obtain mercy.
(Matt. 5:7)

This word *mercy* is rich in its original meanings, among them: "to be gracious; to console; to bring help to the afflicted." Mercy is an action word; it rolls up its sleeves and gets to work when the need arises. Not surprisingly, most of the biblical references dealing with mercy speak of God. Hundreds of verses remind us that the Lord is merciful and long-suffering toward sinners. "Merciful and gracious" is a combination often used to describe Him. All the more awesome, then, is our Saviour's command: "Be ye therefore merciful, as your Father also is merciful" (Luke 6:36). One can hear someone saying, "I should measure up to a standard like that? No way!" The fact is that the whole Christian life contains standards to which we cannot possibly conform, short of a miracle. But that is just what God offers to do for each believer, as the Holy Spirit creates in an otherwise bankrupt and helpless personality the very attributes of our Lord! Paul calls them the fruit of the Spirit (Gal. 5:22-23).

Small thought here
The classic illustration of mercy in action is the parable of the Good Samaritan (Luke 10:25-37). After telling the inquiring lawyer this story about the wounded victim who had been ignored by both priest and Levite, but aided by the Samaritan, Jesus asked, "Which now of these three ... was neighbor unto him that fell among thieves?" Immediately came the reply: "He that showed mercy on him." Show mercy to someone today, dear friend. You'll be a blessing!

FROM DEFILED HEART TO PURE HEART

Scripture, Matthew 5:1-16
Blessed are the pure in heart: for they shall see God.
(Matt. 5:8)

Our Lord Jesus never minced words. When speaking about defilement and its cause, He said, "Not that which goeth into the mouth defileth a man; but that which cometh out of the mouth, this defileth a man" (Matt. 15:11). When the puzzled disciples asked for an explanation, He said, "Those things which proceed out of the mouth *come forth from the heart*; and they defile the man. For out of the heart proceed evil thoughts, murders, adulteries, fornications, thefts, false witness, blasphemies: these are the things which defile a man" (15:18). So, to have a defiled heart in the scriptural sense means that the motives produced by our old sinful natures are evil and result in sinful actions. Therefore, to have a pure heart must involve the same area of motivation. Down deep in our hearts we must really *want* God's will.

The miracle of salvation is that God does indeed give "a new heart" to those who commit themselves to Jesus Christ as Lord and Saviour: "I will give them one heart, and I will put a new spirit within you; and I will take the stony heart out of their flesh, and will give them an heart of flesh: that they may walk in My statutes, and keep Mine ordinances, and do them" (Ezek. 11:19-20).

Small thought here

Alone, you will never be able to manage your heart, that is, your deepest desires and motives. Give your heart to Jesus and let it be "God that worketh in you, both to will and to do of His good pleasure" (Phil. 2:13).

WHAT IS A PEACE-MAKER?

Scripture, Matthew 5:1-16
Blessed are the peacemakers: for they shall be called the children of God.
(Matt. 5:9)

In America's Wild West era, a "peacemaker" meant only one thing: a Colt .45 revolver. With that formidable piece of hardware strapped on his hip, a man could stand up against all his enemies, or so they said. Hardly the meaning of Christ's teaching, you will agree. Making peace is more than exerting force, or using influence, or acting as a referee. No, peacemaking is far more than that. It reaches into the depths of the heart and calls for a dynamic power that will make people want to get along peaceably.

The source of peace for the believer, of course, is the Lord Jesus Christ. "He is our peace," wrote Paul, "who hath made both one . . . having abolished in His flesh the enmity . . . to make in Himself of twain one new man, so making peace" (Eph. 2:14-15). The Saviour Himself said, "These things I have spoken unto you, that in Me ye might have peace" (John 16:33). Furthermore, the Holy Spirit duplicates this attribute of the Saviour in every heart that is filled with Him: "The fruit of the Spirit is love, joy, peace." To be peacemakers means that we do what Jesus did: helping to bring people into a right relationship with God and with each other through what we are, do, and say.

Small thought here

There is more to the fruit of the Spirit than just a list of good qualities to desire and to take by faith. That, of course, is true. However, to be peacemakers, you and I must be so full of God's love and joy that people will feel comfortable with us, will trust us, and will want to be like us. That is an assignment that calls for the work of the Holy Spirit. He is ready when you are.

IS THAT FAIR?

Scripture, Matthew 5:1-16
Blessed are they which are persecuted for righteousness' sake: for theirs is the kingdom of heaven.
(Matt. 5:10)

Peter, ever the businessman, asked our Lord one day about the "bottom line": "We have left all and followed Thee. What shall we have, therefore?" To which Christ replied, "There is no man that hath left house, or brethren, or sisters, or father, or mother, or wife, or children, or lands, for My sake, and the Gospel's, but he shall receive an hundredfold now in this time ... with persecutions; and in the world to come eternal life" (Mark 10:29). Blessings—with persecutions: that's the divine combination.

During a visit to Colombia, South America, I spoke with an old man who for years had been a leader in the local church. "How are things going?" I asked. "Well enough," he replied, "but not as well as when we were under persecution. In those days, the persecution drove us to our knees, and as we prayed together, the church prospered and believers grew spiritually. Now we have it too easy, I am afraid, and the people forget to pray."

Certainly, persecution is impossible to bear with human strength alone. And we would never ask for it. But though you and I do not like trouble, opposition, or loss because of our Christian testimony, we can be sure that the blessing of God attends us through it all. Jesus said so!

Small thought here
The next time you are under the pressure of a difficult situation, trying looking to your Saviour and saying, "Lord Jesus, I don't like this, but I am going to go through it for Thy glory. Help me learn what I should and give me the blessing You promised!"

THE PERSONAL TOUCH

Scripture, Matthew 5:1-16
Blessed are ye, when men shall revile you, and persecute you, and shall say all manner of evil against you falsely, for My sake. (Matt. 5:11)

It is quite possible to believe all of the Beatitudes but to back away from any personal application of them, especially when it comes to suffering for Christ. In this passage, the Saviour seems intent on nailing down a personal application of the truth. How can we be blessed when someone is lying about us or harassing us just because we're Christians? It all depends on: (1) for whom, (2) for what, and (3) in whose company. Let's look at these three concepts:
• "Men shall revile you, etc. *for My sake,*" Jesus said. If we are getting the heat because of our own faults and failings, that is one thing; but if what we are experiencing comes for *His* sake, the matter is viewed in an entirely different light. "Unto you it is given *in the behalf of Christ,*" Paul said to the church at Philippi, "not only to believe on Him, but also to suffer for His sake" (Phil. 1:29).
• "Great is your reward in heaven." We are living not only for the here and now, but also for eternity. The Judgment Seat of Christ is coming, and His rewards will be given to those who have been faithful. Remember: Jesus never minimized or exaggerated. If He said the reward is great, then it is great, and because it is, no suffering is too much for His sake.
• "So persecuted they the prophets which were before you." Those who suffer for Christ are in wonderful company. Indeed, if being persecuted for Christ puts us with the likes of Abraham, David, and Isaiah, we ought to be glad to belong!

Small thought here
Put yourself in the Beatitudes. Not "they" but "I." That makes a difference, doesn't it, dear friend!

PASS THE SALT, PLEASE!

Scripture, Matthew 5:1-16
Ye are the salt of the earth.
(Matt. 5:13)

Salt adds flavor, combats infections, and acts as a preservative. All of which is well and good—unless the salt has lost its saltiness, in which case it is no good at all. According to Dr. Luke, it cannot be used as fill, to build up topsoil, or even as fertilizer. It is just plain useless! "Ye are the salt of the earth," our Lord said. Why did He choose this metaphor to describe the disciples' relationship to the world? Christians add flavor and spice to life. One believer can make a difference! Christians combat evil and act as a godly preservative in society. By virtue of the fact that Christ indwells the believer through the Holy Spirit, the atmosphere of a Christian's life and personality is bound to make a difference wherever he or she may go.

The secret of continued "saltiness" is to be found within one's own heart. Jesus said, "Have salt in yourselves" (Mark 9:50). There is no substitute for daily contact with God through His Word and through prayer to maintain the "salt content" of your life! To neglect these resources is to lose your impact on a stale, polluted, and decaying world. Lot moved to Sodom, but lost his impact because, while there, Sodom got into him! When he went to warn his sons-in-law of impending judgment, they thought he was joking!

Small thought here

Preserve, at all cost, your daily dynamic contact with your Lord! The alternative is probably the saddest phrase ever used to describe a believer: "Good for nothing, but to be cast out, and to be trodden under foot of men" (Matt. 5:13). Paul disciplined himself, lest, he said, "When I have preached to others, I myself should be a castaway" (1 Cor. 9:27).

THIS LITTLE LIGHT OF MINE

Scripture, Matthew 5:1-16
Ye are the light of the world.
(Matt. 5:14)

If you truly know our Lord, there will be a radiance about you that cannot be concealed! "A city that is set on a hill cannot be hid," said the Master. Much of the discomfort experienced by believers, especially teenagers, comes from an effort to disguise the shine of the Christian life, to thus be accepted by those who are still walking in darkness.

Some things keep the spiritual light from shining. They act like the soot which gathered inside the chimneys of kerosene lamps used in my boyhood farm home. By Saturday night, those glass chimneys were dim with the smoke of a week's use. "Time to clean them chimneys, Boy!" my uncle would say. And I would get to work with wads of old newspaper, cleaning the glass until it was clear and glistening. Then the light really did shine! Mark records what our Lord said about the hindrances to shining: "Is a candle brought to be put under a bushel, or under a bed? And not to be set on a candlestick?" (Mark 4:21) The bushel speaks of business and daily routines. It's possible to become so busy making money or achieving success that the light is dimmed and finally concealed entirely. The bed speaks of rest, not to say laziness. Sheer neglect and indolence have accounted for many a lost testimony. "The tendency of the fire is to go out," my old boss, Victor Cory, used to say. Keep the fires of faith burning brightly upon the altar of your soul.

Small thought here
People evaluate, not your speeches or your badges, but your actions. God's light—the Lord Jesus—dwells in you. Raise the shades, clean away the dust and soot, remove the bushel basket, and let your light shine!

FRUIT-BEARING AND OTHER THINGS

Scripture, Galatians 5:19-23
The fruit of the Spirit is love, joy, peace.
(Gal. 5:22)

Jesus spoke of fruit in his "Vine and Branches" discourse (John 15). "Fruit" presupposes organized, reproductive, purposeful, and dependent life. The branch is *in* the Vine: a life relationship. The branch bears fruit: a productive relationship. The branch is pruned: a purposeful and progressive relationship. The branch may be removed if it remains fruitless: a disciplinary relationship. The branch can do nothing at all without the Vine: a dependent relationship. The branch perpetuates and reproduces the life of the Vine: a continuing relationship.

With these concepts in mind, look at Galatians 5:22-23. The "fruit of the Spirit" presupposes a life relationship, one that is dependent, productive, and reproducing the life of the Spirit as He manifests Christ through the individual believer. "Fruit" can never be produced by our own efforts. Indeed, *all* that the human heart is capable of producing in its own strength are the "works of the flesh" (5:19-21). Oh for the fruit that the Holy Spirit can bear in our lives when we yield to Him! If you are tired of "trying to act like a Christian," open your heart to the Spirit of God and let Him begin to bear His blessed fruit in your life.

Small thought here
The key to the change from "works" to "fruit" lies in the concept of surrender. When you were "trying" to live like a Christian, you put forth every effort, but became weary. Finally, you gave up. Now, Paul says, as you gave up to sin, in the same way, give up to Jesus! (Rom. 6:19) Surrender is built into your bones. Ultimately you will give up to something or somebody, so why not surrender to Christ?

THE SHAPE OF LOVE

Scripture, Galatians 5:19-23
But the fruit of the Spirit is love.
(Gal. 5:22)

The word *love* in verse 22 (from the Greek *agape*) is a special kind of love—the John 3:16 kind. Found in many other New Testament passages, it always refers to God's redeeming love in Christ, which is implanted in our hearts by His Holy Spirit when we trust Him as our Saviour.

• *This is a preceding love.* "Herein is love, not that we loved God, but that He loved us, and sent His Son to be the propitiation for our sins" (1 John 4:10). Your Christian life will be deepened considerably when you realize that God has loved you from before the foundation of the world.

• *This is a persistent love.* John writes: "Having loved His own which were in the world, He loved them unto the end" (John 13:1). Jesus will never give up on you!

• *This is a powerful love.* One glimpse of the love of Christ will convince anyone that there is more to live for than self-satisfaction. "Not henceforth live unto themselves" (2 Cor. 5:15) is another way of saying: "If Christ loved me enough to die on the cross for me, I can never be content until I am living for Him!"

• *This is a persuasive love.* God's love, shining through your life, will do more to draw people to Christ than any amount of sermons! And this love will fill your heart by the same process through which you experienced the new birth: through faith!

Small thought here
Give up the thought of achieving this divine miracle of love through your own efforts. When someone says, "I'm trying to love him or her," it is a pretty good sign that the Holy Spirit hasn't had a chance to work. Let Christ love others *through* your yielded life.

JOY! MORE THAN HAPPINESS

Scripture, Galatians 5:19-23
The fruit of the Spirit is . . . joy.
(Gal. 5:22)

The human race has always been obsessed with the desire for happiness. America's founding fathers spoke of "the pursuit of happiness." Defined as "good luck, good fortune, prosperity, a state of well-being and pleasurable satisfaction, bliss," this condition would seem to be most desirable. The problem is that having achieved the experience, or possession, or position we thought would bring happiness, we aren't happy very long; and an unexpected reversal of circumstances can turn happiness into wretchedness in short order! *Joy,* on the other hand, is defined as "the emotion excited by the acquisition or expectation of good; gladness; delight." Quite evidently, there is a connection between one's value system and joy or the lack of it. *Joy* relates to "good" and "glad" while *happy* relates to "happen." Certain "happenings" may make you happy, but only God's goodness can make you joyful.

With this in mind, look with me at some Scriptures that bear on that subject:
- *There is joy in God's Word* (John 15:11; Jer. 15:16).
- *There is joy in knowing God's presence* (Ps. 16:11).
- *There is joy in reaping God's harvest of souls* (Ps. 126:5).
- *There is joy in answered prayer* (John 16:24).

The blessed Holy Spirit is the author of all this joy, and much more. "For the kingdom of God is not meat and drink," said Paul, "but righteousness, and peace, and joy in the Holy Ghost" (Rom 14:17).

Small thought here

Focus one whole day on what God is doing through you and around you, rather than on what is happening to you and how you feel about it. You will be amazed and delighted at the *genuine* joy you experience!

MAKE GOD'S PEACE PERSONAL

Scripture, Galatians 5:19-23
The fruit of the Spirit is . . . peace.
(Gal. 5:22)

Everything about our relationship with the living God turns out to be personal, and the ministry of the blessed Holy Spirit is no exception. He produces God's wonderful peace in the believer's life when He is in control. The fruit (result of His presence and control) of the Spirit is *peace*. The Holy Spirit also reveals Christ, who *is* our peace (Eph. 2:14). He stands between us and a holy God and unites us with those human beings with whom, because of our sin, we were at enmity.

• *This peace involves a new focus of attention.* "Thou wilt keep him in perfect peace," said Isaiah, "whose mind is stayed on Thee, because he trusteth in Thee" (Isa. 26:3). Get your mind on God and what He can do, and you will spend a lot less time worrying!

• *This peace also involves a new procedure.* "Don't worry about anything," said Paul, "but pray about everything! And the peace of God which passeth all understanding, shall keep your hearts and minds through Christ Jesus" (Phil. 4:6-7). Specific praying tends to defuse worry that otherwise can crush you. When, by faith, you place God in control of a situation, the storm may rage on the outside, but you have His peace within!

Small thought here
The heart that is at peace is also one that loves God's Word: "Great peace have they that love Thy Law, and nothing shall offend them" (Ps. 119:165). Fill your mind and heart with God's blessed Word, and see for yourself how it protects you from life's bumps and bruises! Why be a victim, when you can be "offense-proof"!

MAKE ROOM IN YOUR HEART

Scripture, Galatians 5:19-23
The fruit of the Spirit is . . . long-suffering.
(Gal. 5:22)

The word *long-suffering* literally means "long-spirited" or "large-hearted." The emphasis is on patience and willingness to endure. Underlying this patient willingness to put up with people is the concept of large-heartedness: room in your heart for people . . . as they are, not as you wish they were, or as they ought to be! In other words, this fruit of the Spirit involves a great deal more than just "coping" with people. It involves love and acceptance of another human being.

Dr. Dick Hillis told the story of an interpreter whom he had hired to help him get the Gospel message to some mountain tribes in Formosa. There was some genuine doubt in Hillis' mind as to whether this interpreter really was committed to Christ; however, he was quite conversant with the Gospel message, so they began the journey. One day, this interpreter came to Dr. Hillis and said, "I am now a Christian. Your God is my God and your Saviour is my Saviour." "When did this happen?" asked the missionary. "Do you remember that cold night when we had nowhere to stay and had to sleep in a farmer's barn?" "Oh, I remember it well!" Hillis replied. "And do you remember that we only had one blanket—yours—and that you shared it with me?" "Yes, I remember." "And do you remember that in the morning, *I* had the blanket, and you were just about frozen?" Laughing, Hillis said, "Yes, I remember!" "That was when I decided to become a Christian. I had your blanket; you were very cold; and you weren't even angry!"

Small thought here
The most effective sermons are often preached by "long-suffering"—large-hearted conduct.

A HEAVENLY VIRTUE

Scripture, Galatians 5:19-23
The fruit of the Spirit is . . . gentleness.
(Gal. 5:22)

W e ought to count it one of the supreme gifts of God's grace that He designs to take something that is part of His nature, such as gentleness, and makes it ours through the indwelling Holy Spirit! *There is a gentleness that is yielding and pliable,* as in Titus 3:2—"To speak evil of no man, to be no brawlers, but gentle, showing all meekness unto all men." *Then there is a gentleness characterized by mildness and affection,* as in 1 Thessalonians 2:7, where Paul spoke of his ministry: "We were gentle among you, even as a nurse cherisheth her children." *There is also a gentleness that prepares the way for effective teaching:* Paul exhorted young Timothy, "The servant of the Lord must not strive; but be gentle unto all men, apt to teach, patient, in meekness instructing those that oppose themselves" (2 Tim. 2:24).

Advancement and greatness evidently come through gentleness: "Thy gentleness hath made me great," said the psalmist (Ps. 18:35). As anyone knows who has walked with the Lord for a while, the way up . . . is down! "Humble yourselves in the sight of the Lord," said James, "and He shall lift you up" (James 4:10). Peter echoed the same sentiment: "Humble yourselves therefore under the mighty hand of God, that He may exalt you in due time" (1 Peter 5:6).

Small thought here

Interestingly enough, the word we find in Galatians 5:22 comes from a root that means useful! You want God to use you? Let His Holy Spirit make you gentle!

GOOD FOR WHAT?

Scripture, Galatians 5:19-23
The fruit of the Spirit is . . . goodness.
(Gal. 5:22)

The Greek word translated *goodness* here means uprightness of heart and life. Paul uses the same word in speaking of God (2 Thes. 1:11). Goodness has a number of famous neighbors! Paul wrote that "the fruit of the Spirit is in all goodness and righteousness and truth" (Eph. 5:9). And in writing to the Romans he said, "Now the God of hope fill you with all joy and peace in believing, that ye may abound in hope, through the power of the Holy Ghost. And I myself also am persuaded . . . that ye are full of goodness, filled with all knowledge, able also to admonish one another" (Rom. 15:13-14). Yes, next door to goodness dwells righteousness, truth, hope, joy, peace, power, knowledge, and the ability to admonish. And we receive them all when we yield to the blessed Holy Spirit!

God has something eternally significant in mind when He offers us His goodness. And God's purpose for us is always connected with His plan to glorify the Lord Jesus Christ: "That the name of our Lord Jesus Christ may be glorified in you, and ye in Him, according to the grace of our God and the Lord Jesus Christ" (1 Thes. 1:12).

Small thought here
God wants you to be characterized by His goodness, but not for goodness' sake alone. You are to be "good for something"! This heavenly goodness, produced within your redeemed heart and life by the Holy Spirit, is designed to bring honor to your wonderful Lord.

RISK IT ON GOD!

Scripture, Galatians 5:19-23
The fruit of the Spirit is . . . faith.
(Gal. 5:22)

Faith is confidence in a Person. Jesus exhorted His disciples, "Have faith in God!" (Mark 11:22) The background of this divine plea was the disciples' amazement that the fig tree to which Christ had spoken the day before was already withered. Those who knew Scripture realized that He was giving an object lesson pointed at God's fig-tree nation, Israel, which had been without spiritual fruit and was now about to be judged. Peter, however, missed the point and Jesus had to remind him that he was dealing, not with ordinary situations, but *with God!*

Have you learned, dear friend, to relate the circumstances and challenges of life to the fact that you are a partner with Almighty God? "We are laborers together with God," said Paul (1 Cor. 3:9). Meditate on this truth until it stirs your heart with a holy thrill: you and God are working *together* on things!

Faith is based not only on a wonderful Person, but also on His Word (Luke 11:9). Discover the joy of praying on the authority of God's promises. Dig deeply into God's Word until you have found some promises relating to your prayer concern. Now pray, not on the basis of *what you want*, but on the basis of what *God* wants, as revealed in His Word. "If we ask anything according to His will . . . we know that we *have* the petitions that we desired of Him" (1 John 5:14-15).

Small thought here

Faith is not really faith unless it is willing to risk the outcome of the situation on obedience to God's command. "Whatsoever He saith unto you," said his mother Mary to the servants at the wedding feast, "do it" (John 2:5). And when they obeyed Jesus' command, water became wine. Obedience by faith opens the door to miracles.

HOW HE GOT THAT WAY

Scripture, Galatians 5:19-23
The fruit of the Spirit is . . . meekness.
(Gal. 5:23)

Look with me at some of the factors that contribute to meekness. We read that "Moses was very meek, above all the men which were upon the face of the earth" (Num. 12:3). When and how did this trait develop? In early childhood, Moses certainly must have heard from his mother and sister the story of how he was rescued from the river by Pharaoh's daughter. He probably thought, "I must be pretty special." Later, when he went back to live at the palace, he was schooled in all the learning of the Egyptians (Acts 7:22). He probably thought, "I'm very wise." Even when Moses came of age and "chose rather to endure affliction with the people of God" (Heb. 11:25) than to enjoy the pleasure of ruling over a vast empire, we find no hint of meekness. There came the day when, having thrown in his lot with God's people and having been trained in the authority of the royal household, he began to exert that authority by killing and hiding the body of an Egyptian who had beaten one of the Hebrew slaves. Still no evidence of meekness. Not until Moses was confronted by the very presence of God at the burning bush did he show signs of humility and meekness. When God commissioned him, saying, "Come now therefore, and I will send thee unto Pharaoh, that thou mayest bring forth My people . . . out of Egypt," Moses must have remembered the failure and fleeing . . . and the skepticism of his own people.

The path to meekness is to face your shortcomings and failures with God (Ps. 69:5). When Moses came face to face with God, he began to realize what an impossible task godly leadership is apart from the Lord's enablement.

Small thought here

Point of view means everything. If you look only at your own weakness and need, you may get discouraged, but you will not necessarily be meek. But if you look to God and to His promises, your awareness of human frailty will make you kind, gentle, and meek toward others.

WHO'S IN CONTROL?

Scripture, Galatians 5:19-23
The fruit of the Spirit is . . . temperance.
(Gal. 5:23)

Suffer a little word study here, will you? The Greek word translated *temperance* is a compound word meaning "inner strength." First, we have a little prefix, *en*, followed by *krateia*, a word related to *kratos*, meaning "force, power, or dominion." What Paul is saying is that when the Holy Spirit is in control of your life, there will be force to drive you, power to keep you in line, and dominion to make your life an experience of victory, not defeat.

The Holy Spirit provides the power to keep you going in God's will. The Spirit-filled Christian need not experience burnout! "If the Spirit of Him that raised up Jesus from the dead dwell in you," Paul wrote, "He that raised up Christ from the dead shall also quicken your mortal bodies by His Spirit that dwelleth in you" (Rom. 8:11). *Mortal* means "still alive, but capable of dying." *Quicken* means "give life to." When the Holy Spirit provides the power there's no need to worry about collapsing! When He gives that inner strength of which our text speaks, life is filled with dominion instead of drudgery. To be blessedly in control of one's life because God is running things— that is joy indeed! And it all begins when you trust God to supply the lacking dimensions of your redeemed personality.

Small thought here

"Inner strength"—what the Bible calls temperance—is achieved by faith. Confess your need, ask for His supply, and receive it by faith. Our Heavenly Father says, "Fear thou not; for I am with thee; be not dismayed; for I am thy God; I will strengthen thee; yea, I will help thee; yea I will uphold thee with the right hand of My righteousness" (Isa. 41:10).

Be thou an example of the believer in word, in conversation, in charity, in spirit in faith, in purity.
(1 Tim. 4:12)

Be a Blessing
BY ENCOURAGING CHRISTIAN GROWTH!

To begin the Christian life is one thing, but to continue and to grow may be quite another. Few of us can accomplish this desired growth without the encouragement of another believer, be it pastor, friend, or loved one. You can be a blessing to others if you will develop the ability to encourage them.

• *Spend time with the individual.* It can be very lonely to be the only Christian in a home or office. Just to have someone who cares enough to spend time together means so much.

• *Show an interest in what concerns the other person.* As a mature Christian, you may not think it important, but it matters greatly to him.

• *Spend time in prayer, mentioning specific requests before the Father.* Teach your friend to pray specifically and to look for definite answers.

Robert A. Cook

November

"What a character!" You've heard that said about someone, haven't you? Yes—and usually in a tone of voice that suggests the person may be a bit lacking in some desirable human quality. This month I want to talk with you about a number of characters in the Bible. To start with, we'll get acquainted with some dear folk from Romans 16 whom God used to help and encourage the Apostle Paul. Then for the rest of the month we'll look into the lives of some other Bible people. Perhaps if you *learn* and *live* the lessons these characters can teach us, others will say of you, "What a *godly* character!"

PHEBE AND I, WITH OTHER FRIENDS

Scripture, Romans 16:1-27
I commend unto you Phebe our sister, which [who] is a servant of the church which is at Cenchrea.
(Rom. 16:1)

Let's construct a composite picture, putting together memories familiar to each of us. We are at a wedding reception. Long white tables display beautiful gifts. The young bride, her face aglow, passes from item to item, admiring and expressing thanks. Her fingers gently touch the monogrammed crystal, or the initialed linen, or the smooth, shining surface of a handcrafted table that bears beneath its edge the initials of the bride and groom. We admire all of the gifts, but go away thinking: those bearing names add a *distinctively personal touch.* Perhaps Paul had similar thoughts about people's names. At any rate, in the last chapter of the Book of Romans he introduces us to several individuals whose histories and/or characteristics have special meaning for believers of every generation, including our own. For we read elsewhere in Scripture: "All these things happened unto *them* for ensamples, and they are written for *our* admonition, upon whom the ends of the world are come" (1 Cor. 10:11).

First, here is Phebe. Not just Phebe standing alone, but Phebe and I . . . Phebe and every other believer . . . each of us singled out for instruction and blessing in a particular way. Listen to what Paul says: "I commend unto you Phebe our sister, who is a servant of the church which is at Cenchrea: that ye receive her in the Lord, as becometh saints, and that ye assist her in whatsoever business she hath need of you; for she hath been a succorer of many, and of myself also" (Rom. 16:1-2).

Small thought here
What are some of the concepts these friends of long ago can share with us? We'll examine them in the days ahead.

A WARM COMMENDATION HELPS

Scripture, Romans 16:1-27
I commend . . . Phebe.
(Rom. 16:1)

Don't be afraid to say a good word about somebody. Very often it will smooth the way for him or her. If you know a family that is moving to another community, write a letter to a local pastor there, telling him about these people (their children, their interests, etc.) and ask him to look out for them. Presumably, he will be glad to follow through. Before long a knock will sound at the newcomers' door and the pastor will be there to greet them. "John Doe wrote me about you," he will say, "and I've come to welcome you." These dear friends of yours have thus been *commended* by you to a new community of believers. That's what it's all about.

Or suppose you are having coffee with an executive from another company. Knowing he has recently hired a young man from your church or school, you might say, "Bill, I understand you have on staff a young fellow I know well. He recently was graduated with honors from college. I'm so proud of him! I think he's a comer. Keep your eye on him, will you?" You haven't told your executive friend how to run his business. You have merely said a good word on behalf of a lad just starting his career. Six months later, your friend may call this young man into his office and say, "You know, I've had my eye on you ever since So-and-so (that's you) said a good word about you. I'm pleased with your progress." That young man has been *commended* . . . and made stronger in the process.

Small thought here

Often a small word of commendation will ease a burden or open a door of opportunity. Say that word. Write that letter. Don't hold back because you fear the result of such praise. God will take care of that!

PEOPLE NEED EACH OTHER

Scripture, Romans 16:1-27
Phebe our sister.
(Rom. 16:1)

We believers in the Lord Jesus Christ are not isolated human beings, but part of a close-knit fellowship. Indeed, we belong to one another as members of the body of Christ (1 Cor. 12:12-20), yet each person has his separate and distinct function. Years ago, while taking courses in management, I read that every committee has on it one or more of the following: an initiator, an innovator, a proclaimer, an evaluator, an accountant, and somebody who is against everything!

We all have God-given roles to play. I remember praying in a Los Angeles hotel room, though I was actually complaining to God about certain people who were intensely critical of my work for Him. When I paused for breath, the faithful Lord Jesus spoke to my heart: "Son, let those people alone. They're Mine and they're serving My purpose. I use them as My gadflies." I looked up the word *gadfly* in the dictionary and found among other meanings that it is "a person who annoys or stirs from lethargy." As soon as I accepted that verdict, my heart was at rest regarding those dear brothers about whom I had complained so bitterly.

Small thought here
It's not necessary that everybody, or anybody, should approve of you or me. And it's impossible to always avoid criticism. God has different kinds of people to do His work. Let them do it. Just be sure you fit into God's plans for you.

THE CHURCH NEEDS SAINTS

Scripture, Romans 16:1-27
Phebe . . . a servant of the church.
(Rom. 16:1)

I firmly believe the Bible teaches that God has something for every believer to do in the local church. That being the case, how can each of us become an effective servant in the church? Here is where common sense as well as zeal come in. We must be honest and realistic about our fitness for particular tasks. For example, if the Lord hasn't given you a solo voice, don't press to "help" the church by singing solos. If you are not gifted in public speaking, don't expect to be the voice of the congregation.

Dr. Ted Place, a precious man of God who has a ministry of preaching, counseling, and writing, told me that as a high school student he had gotten down on his knees one day and said, "Jesus, I want to give You my life. But I don't have any abilities. I stammer. I get embarrassed when I try to speak to a group. I can't sing. The only thing I can do is gymnastics. So I'm going to give you that." The following day he went to the park to work on his tumbling routine. When he paused, he was surprised to find an audience had gathered. The Holy Spirit prompted him: "Tell them about Jesus." Though he thought he couldn't, in a moment he was facing the crowd and explaining: "You're watching me do these tumbling tricks and gymnastic exercises. I want you to know that just yesterday I gave my ability to do this to Jesus, my Saviour, and I want to recommend Him to each one of you."

Small thought here

That was the beginning of Ted's ministry. He later learned to lead music, to speak in public, and, after seminary, to direct overseas Gospel teams. All because he had given his gift to Jesus. He became a true servant of the church just like Phebe.

A WORD ABOUT RESPONSI-BILITY

Scripture, Romans 16:1-27
Phebe . . . a succorer of many.
(Rom. 16:1-2)

The word *succorer* suggests one who takes assigned responsibility for caring for the needs of others, even to the expenditure of his or her own resources. Such caring need not be publicized. People shy away from those who are officiously helpful.

All of us have God-given opportunities for small, impulsive, generous actions. We ought not stifle them. I received a letter from a person who had heard me say this and shortly thereafter had an opportunity to put it into practice. On a wintry day, he saw an elderly lady carrying several bags of groceries. He thought, "I'm in a hurry," but nevertheless he brought his car around to where the woman was plodding through the snow. "May I help you?" he asked. "Oh, bless you!" she replied. "I was just praying that God would send someone to help me."

That's being a *succorer*. One person showing a caring heart to another person in need. The worth of our giving is measured by what we have right now: in our bank accounts or in our toolsheds or in our pantries. King Solomon wrote, "Withhold not good from them to whom it is due, when it is in the power of thine hand to do it. Say not unto thy neighbor, 'Go and come again, and tomorrow I will give'" (Prov. 3:27-28).

Small thought here
Phebe must have been a "right now" person. I ask myself: Am I like her? Or do I procrastinate easily? Is the oneness among believers more than an essential doctrine to me? Is it an everyday reality?

NEEDED: PEOPLE WHO WORK TOGETHER

Scripture, Romans 16:1-27
Greet Priscilla and Aquila, my helpers in Christ Jesus.
(Rom. 16:3)

In effect, Paul is saying, "These two people really know how to work with others. I wonder: Could that be said about you and me? And if not, how do we go about becoming that kind of helper? First, the helper must establish good rapport. He must look for what challenges or burdens the person he is seeking to help. Before you "witness," help pull weeds, or repair a fence, or fix your neighbor's lawn mower. People need to feel at ease with you.

Second, look for opportunities to lift a burden or to share a heartache. You don't have to know all about a person's work in order to show him you appreciate it. I was invited to dinner at a friend's home and gave a quick look around, as anyone would do. It struck me that everything in that house was shining. So I turned to the hostess and said, "You've worked hard getting ready for this visit. Everything is shining and beautiful." She seemed surprised that I had noticed. "Well, yes, Mr. Cook, I did work, but I wanted things to be nice when you came." There was a sense of relaxation at that point; we understood each other—so it was easy to go on to talk of spiritual things.

Third, make sure that you get something fresh from the Lord every day that thrills and excites you—to pass on to others. Priscilla and Aquila had something to share with Apollos, the brilliant young preacher who, at first, was not properly oriented to the Gospel.

Small thought here
What did these "helpers" do? They took Apollos "unto them and expounded unto him the way of God more perfectly" (Acts 18:26). See how they worked: quietly, lovingly, thoroughly, in the warmth and privacy of their own home. Paul says they were "helpers in Christ Jesus."

WILLING TO COUNT THE COST

Scripture, Romans 16:1-27
Who for my life laid down their own necks.
(Rom. 16:4)

A good index of a Christian's usefulness is how much he is willing to let *another person's* need cost *him?* "Laid down their *own* necks." I like that! Most of us are quick to lay down someone else's neck for our pet projects, aren't we? But Priscilla and Aquila risked everything for Paul and the Gospel. Evidently, at some point in time they were in grave danger because of their friendship and association with Paul in the ministry. They had welcomed him at Corinth when all of them needed to work at their tent-making trade. Later they opened their home to believers and an infant church. We are not told what opposition may have followed. But somewhere along the line this husband and wife had made a commitment: "We don't care what it costs us; we're with Paul and the Gospel."

It may not be a life-or-death matter with us, but somewhere along the line true friendship will require that we take a stand as definite as that of Priscilla and Aquila. That person must know that we accept him unconditionally. We may not agree with him about everything. We may deplore his faults. Yet we deeply love him as he is and we will lay down our own necks to help him.

Small thought here

Most of us will respond readily to the needs of our own family or loved ones. But does our compassion and commitment spread far enough to reach "ordinary people"? Ask yourself: "How much am I willing to let another person's need cost me?" That gets right down to the quick, doesn't it, underneath the calluses we so often allow to grow over our spiritual sensibilities.

WILLING TO BE VULNERABLE

Scripture, Romans 16:1-27
*Priscilla and Aquila my helpers in Christ Jesus
. . . laid down their own necks: unto whom
. . . I give thanks.
(Rom. 16:3-4)*

W hen you accept a person into your life and are concerned for him, you become vulnerable, don't you? It is practically certain that this relationship will cost you considerable time, effort, and emotional stress, not to mention money or other personal resources. The question again is: "How great a cost am I willing to pay, for Christ's sake and the Gospel?"

Aquila and Priscilla had been helpful not only to the Apostle Paul but also to many others. I wonder: Who is thankful for you? For me? If that's a disturbing question, so be it. We can very well afford to give a good deal of serious thought to being the kind of people for whom others can thank God. Paul said elsewhere, "I thank my God upon *every remembrance* of you" (Phil. 1:3). In other words, he said, "Every time I think about you I thank God for you!" How do we get into that special category of thanked-for-Christians? If we want others to thank God for us, we will be helpful without being officious or patronizing. We will be sympathetic without being maudlin. We'll express love without selfishness and give aid or counsel without intruding on the other person's mental and emotional privacy or laying a heavy guilt trip on him. A fine line exists between counsel and advice. Most people don't want our advice, but they do hunger for loving counsel.

Small thought here
One who counsels may not be particularly religious or pious, but he demonstrates the genius of bringing the presence of God into the situation. So here we are, sharing with Paul his appreciation of fellow workers: Phebe, Aquila and Priscilla, and tomorrow . . . a man whose name is not well known.

CHERISHING THE "FIRSTBORN"

Scripture, Romans 16:1-27
Salute my well-beloved Epaenetus, who is the firstfruits of Achaia unto Christ.
(Rom. 16:5)

There is a special relationship between you and the one you win to Christ, particularly if he or she is the first in a locality where you live or have been ministering. When Paul came into Achaia and preached the Gospel, the first one to respond, Epaenetus, became special to him.

Let me share a similar experience, which occurred in Caracas, Venezuela during a great evangelistic World Congress. The daytime meetings were held in a large convention hotel and attendance was encouraging. But it took a bold leap of faith to engage the local bull ring which could accommodate thousands of people for the evening meetings. That first night, there was beautiful music and a message from the Word. Then, speaking through an interpreter, it was my assignment to give the invitation to receive Christ. Everybody waited. In some panic I thought: "What if no one responds? What if we have contracted for the use of this immense structure, all for no purpose?" Then from the far side of the arena I saw him: a tall man dressed in a neat business suit, erect, purposeful, coming to make his commitment to Jesus Christ. He was the "firstfruits" of my stumbling efforts. Though hundreds followed that night and on the succeeding eight nights, I will always recall with profound thanks that man who was first to respond to God's call.

Small thought here

Can you recall a "firstfruits" experience in your life? If you can, have you kept in touch with that person? Is his or her name on your lips and in your prayers as the name of Epaenetus was in Paul's case?

THE GIFT OF WORK

Scripture, Romans 16:1-27
Greet Mary, who bestowed much labor on us.
(Rom. 16:6)

Several women named Mary are mentioned in the New Testament and we don't know for certain which one is referred to here. However, since this letter of Paul's was written to people in Rome, she must have lived there at that time. Who is this person? Is she the wife of a rich man or some government official? Is she a servant? We are not told. But of one thing we can be sure: she had a place in Paul's heart because of something she had done, something Paul describes as bestowing "much labor."

Centuries later we still find this lady memorialized in God's Word as being somebody who *worked*, who did not demand recognition, who ministered to the Lord and to His servants out of a heart of love. She may have welcomed Paul's missionary team into her house. She may have cooked meals for them. Perhaps she washed their clothes. She may have run errands for them or done any of the routine things that no one else was willing to do. We do not know. But whatever she did, she did *willingly*; it was "bestowed." The verb *bestow* means to "give as a gift." Her work was performed in loving self-forgetfulness. But Paul remembered—and God did too!

Small thought here
Have you stopped to think that what you do today, dear friend—the ordinary, routine things that may not be "religious" in nature—are remembered by our blessed Lord? Being a Christian glorifies and dignifies all of life. Think about it, will you?

THE FELLOWSHIP OF SHARING

Scripture, Romans 16:1-27
Salute Andronicus and Junia, my kinsmen, and my fellow prisoners, who are of note among the apostles, who also were in Christ before me.
(Rom. 16:7)

What makes you valuable to other Christians? We find four clues here about Andronicus and Junia which, taken together, provide an answer to our question:

• *First, they belonged.* In a particularly close and tender way they were "kinsmen." It isn't what you do, what you give, or your successes which endear you to fellow believers. For the kind of closeness the Apostle Paul is talking about, people must feel that you belong to them, and they to you, in the bonds of Christian love.

• *Second, they were involved.* Paul calls Andronicus and Junia "my fellow prisoners," because at some point they had been imprisoned, along with Paul, for their faith. If you want to be valued as a Christian friend, you must be willing to become involved in another person's needs, burdens, heartaches, laughter, and tears.

• *Third, they worked.* Andronicus and Junia were "of note among the apostles" and such notoriety could only be gained by spiritual service. I remember a man who showed up at every business meeting of an organization with which I was associated. He would go around telling everybody, "You know, I'd really make a good president." Well, he was never even *nominated*, much less *elected!* Why? Because he never *did* anything.

• *Fourth, they were respected.* Paul said these spiritual kinsmen were to be honored because they had walked longer with the Lord Jesus than he had.

Small thought here
We cannot demand respect; we earn it. It's true that respect isn't always forthcoming, but service is the soul out of which it must spring.

A NEW START

Scripture, Romans 16:1-27
Salute Apelles approved in Christ.
(Rom. 16:10)

We know nothing of Apelles except that he was "approved in Christ." What do these words mean? They suggest, first, that a story must be behind them, an explanation that we will not receive in full until we get to Glory. There must have been a time when Apelles was not approved. This would be true of him, as it is of all of us, while he was yet unsaved. Perhaps even as a believer Apelles was a difficult person to get along with and therefore not readily accepted. Maybe he was an off-and-on-again type, totally undependable. It's possible that he often got discouraged and quit. The summation of all these qualities, whether or not they applied to Apelles, would be: *not approved*. However, the day arrived in Apelles' life when the power of Christ and of the indwelling Holy Spirit began to produce a character so different, so unlike his old self that Paul was impelled to write of him, "Salute Apelles *approved in Christ*." I'd like to have that designation, wouldn't you?

What does it mean to be approved as a Christian? Are you comfortable in the presence of God or do you flinch a little when someone says, "Let's pray"? Are you witnessing for your Saviour and giving sacrificially of your time, talent, and treasure to His work in the world? Elsewhere Paul told young Timothy to give diligence to show himself approved of God (2 Tim. 2:15). Divine approval involves a new nature, a new work ethic, and a new commitment to God's Word.

Small thought here
By the grace of the Lord Jesus and the sweet ministry of God's Spirit in your life, you too can share that blessed commendation accorded Apelles: "approved in Christ."

THOUGHTS ON BEING QUIET

Scripture, Jeremiah 51:59-64
The word which Jeremiah the prophet commanded Seraiah the son of Neriah. . . . And this Seraiah was a quiet prince. (Jer. 51:59)

Seraiah was chief chamberlain. Today he might be likened to an army quartermaster. In any case, he was a "quiet prince." There is something to be said in defense of quietness. In our fast-paced, noisy culture this virtue is often maligned and tagged as a weakness. The macho man and the assertive woman find no time for quietness in the day's activities, no place for a quiet spirit in the inner universe of their thoughts. The Apostle Peter wrote, however, that a meek and quiet spirit is "in the sight of God of great price" (1 Peter 3:4). As a matter of fact, there is some doubt as to whether one ever really knows God until he or she becomes quiet before Him. The Lord Himself commands, "Be still, and know that I am God" (Ps. 46:10).

Every warrior of the Cross knows that sometimes the victory is won, not by *doing* something, but by *waiting* on God. The classic illustration of this truth is found in Exodus 14:13. "Fear ye not," said Moses to the Israelites who were being pursued by Pharoah's chariots. "Stand still, and see the salvation of the Lord." Indeed, Egyptians by the thousands who were one day menacing and intent on Israel's destruction were forever beneath the waters of the Red Sea the next!

So we come back to Seraiah, the quiet prince. That blessed combination of royalty and poise is the birthright of every Christian! We can be quiet because when we pray about everything we have the "peace of God, which passeth all understanding" (Phil. 4:7). And we are "a chosen generation, a *royal priesthood*, an holy nation, a peculiar people (1 Peter 2:9).

Small thought here

Quietness is no accident; you have to plan for it. Carve out some minutes every day during which you will be absolutely still before God, allowing Him to speak to your heart.

I WENT OUT AFTER HIM!

Scripture, 1 Samuel 17:32-37
There came a lion . . . and took a lamb out of the block: and I went out after him . . . and smote him, and slew him.
(1 Sam. 17:34-35)

If you want to avoid responsibility, an alibi is always handy. In David's case, all he would have needed to report was that a lion had appeared, snatched a lamb from the flock, and "how sad, too bad!" David, however, was built of sterner stuff. "I went out after him!" he said. Next came Goliath: nine feet tall, heavily armed, and seemingly unbeatable. David, who had just arrived at the military encampment with food for his brothers and for their captain, heard the giant's cursing challenge and immediately asserted himself: "Who is this Philistine, that he should defy the armies of the living God?" (17:26) Saul and his people were saying, "He's too big to kill!" David was saying, "He's too big to miss!"

David combined several qualities which we may well emulate. First, he faced challenges with God. "The Lord that delivered me out of the paw of the lion and out of the paw of the bear . . . will deliver me out of the hand of this Philistine" (17:37). God did it before; He could do it again! Second, our young hero was wise enough to work with familiar equipment. When King Saul pressed the royal suit of armor upon him, David said, "I cannot go with these; for I have not proved them" (17:39). Instead, he "took his staff in his hand, and chose him five smooth stones out of the brook, and put them in a shepherd's bag which he had . . . and his sling was in his hand" (17:40). Why five stones? Someone suggested that David believed in being prepared: the giant had four brothers! (2 Sam. 21:19) Third, David used his skill (aiming at the one unprotected place on Goliath's exterior, his forehead) while depending on God: "The battle is the Lord's!" he said (1 Sam. 17:47).

Small thought here

In any crisis, there is always a way to win. Use your human best, while depending absolutely on your blessed Lord!

JOB NEVER GOT AN ANSWER

Scripture, Job 3:1-26
The thing which I greatly feared is come upon me, and that which I was afraid of is come unto me.
(Job 3:25)

Satan's sneering accusation that Job served God for what he could get out of it led to God's permission to touch, first, Job's possessions and family, and finally, his body. Afflicted with boils from head to toe, heartbroken by sorrow, Job looked heavenward and asked, "Why?"

Certainly Job's three friends were no help. Their presupposition was that God only allows suffering to come to bad people; therefore Job must be a great sinner, to be suffering so greatly. Time dragged. How long these speeches and Job's answers must have taken is anybody's guess. Finally, God spoke to Job and revealed Himself as the Creator, the Sustainer, the Controller of the universe *and* Job's destiny! Shaken and crestfallen, Job confessed, "I have heard of Thee by the hearing of the ear; but now mine eye seeth Thee. Wherefore I abhor myself, and repent in dust and ashes" (Job 42:5-6). The *real* change occurred, however, when instead of asking "Why?" or attempting to answer the criticisms of his friends, Job learned the art of intercession. "The Lord turned the captivity of Job (in other words, changed his circumstances) when he prayed for his friends" (42:20). If you want your situation to change, start praying for others!

Small thought here
If you worry about a thing long enough, you help it to happen! Job lived amid worry that something would happen to his family and his property; and when everything came crashing down around him, he said, "The thing which I greatly feared is come upon me." Worry helps bad things happen. Positive faith and trust help good things happen.

WHEN THE FEVER LEFT AT 1 P.M.

Scripture, John 4:46-53
The man believed the word that Jesus had spoken unto him.
(John 4:50)

News gets around! As it was in the days of His earthly ministry, so it is today: when Jesus is working, the news is carried far and wide. The miracle of water turned to wine at Cana of Galilee was told in towns and hamlets up and down the region; the nobleman at Capernaum was certainly among those who knew about it. When he heard that Jesus was returning to the area, he thought, "I'll get Him to come down and heal my boy!" There was probably no thought at this point whether Jesus was indeed the Messiah—only the grinding agony of knowing that his precious son was about to die and that something must be done, and *quickly*.

Walk with this burdened father, past the curious crowds, past the protective disciples, into the presence of the Master. "Please come to Capernaum, Sir, and heal my son—he's dying!" Almost curtly, it would appear, Jesus answered, "Except ye see signs and wonders, ye will not believe!" The Saviour's response, seemingly unfeeling, gives us nevertheless a look into the very heart of God. Jesus had just told the Samaritan woman (John 4:23-24) that true worship of God must be in spirit and truth, that is, apart from any of the externals which people build around their religions: custom, location, ritual. In the case of the nobleman, his heart attitude was more important to Jesus than the miracle about to be performed. Happily, the nobleman caught the impact of this truth; for when Jesus said, "Go thy way; thy son liveth," he *believed* the word.

Small thought here

God wants *you* more than He wants anything you can do for Him. Commit yourself to Christ and leave the miracle to Him.

WORSHIP— WITH AN ANGLE

Scripture, Matthew 20:20-28
And whosoever will be chief among you, let him be your servant.
(Matt. 20:27)

The mother of James and John was a faithful follower of the Lord Jesus Christ. She firmly believed that He was the One who would establish His kingdom; and believing thus, came to the conclusion that Jesus would delegate His authority to the apostles. That being true, she thought, what would be more reasonable than "my son, the Prime Minister," or "my son, the Chancellor of the Exchequer"? And because she was a woman of action (James and John came by their vigorous nature quite legitimately!), she took the young men and approached our Lord with her request: "Grant that these my two sons may sit, the one on Thy right hand, and the other on the left, in Thy kingdom" (Matt. 20:21).

Salome seems to have had an "angle" when she combined worship with petition. Is this wrong? Certainly not. Paul says that "in everything, by prayer *and* supplication," we are to make our requests known to God. Her problem lay in the emphasis on "my two sons." The way to leadership, Jesus explained, is service; and the prime motivation for service is the example of Christ Himself, who came "not to be ministered unto, but to minister, and to give His life a ransom for many" (20:28).

Small thought here

Look again at the contrast in concepts of leadership: according to verse 25, heathen nations "exercise dominion" (I am greater than you!) and "exercise authority" (I can tell you what to do!). Christ's followers minister and serve others for *His* sake (2 Cor. 4:5) .

FIRST, BUT WITH NOTHING TO SAY!

Scripture, 2 Samuel 18:9-33
Let me now run, and bear the king tidings. . . . I saw a great tumult, but I knew not what it was.
(2 Sam. 18:19, 29)

When Absalom literally was brought down by his own crowning glory—his beautiful hair—and killed by General Joab, someone needed to bring news to King David that his son's rebellion against him had ended. Ahimaaz requested that he might be the chosen messenger, but Joab said no and sent Cushi instead. Nonetheless Ahimaaz persisted until Joab at last gave in and said, "Oh, go on!" Fleeter of foot than Cushi, Ahimaaz got to David first (18:23). He had been identified by watchmen while he was yet a good distance away and arrived sweaty and breathless. But, when David asked the crucial question, "What about Absalom?" Ahimaaz had nothing to say . . . nothing but "I saw a great tumult, but I knew not what it was" (18:29). Only when Cushi arrived did David learn the sad truth about Absalom.

Mark well the importance of having something to say! Activity, which Ahimaaz demonstrated, and a good reputation, which he surely had, are no substitutes for knowing the truth and communicating it! For the believer, the essence of having something to say to our world is found in God's infallible Word, the Bible. Dr. James M. Gray, of beloved memory at the Moody Bible Institute, used to say, "Master the English Bible! If you know what the Bible says, you will have no trouble with what it means."

Small thought here
Learn from Absalom that your gifts and talents can be your undoing; and learn from Ahimaaz that it is more important to have something to say than to be first.

CURE FOR THE BLUES

Scripture, 1 Kings 19:1-18
But he himself went a day's journey into the wilderness, and came and sat down under a juniper tree: and he requested for himself that he might die; and said, "It is enough; now, O Lord, take away my life."
(1 Kings 19:4)

$\mathbf{T}$he background of this passage is the three-year drought in Israel, the day-long confrontation between Elijah and the prophets of Baal, the fire from heaven, and the rain that came in answer to Elijah's persistent prayers. When King Ahab told wicked Queen Jezebel all about the events at Mount Carmel and how Elijah had presided at the execution of the prophets of Baal, she sent a messenger to tell him that he was a "dead man." And Elijah ran to the wilderness for safety, deeply depressed and wanting to die.

Have you ever ben so discouraged that you wanted to die? I suppose every child of God experiences "the blues" at one time or other. But there is a cure for your discouragement, just as there was for Elijah. The cure involves a second look at the facts, rest, nutrition, a new vision of God, and a new touch for service. Elijah needed to look again at the facts: he wasn't alone, for 7,000 faithful people had never bowed down to Baal. He needn't have feared Jezebel because the God who had demonstrated His power forty-eight hours before could certainly take care of one pagan queen. Furthermore, he had received no divine word that his career was ended, and was jumping to conclusions when he said, "It is enough . . . take away my life." For Elijah, there were also the long sleep, the fresh food, the revelation of God's presence in "the still, small voice," and the new commission for further service. You and I can likewise conquer even the worst case of discouragement if we let our Father minister to us in the same way.

Small thought here
Isaiah wrote, "When thou passest *through* the waters, I will be with thee" (Isa. 43:2). Keep on: even in tough times trust God and let Him lead you through.

THERE IS A GOD IN HEAVEN!

Scripture, Daniel 2:1-49
But there is a God in heaven that revealeth secrets.
(Dan. 2:28)

Daniel's story is that of a man who throughout his life looked heavenward. Carried away from his homeland with other Jewish young people to Babylon, he first made his mark on that pagan culture when he and his three friends refused the king's food and stuck to their God-appointed diet. The result? After ten days, these four young men were in better shape physically and intellectually than any of their companions because "God gave them knowledge and skill in all learning and wisdom" (1:17).

Next we come to Nebuchadnezzar's dream and the impossible demand which he made: "Tell me what I dreamed and then tell me what it means." No one could come up with the answer until Daniel said, "Bring me in before the king, and I will show unto the king the interpretation. . . . There is a God in heaven that revealeth secrets" (2:24, 28). The result? Daniel interpreted the dream and Nebuchadnezzar responded by praising God and giving Daniel a high position in the kingdom.

Many years later a law was passed that no one might pray to anyone save the king for thirty days. Daniel went home and did what he had done all his life: he prayed to Jehovah. The result? Into the den of lions he was thrown, but when morning came, he was able to say, "My God hath sent His angel, and hath shut the lions' mouths!" (7:22)

Small thought here
Learn to look heavenward during life's tests and crises. You will never fail as long as you can say with utter trust, "There is a God in heaven!"

THE DIOTREPHES SYNDROME

Scripture, 3 John 9-10
Diotrephes . . . loveth to have the preeminence among them.
(3 John 9)

There is a Pennsylvania Dutch proverb which goes something like this: "First me, then me again, and after that you, but not for a long time!" The desire to excel and be recognized is part of the whole creation. A wolf pack has a leader and every pride of lions has one older lion who is "preeminent." In its beneficial sense, this trait in human beings results in competition, which stimulates us to do our best. The problem with Diotrephes seems to have been a matter not of excellence but of prominence. John said of him that he *"loveth"* to have the preeminence. Being first and foremost among the believers had gotten into his heart.

Once the Diotrephes syndrome has taken hold, other things inevitably follow. John spoke of "his deeds which he doeth, prating against us with malicious words, and . . . neither doth he himself receive the brethren, and forbiddeth them that would, and casteth them out of the church." Let us take a quick look at this list. First, there is an undue emphasis on works: "his deeds which he doeth." Next, there is an increase of destructive criticism: "prating . . . malicious words." Third, there is exclusivism, where other believers who posed a threat to Diotrephes' leadership are cast out of the church. Interestingly, there are only two places in the New Testament where the English word *preeminence* is used: once here, of Diotrephes, and in Colossians 1:18, referring to the Lord Jesus. Take your choice!

Small thought here

The way to avoid the Diotrephes syndrome is to make—and keep— Christ preeminent in your life.

DID GOD REALLY FAIL HIM?

Scripture, Jeremiah 19:15—20:18
His Word was in mine heart as a burning fire shut up in my bones, and I was weary with forbearing, and I could not stay.
(Jer. 20:9)

Jeremiah, the Weeping Prophet, brought a message of unmitigated judgment against Judah, punctuated by earnest calls for repentance. All of his ministry, it seemed, was to no avail. He was constantly rejected and, on the occasion of our text, had just spent a night in prison with his feet fastened in the stocks. During these moments of stress, the memory of Jeremiah's original call came back to mock him. In those earlier days, Josiah was king of Judah and was true to the Lord and His Word. God's call to Jeremiah, then, must have been particularly attractive, even though he demurred at first because of his youth. But the Lord said, "Say not, 'I am a child': for thou shalt go to all that I shall send thee, and whatsoever I command thee, thou shalt speak. Be not afraid of their faces: for I am with thee, to deliver thee" (1:7).

A great beginning, wouldn't you say? Now look at Jeremiah. Dirty, disheveled, weary from a sleepless night in the stocks, rejected by the religious authorities, his very life threatened. What would you have done? Exactly what Jeremiah did. He said, "I quit. I am not going to preach anymore because all I get is abuse." But Jeremiah also realized deep inside that God had privileged him with His message and there was no giving up. So he confessed, "His Word was in mine heart as a burning fire shut up in my bones, and I was weary with forbearing, and I could not stay (keep silent, that is)" (20:9).

Yes, God's call is for always. But so is God's presence. God will take care of your enemies. All you have to do is praise Him and keep on speaking His Word!

Small thought there

The Bible records Jeremiah's complaints to remind us that God's prophets were human enough to get discouraged and to complain, but protected by a great God who never failed them.

WHAT MAKES A GREAT MAN?

Scripture, Isaiah 6:1-8
Then said I, "Here am I; send me."
(Isa. 6:8)

There is an experience in the life of every great man or woman that marks the beginning of his or her rise to the top. Perhaps it is a time of crisis or suffering; perhaps it is an occasion when he or she comes in contact with another person and is so challenged that all of life is transformed from that point on. This was the case with Isaiah. King Uzziah he knew—and what a disappointment! Uzziah had begun so well; indeed, "as long as he sought the Lord, God made him to prosper" (2 Chron. 26:5). "But when he was strong, his heart was lifted up to his destruction: for he transgressed against the Lord his God" (26:16). The consequence of that kingly rebellion against God was that Uzziah became a leper and lived apart from society until his death. What could have been glorious ended in ignominy and failure, and Isaiah needed a new vision of a new kind of King. "I saw the Lord," he wrote, "sitting upon a throne, high and lifted up" (Isa. 6:1). Isaiah's vision was marked by three things: the awe-inspiring spectacle of God's holiness; the heartbroken confession of his own sin and need; and the divine touch of cleansing.

Real greatness, beloved, starts right here, at the throne of God, where our sin and need are exposed in the light of His glorious holiness; and where His cleansing touch is applied to our needy hearts. *Then* God can do something with us! *Then* our hearts can respond to His call with eager acceptance: "Here am I; send me!"

Small thought here

Isaiah's distress was not over what he had done, but because of what he *was*. Let God transform the person and the service will take care of itself.

LESSONS PETER LEARNED

Scripture, 1 Peter 1:1-9
An inheritance . . . reserved in heaven for you who are kept by the power of God through faith unto salvation.
(1 Peter 1:4-5)

When we first met him (in the Gospels), Peter was brash, outspoken, and overconfident. He always had something to prove: "Lord, if it be Thou, bid me come unto Thee on the water." He always had something to promise: "Though all men shall be offended because of Thee, yet will I never be offended." He always had something to promote: "Lord . . . let us make here three tabernacles; one for Thee, and one for Moses, and one for Elias."

But Peter's epistles show that he learned a great deal from his Master and from the Holy Spirit. These truths include:

• God's plans for the believer precede the actual experience of salvation. How blessed and motivating it should be to know we are "elect according to the foreknowledge of God" (1 Peter 1:2).

• God is able to keep the believer as he lives in a sinful world, looking toward that "inheritance incorruptible and undefiled . . . reserved in heaven for you who are kept by the power of God" (vv. 4-5).

• Trials and temptations are also part of God's plan. Like fire that purifies precious gold, trials purify our faith and get us ready to bring "praise and honor and glory at the appearing of Jesus Christ" (v. 7).

• Love for Christ (Peter had some experience with that subject. See John 21:15) depends not on His physical presence, but on the faith that makes Him Lord of one's life (v. 8).

• When a person commits himself to Christ, God's love (placed within him by the Spirit) gives rise to "joy unspeakable" (v. 8).

Peter also learned the transitory nature of the things around us, including human nature itself! "All flesh is as grass, and all the glory of man . . . but the Word of the Lord endureth forever" (vv. 24-25).

Small thought here

Give more time and attention to listening for what God wants to say to you through His Word. Peter finally learned to listen and the transformation in his life made him a man God could mightily use.

LESSONS FROM A CHURCH FUSS

Scripture, Acts 6:1-8
Seven men of honest report, full of the Holy Ghost and wisdom . . . faith and power.
(Acts 6:3, 8)

A good many church fights have originated in the kitchen. People tend to be less patient, more demanding, and more easily polarized when they are hungry. And of course, it is always a mistake for the minister to attempt to arbitrate these disagreements. One of the by-products of "equipping the saints for the work of the ministry" (Eph. 4:12) is that management details can be handled by people who are particularly fitted to cope with them. That, however, is not the whole story. The men who were to defuse this potentially explosive situation of feeding the widows of the early church were to be men of honest report (that is, they required a good reputation), full of the Holy Spirit (in contrast with some who may have been able, but not Spirit-filled), and full of wisdom (people, in other words, who had common sense).

A good name—everyone from Solomon to Spinoza agrees that it is important. But the Apostle Paul sums it up best when he remarks that if one desires leadership in the local church, "he must have a good report of them which are without (that is, people in the community)" (1 Tim. 3:7).

To be full of the Holy Spirit is the privilege of every believer. Christian service without Him ends up being boring, demanding, and exhausting. *With Him, it is an adventure with Deity!*

There is no substitute for good sense. Some seem to be born with it, others without it. If you consider yourself one of the latter, there is hope for you in James 1:5. God will always answer the prayer for wisdom. Pray your way through the day and just obey when God whispers answers to your heart.

Small thought here
Be a New Testament kind of leader! Keep your testimony crystal clear, your heart filled with God's Spirit, and your mind in high gear.

JONAH— AND THE THINGS GOD PREPARED

Scripture, Jonah 1—4
The Lord sent out a great wind. . . .
The Lord had prepared a great fish. . . .
The Lord prepared a gourd. . . . God
prepared a worm. . . . God prepared
a vehement east wind.
(Jonah 1:4, 17; 4:6-8)

Jonah was a prophet of God to whom the Lord spoke regularly. On one such occasion God commanded: "Go to Nineveh and cry against it." But Jonah decided, even at his own risk, to disobey God, in order that no opportunity for mercy might be given to the wicked Ninevites. We all know what happened from that point. We also know that the God "who is there" had not forgotten his erring prophet. He prepared a great fish to swallow Jonah and to provide him with a three-day prayer meeting, during which he got right with God and became willing to obey His command. But had Jonah really learned his lesson? No. When the people of Nineveh repented, instead of rejoicing, Jonah began to pout: "I told You so! These awful people repent and You give them another chance!" And God had to take His sulking prophet "back to the drawing board."

What do you make of the story of Jonah?
• You can be officially in touch with God and busy for Him, and still not be willing to do His will. You may pray and receive answers to prayer, but never mean business until you "cry unto the Lord."
• You can give out God's message (sermon, Sunday School lesson, testimony, casual conversation geared to eternal matters) and still not have a heart for the lost; in fact, you may be resentful of the very people with whom you are dealing, just as Jonah was!
• God's logic is inescapable. Why shouldn't His heart be touched when a sinner repents? And if your life is full of God's Spirit, why shouldn't you be equally touched?
• The turning point in any situation where God is disciplining you is the point at which, like Jonah, you say, "I will pay what I have vowed."

Small thought here

Learn from Jonah to obey God and to care about the lost. Humanly you may not like them, but God, through you, wants to love them.

ANDREW — A VERY SPECIAL PERSON

Scripture, John 1:29-42
He first findeth his own brother Simon, and saith unto him, "We have found the Messiah." . . . And he brought him to Jesus. (John 1:41-42)

Andrew was always known as "Simon Peter's brother." He never seemed to have any special recognition of his own. But chances are that Andrew was so busy helping other people that he never noticed the lack of medals! His first act after having spent a day with Jesus was to look up his brother and bring him to the Saviour! While Philip was sputtering about how much it would cost to feed the 5,000, Andrew was surveying the situation and discovering that indeed something could be done, provided that a certain little boy's lunch was placed in Divine Hands. And when the Greeks came seeking Jesus, Andrew, with Philip, were the ones who brought them to the Lord. Certainly, there was never any question about Andrew's willing spirit. When Christ called the fishermen to be His disciples, Andrew responded immediately, even though it meant leaving the ship and its nets. And three years later when the cloud had received the risen Saviour out of their sight, Andrew was among those who returned to Jerusalem to await the outpoured Holy Spirit.

   Why do we remember this man? Because he was a soul-winner, and because he *did* something about a situation involving need, instead of just talking about it. That's a pretty good example to follow, wouldn't you say?

Small thought here
Don't be afraid to offer God something for Him to use. It may seem ridiculously small, just as the little boy's lunch must have seemed in the face of 5,000 hungry men; but Jesus makes the difference!

HOW TO PLAY SECOND FIDDLE

Scripture, Acts 13:1-13, 43
The Holy Ghost said, "Separate Me Barnabas and Saul for the work whereunto I have called them."
(Acts 13:2)

His nickname was "the Son of Consolation." Barnabas must have been a comfortable person to be with. Surely he had a heart for God and for His people, demonstrated by his prompt action in selling a piece of land and giving the proceeds to the apostles. Furthermore, Barnabas was not afraid to stand up for the new convert, Saul of Tarsus, lately arrived in Jerusalem from Damascus. "They were all afraid of him, and believed not that he was a disciple. But Barnabas took him, and brought him to the apostles" (Acts 9:26-27).

Now came the Holy Spirit's call which launched Barnabas and Saul on their first missionary journey. Barnabas, as the elder and more experienced brother, was captain of the team. The trip began as "Barnabas and Saul" (13:2). But by the end of Acts 13, we read about "Paul and Barnabas" (vv. 43, 46). Something had happened: Paul was now the leader or spokesman and Barnabas was second in importance. It was a tribute to Barnabas' grace and humility that he did not resent the sudden prominence of one who might ordinarily be called a novice, not to say an upstart. Barnabas, bless him, was willing to play second fiddle. But his determination to help the underdog resulted finally in separation from Paul. Paul had called John Mark a quitter after he left the team at Perga. Barnabas, however, was not willing to give up on the young man, and took Mark right back along the same route which he had traveled before. He helped Mark face the fact of his failures and to become an effective soul-winner. Later, Paul could write of Mark, "He is profitable to me for the ministry."

Small thought here
Be willing to play second fiddle, as long as you can help someone else to succeed for God!

A PRAYER, A SWORD, AND A TROWEL

Scripture, Nehemiah 4:6-21
We made our prayer unto our God, and set a watch against them day and night . . . for the builders, every one had his sword girded by his side, and so builded.
(Neh. 4:9, 18)

Nehemiah's story might well be titled, "From bartender for Artaxerxes to builder for God." One day Nehemiah received news that the walls of Jerusalem were broken down, the gates burned with fire, and that the poor people left were in distress. Even though, as a captive in this strange land, he was in a somewhat favored position as the king's cupbearer, his heart ached for his brothers and sisters back home. True to his lifetime habit, the first thing Nehemiah did was pray. In answer to that prayer, Artaxerxes sent him with a delegation and supplies back to Jerusalem to rebuild the walls and to create order in the city. Not everyone was glad about this development, however. Indeed, some devious characters immediately conspired to keep God's people from regaining any part of their former prosperity and influence. Throughout various episodes of conspiracy and intrigue, Nehemiah again and again turned to the Lord.

Along with his praying, Nehemiah mixed courage and good sense. To the suggestion that he hold a "summit conference," he said, "I am doing a great work. Why should the work cease while I come down to you?" To the whispered warning that someone was coming to kill him, and that he had better run and hide, he exclaimed, "Should such a man as I flee!" And to emphasize the strength of their determination to finish building the walls, Nehemiah put a trowel in one hand of his workers and a sword in the other. Watchfulness, prayer, and courage combined to give the victory!

Small thought here

You simply cannot improve on Nehemiah's formula for success: pray about things; face the facts; get people working; and don't scare easily. And when you have finished a job, give God the glory! (See Neh. 9:5.)

FROM GILGAL TO GLORY!

Scripture, 2 Kings 2:1-15
And Elisha said, "I pray thee, let a double portion of thy spirit be upon me."
(2 Kings 2:9)

God often tests us to see whether we really desire His blessing. So it was in the case of Elisha on the day that Elijah was taken up to Glory. At each stop, Elijah said, "Stay here, I have to go." Elisha, however, would not be deterred. With probably more determination than he had ever dared to use with his master before, he declared, "As the Lord liveth, and as thy soul liveth, I will not leave thee!" (2:6) Three times this confrontation occurred, until the two of them stood by the River Jordan. There the Prophet Elijah wrapped his mantle together, smote the waters, and they divided to let the two men of God cross over on dry ground. Elijah turned to his erstwhile servant and said, "Ask what I shall do for thee, before I be taken away from thee." Instantly Elisha replied, "Let a double portion of thy spirit be upon me." As they talked, the chariot and horses of fire appeared and Elijah "went up by a whirlwind into heaven" (2:11). What followed was simply confirmation of the fact that Elisha's persistence and faith had paid off. The waters of the Jordan parted for him just as they had for Elijah, and the sons of the prophets who saw it exclaimed, "The spirit of Elijah doth rest on Elisha" (2:15).

Small thought here

Elisha kept close to his contact with God. He asked for God's Spirit, not power or advantage . . . and he never hesitated to put the Lord to the test. Try it on for size in your own life.

December

My heart leaps a little every time I hear the blessed words, "Behold, I bring you good tidings of great joy, which shall be to all people" (Luke 2:10). But for many the Christmas season is a time of *pressure* and depression. This month, in Psalm 107, we'll see that God's prescription for pressure is prayer and praise. Also this month are insights from answers Jesus gave the scribes and Pharisees to three leading questions. In addition are lessons about living—learned from my God-fearing father. And finally, to help us walk a little closer to our blessed Lord, are comments from 2 Peter on God's gifts and faith's "additives."

PRESSURE, PRAYER, AND PRAISE

Scripture, Psalm 107:1-43
Hungry and thirsty, their soul fainted in them. Then they cried unto the Lord in their trouble, and He delivered them out of their distresses.
(Ps. 107:5-6)

Y ou want to experience victorious living, don't you? Of course you do! Our gracious Heavenly Father wants all believers to enjoy that kind of life and has set forth, especially in Psalm 107, three main elements related to a vital, victorious walk with Him. They are: *pressure, prayer,* and *praise.* I'll be talking about these important Ps for the next few days.

Psalm 107 begins with *praise.* It is not only the happy conclusion to the process of walking with God; it is the glorious beginning. But you say, "How can I praise God for the trauma I'm suffering right now?" Yours may be a broken home, a wayward child, an ailing body, a thwarted hope, an undermined position, or a financial crisis. Dear friend, God allows you to get into pressure situations so that He can show Himself strong on your behalf. Your difficulties are calculated to turn you toward Him, to bring you to your knees in worship, love, surrender—and finally, in *praise.* Our God isn't some sadistic deity who delights in punishing people. No, He is a loving Father (Heb. 12:6). The whole purpose of your trials and tears is that you will obediently run to Him and whisper in childlike trust, "Abba, Father."

Small thought here
Notice two recurring expressions: "They cried" (just as you may be crying today), and "The Lord is good." Psalm 107 teaches us to face pressure honestly, to pray with intensity, and to praise the Lord continually.

FACE PRESSURE HONESTLY

Scripture, Psalm 107:1-43
They wandered . . . in a solitary way.
(Ps. 107:4)

In our day, the word *pressure* has come to be commonly used and understood. Among other definitions, the dictionary offers these: (1) the burden of physical and/or mental distress; and (2) the constraint of circumstances. We have noted that this kind of pressure is designed by a loving Heavenly Father to be an effective means of bringing blessing into the lives of His children. But to obtain the fullness of that blessing we must admit, with utter honesty, the fact and manner of our hurting. Is this negative thinking? No, it is a realistic recognition of that which God will use to bring us deliverance and joy. Psalm 107 speaks of three kinds of pressure: loneliness, unfulfilled desires, and despair. Let's look today at the first of these: *loneliness.*

There is indescribable loneliness in the life that has not found fulfillment in God. If you have lived for any length of time you can testify to the fact that one can experience feelings of loneliness in a crowd or in a small, intimate group of people. Loneliness is also linked to purposelessness (v. 4). For many, life is a series of wanderings from one situation to another. But, thanks be to God, you don't have to live aimlessly shifting from one crisis to the next; from one series of hopes and dreams to another; from one marriage to another.

Small thought here

Aimlessness and a lack of direction in life show up clearly in many an otherwise successful person. If this describes you, dear friend, allow our blessed Lord to put purpose in your life. Invite Him today to inject His presence into your circumstances. Then the loneliness and wandering will be dissipated and replaced by His peace and joy.

NEED FOR FELLOWSHIP

Scripture, Psalm 107:1-43
They found no city to dwell in.
(Ps. 107:4)

True fellowship is three-sided; you, God, and others. Let me illustrate from the field of technology. For two computers to communicate information to each other, a device is used called a multiplexer. It allows incoming data to be fed to either one computer *or* the other or from one computer *to* the other. You and I need a multiplexer, so to speak, to operate between the separate "computers" of our brains and our spirits. That function is served by the blessed Holy Spirit. Apart from the mediating work of the Spirit, which allows communication to flow freely between us and God, He also helps us to get along amicably with other human beings, a task that often seems to be a mission impossible! If you want to know how quickly people can tire of one another, put a dozen or so in an elevator and arrange for it to be stuck between floors for several hours!

Instead of engaging each other's personalities head on, with the inevitable conflict and abrasion that results, we need to allow God to bring *His own presence* into those relationships. In the "city" of our lives (v. 4), we sorely need the kind of fellowship that only God can make possible.

Small thought here
The Apostle John expressed it this way: "That which we have seen and heard declare we unto you, that ye also may have *fellowship* with us; and truly our *fellowship* is with the Father, and with His Son Jesus Christ" (1 John 1:3). Put that to work, will you, on Main Street of your life? As you do, you'll discover a new zest for loving and living!

THE PRESSURE OF UNFULFILLED DESIRES

Scripture, Psalm 107:1-43
Hungry and thirsty, their soul fainted in them.
(Ps. 107:5)

One of my saddest observations is the constant effort among people of every rank to satisfy their longings with something less than the presence and provision of God. They may try alcohol, drugs, sex, or simply the pursuit of things, but none of these suffices. They may be chronic "joiners," going from club to club; or "do-gooders," working hard at a dozen projects; or inveterate travelers, intent on seeing the world. But all this activity is not enough. On the other hand, how marvelously sustaining and satisfying the grace of God is to anyone who is open to Him!

In my library is a book written by a journalist who followed the stories of people who experienced wartime brainwashing experiments. In a certain camp he noticed that those prisoners who came in strong and healthy but with "no special commitment" had great difficulty. Educated in a humanistic tradition that saw no need for God and His Word, they began to wither and die at an alarming rate. When the pressure of their situation bore down on them, they had no inner strength or will to live. But one frail and somewhat sickly soldier also entered that prison camp and survived. He had spiritual convictions based on the Word of God and declared unabashedly, "My God is as real to me as the back of my hand, and as near." With a faith like that, he lived to tell the story!

Small thought here
Solomon sought satisfaction in money, culture, and pleasure of every sort. But at the end he said, "All is vanity." The words of the old song are still true: "Only Jesus, only Jesus, only He can satisfy."

THE PRESSURE OF DESPAIR

Scripture, Psalm 107:1-43
Their soul fainted in them.
(Ps. 107:5)

Have you noticed that people give up *within themselves* long before the formal "surrender"? Long before you say, "I quit," you have said it inside. That is why it is so important to have an inner peace, a deep-seated stability that comes only through the blessed Holy Spirit's work within you. Paul prayed for the church at Ephesus that they might be "strengthened with might by [God's] Spirit in the *inner man*" (Eph. 3:16).

How do you achieve this inner tranquility? You begin by acknowledging yourself as a needy sinner and trusting Jesus as your Saviour and Lord. You go on by consciously committing yourself to the Holy Spirit's direction. Of course, the tendency of every human heart is to want its own way. Look at Psalm 107:11: "They rebelled against the words of God and [spurned] the counsel of the Most High." Indeed, when you resist God's commands, yours becomes the longing soul, the hungry heart. Even when you attain your dearest desires, you are dissatisfied and ultimately will experience despair and utter defeat. The only way out is to plead for God's mercy and forgiveness. Ask Him to deliver you out of all your distresses (107:6), and He will.

Small thought here
What does God do when you rebel? He brings you "down ... with labor" (107:12), that is, the firm hand of correction. The pressure you feel now, the fact that you are working your fingers to the bone and getting nowhere may be God's wise and gentle way of nudging you toward Himself. Don't fight it! Run to Jesus.

PRAY WITH INTENSITY

Scripture, Psalm 107:1-43
They cried unto the Lord in their trouble.
(Ps. 107:6)

When you have faced your particular pressure situation with candor, what then? Pray! The whole thrust of our passage is that you are headed for collapse unless you bring your need to the Lord and experience His deliverance. When people pray, they often use general terms: "Lord, bless me. . . . Help me. . . . Get me (or my loved one) out of the trouble I'm in." There is nothing particularly wrong with that kind of prayer. In fact, sometimes it is the only kind possible.

Matthew 14 records an experience Peter had with a one-sentence petition that brought quick results. You remember that as Peter began to sink (after being the only mortal in history to walk on water), he cried out, "Lord, save me!" And immediately our blessed Lord "stretched forth His hand, and caught him, and said unto him, 'O thou of little faith, wherefore didst thou doubt?' " (Matt. 14:31) Jesus' purpose was, first, to get Peter's faith on track. And second, it was to calm the wind and waves. Notice the order. God wants to deal with your inner tempest first. Then, if necessary, He will change your circumstances—all to conform to His own perfect purpose. Are you overwhelmed with a burden of sorrow? Are you brokenhearted over the betrayal of someone dear to you? Crushed by resentment? Outfoxed in the business jungle by somebody who has taken your job? Utterly nonplussed over what to do with aging parents when neither they nor you has adequate financial or emotional resources? Pray!

Small thought here
When the sorrows of life sweep over your spirit and threaten to engulf you, when the results of your own foolish rebellion catch up with you, don't give up on God! And don't give up on yourself either.

THE HEALING VALUE OF PRAYER

Scripture, Psalm 107:1-43
He sent His word and healed them.
(Ps. 107:20)

Feelings may be either powerful friends or fearsome foes. It's the latter type that can practically paralyze a person, causing almost unbearable distress. I have a physician friend who told me that he has case records of people who quite literally were scared to death. They were so afraid in some situation that terror actually affected their bodily functions to the extent that they died.

Whatever your distress, tell God exactly how you feel. When you do, He will dispel your panic through His Word and give you His healing peace. Verses 23 to 29 of Psalm 107 present a nautical illustration of this truth: "They that go down to the sea in ships, that do business in great waters; these see the works of the Lord, and His wonders in the deep. For He commandeth, and raiseth the stormy wind, which lifteth up the waves thereof. They mount up to heaven, and they go down again to the depths. . . . They reel to and fro . . . and are *at their wit's end.* Then they cry unto the Lord . . . and He bringeth them out of their distresses. He maketh the storm a calm, so that the waves thereof are still."

Small thought here
If you will pray in the midst of a wit's-end-corner situation, two things will happen: God will quiet the storm and He will direct your next step. Remember: He may not change everything at once. But your obedience to Him no matter what the circumstances is the key to victory over your feelings.

PRAISE GOD CONTIN- UALLY

Scripture, Psalm 107:1-43
Oh, that men would praise the Lord for His goodness, and for His wonderful works to the children of men! (Ps. 107:8, 15, 21, 31)

The third element in successful Christian living, after *pressure* and *prayer*, is *praise*. Psalm 107 demonstrates that praise belongs at the beginning *and throughout* the process. Have you tried praising God recently? Have you come to your blessed Lord in prayer, not asking for anything but just exalting His name, just expressing your love for Him? This will bring you into touch with the Almighty in a way nothing else can. Of course, such a prescription does not preclude the necessity of your telling God the truth about yourself, so bring your needs to Him also. Then start praising Him for His goodness. Praise unleashes the mighty delivering power of God. A gentleman from Pittsburgh once wrote to me, saying: "When I first heard you, I was a bit offended. You said, 'If there is somebody who is a slave to alcohol, Jesus will deliver you if you will ask Him to.'

"Then I thought to myself: Why shouldn't I ask? So I got down on my knees and told God I was a slave to this thing, that I was powerless, and that I wanted Him to free me. I began to praise and thank Him for what He had done, though I didn't feel any great change at the time. But soon things began to shape up, little by little. I've turned clear around in my life. I am free and delivered." His wife added a postscript: "I want to say 'amen' to what my husband has written. Ours is a whole new ball game. It's like having a second honeymoon."

Small thought here

Where are you in the pressure-prayer-praise process? Crushed by some circumstance? If so, move on to intense prayer that matches the seriousness of your need. Then begin to praise God—lifting your eyes from what troubles you—to focus on His goodness . . . His mercy . . . His loving-kindness.

<table>
</table>

THREE QUESTIONS, THREE ANSWERS

Scripture, Mark 2:13-28
The scribes and Pharisees saw Him [Jesus] eat with publicans and sinners.
(Mark 2:16)

Three questions asked of our Saviour and His disciples accurately pinpoint the areas which perplex the average human being until he comes to know the Lord Jesus Christ for himself. I'll be spending about a week with you on these questions, the first of which is found in Mark 2:16:

• *"How is it that He eateth and drinketh with publicans and sinners?"* This question was a natural, seeing that Jesus had just called Matthew—a despised tax collector—to be one of His disciples, and was now dining in his home.

The second question asked of our Lord (2:18) had to do with the fact that Jesus' disciples did not observe routine religious customs such as fasting:

• *"Why do the disciples of John and of the Pharisees fast, but Thy disciples fast not?"*

The third question asked of our Lord Jesus is recorded in verse 24:

• *"Why do they (the disciples) on the Sabbath Day that which is not lawful?"* In those days the paths from one village to another wound their way through grain fields. When the harvest was ripe, it was permissible for a passerby to take a few handfuls of grain, rub the kernels between his palms, blow away the chaff, and have a snack to hold him over until lunchtime!

Small thought here

What's more important: to be fastidiously correct in matters religious or to be real before God in matters of the heart? The answer is obvious. Ask God to make your heart warm and tender to His Word today.

CHRIST: GREATER THAN SOCIETAL BARRIERS

Scripture: Mark 2:13-17
How is it that He eateth and drinketh with publicans and sinners?
(Mark 2:16)

When our Lord Jesus asked Matthew to commit his life to Him and to become His disciple, one of the first things Matthew did was to get all of his friends together so they too could meet the Master. Of course, the people in Matthew's circle of friends included folks whose lifestyles were publicly out of line with the Law of God: the drunk, the prostitute, the petty thief, the pickpocket—you name it—they were "publicans and sinners." Matthew started where he was, with people he knew, and shared his faith in Jesus with them. An admirable thing, yet the pious scribes and Pharisees inquired, "How is it that He eateth and drinketh with publicans and sinners?" In other words, "How could You stoop so low?"

I remember one of our Arab students at The King's College who went to a student conference attended by thousands of college students from around the world. Sitting next to this young man on the platform was an Israeli who had also trusted Christ as his Messiah. When it was his turn to speak, our young student said, "One of the most wonderful things about being a Christian is the love the Lord Jesus has given me for my brother from Israel." And the two of them stood there with their arms around each other's shoulders, the tears running down their faces—living proof that God breaks down man-made barriers.

Small thought here

Jesus' answer to the question put to Him was simple and direct. In essence, He said, "I'm eating with them because they *need* Me" (Mark 2:17). Somebody *needs* you today. Forget the man-made barriers that divide people, find that someone, and introduce him or her to your Saviour!

CHRIST: ETERNAL DIMENSION FOR LIVING

Scripture, Mark 2:18-22
Why do the disciples of John and of the Pharisees fast, but Thy disciples fast not? (Mark 2:18)

Just as secular society is often built on barriers that divide people, so religious society is often built on rituals which soothe and give status to people. Fasting is one such misused observance. In Bible times, a good Pharisee would deprive himself of food for certain hours on two or even three days each week, thereby gaining status in the eyes of his fellowmen, and assuring himself that he was indeed a very holy person! Nice gesture, wrong motive!

Christ's answer to the second question asked by the scribes and Pharisees (Mark 2:18) was disarmingly simple. In effect, He told them, "Really now, gentlemen, you don't fast when you go to a wedding reception, do you? I'm here, and for My disciples, life is a feast of good things. They may not have much, but they have Me!" Using the twin figures of speech of new wine in old wineskins, and new, unshrunk cloth sewed on an old garment, Jesus taught again the truth that He is the new dimension in living—greater than the old observances which serve merely as crutches for one's self-esteem; greater than the old wineskins of past enjoyments and achievements; greater than the old fabric of dogma and custom! Institutional religion tends to exist by and for itself, rather than as an evidence of God's presence and power. The presence of the Lord Jesus Christ creates a dynamic power *within* the individual that is far greater than any kind of religious regimentation.

Small thought here

Did Jesus condemn fasting? No! It can be useful as a means for breaking through the crust of your own soul to a greater spiritual awareness. But God wants a life that is right with Him more than He wants perfunctory prayer and fasting. There isn't room for new wine in old wineskins.

CHRIST: LORD OF ALL

Scripture, Mark 2:23-28
Why do they on the Sabbath Day that which is not lawful?
(Mark 2:24)

The scribes and Pharisees were certainly "letter-of-the-Law" kind of people. Unfortunately, the Law became such an obsession with them that they became totally oblivious to its intent. Because the Law of Moses commanded that no work be done on the Sabbath, they accused Jesus' disciples of harvesting grain for merely picking a few ripe ears of corn—a perfectly legal practice. Jesus did not argue this point, except to remind the scribes and Pharisees that King David, in an instance of extreme need, had dined on the showbread, something reserved exclusively for the priests. In effect, our Lord said, "The Sabbath was given to provide rest and worship for man, not to bind him with petty rules." The entire conversation turned, however, on our Lord's comment, "The Son of man is Lord also of the Sabbath" (Mark 2:28). It is Christ's lordship that makes all the difference! He is Lord of forgiven sin (2:5). He is Lord of renewed strength and health (v. 11). He is Lord of a changed life (v. 14). He is Lord of fulfillment and joy (vv. 18-22). Indeed, when Jesus Christ is in total control, He puts everything in true perspective—personal, interpersonal, and religious.

Small thought here
Learn today the meaning of "Lord also" (v. 28). Let Jesus be Lord of your career, your education, your family, your budget, your recreation ... Lord of all! When He is Lord, you can begin to experience the joy of really living (Col. 3:23), and petty, everyday burdens will never again enslave you.

THE FUTURE BELONGS TO YOU

Scripture, 1 Corinthians 3:9-16
Let every man take heed how he buildeth thereupon.
(1 Cor. 3:10)

Leonardo da Vinci once said, "In rivers, the water that you touch is the last of what has passed and the first of that which comes: so with time present." It is important to stop thinking of the future as something apart, something that is yet to arrive in your experience. Today is yesterday, bearing fruit; and tomorrow is already here, in embryo form. In nautical language, your course direction for tomorrow is generally revealed by the set of your sails today. In other words, your future is already packaged—in your body and mind; forces and faculties; appetites and aptitudes. Most of us know this. But not everyone knows how to apply it. Here are some thoughts that may prove helpful:

• *Check your values.* Today's value system will shape tomorrow's choices. How do you rate the word *duty*, for instance, with *dollar*? Or how does *popularity* compare with *prayer*? Can *faith* hold its own with *fun* or *food*?

• *Examine your habits.* Your mental, physical, and spiritual habits today will set your thought and performance patterns for years to come.

• *List your skills.* Are you learning skills that have a future in our new and complex technological world? If not, start acquiring some!

• *Watch your reactions.* Do you lash out at people? Sulk when corrected? Quit easily? Insist on your own way? Or try to solve problems through careful thought and prayer?

• *Learn that life is "for keeps."* Nothing you do or say is ever lost. Everything counts.

Small thought here

Learn early that the things that harm as well as build you up are spiritual in nature. Success in the future depends on a heart and will surrendered to the lordship of Jesus Christ!

WHAT'S WRONG WITH WORK?

Scripture, 2 Thessalonians 3:6-14
We ... wrought with labor and travail night and day, that we might not be chargeable to any of you.
(2 Thes. 3:8)

The way it looks to me, you'd think the greatest human dream is to get paid for doing nothing. The formula is simple enough: a shorter work week with higher pay so we can have more time off to relax. Of course, how it really works is that we get shorter hours and higher pay, but we also get a higher priced set of needs and wants. So we take a second job in our time off to pay for the obligations we assumed when we got our time off. It just doesn't figure, does it?

To begin with, *God instituted work as the way human nature functions best:* "Six days shalt thou labor and do all thy work" (Ex. 20:9). Work for six days; rest and worship for one—that is God's schedule for us. Next, *work is part of God's nature:* "On the seventh day God ended His work which He had made; and He rested" (Gen. 2:2). Third, *work is God's plan for the Christian:* "We are His workmanship created in Christ Jesus unto good works, which God hath before ordained that we should walk in them" (Eph. 2:10). Today's text urges a similar response on a day in-day out level: "that with quietness they work and eat their own bread" (2 Thes. 3:12) Finally, *work is the stuff of which a successful testimony is made:* "Let your light so shine before men that they may see your good works, and glorify your Father which is in heaven" (Matt. 5:16).

Small thought here
Work is especially productive when it is harnessed to eternity. Do all you do as unto the Lord and nothing you do will lack significance.

IN DEFENSE OF GRATITUDE

Scripture, Ephesians 5:15-20
Giving thanks always for all things unto God and the Father in the name of our Lord Jesus Christ.
(Eph. 5:20)

Saying "thank you" seems to have gone the way of the Model T and the Nehru jacket. As one religious leader said to me, "As long as you produce, you don't have to fool with that stuff." Certainly, lack of gratitude on the part of children is high on the list of parental complaints. A mother said to me, "I saved and scrimped so I could buy my daughter a new buggy for her doll baby, and what did she do? She just said, 'Oh, good,' and walked off with it!"

Ingratitude isn't new. Roman 1:21 mentions it as one of the sins of the heathen. Repeatedly in the Psalms and the Prophets, the Lord complained that His people soon forgot the mighty works that He had done for them. Ten lepers were cleansed, but only one returned to thank the Saviour. Paul wrote that in the last days, "Men shall be . . . unthankful, unholy" (2 Tim. 3:2). What a pity that the sin of the heathen and the backsliding of God's ancient people should be duplicated in believers today and accepted as par for the course! So take some quality time, will you, to be thankful? Being busy in the Lord's work doesn't give you a permit to be grabby! He longs for a word of appreciation from you and me: "Whoso offereth praise glorifieth Me" (Ps. 50:23).

Small thought here

Adopt gratitude as a way of life. Your family and friends will appreciate the new consideration you show them. Best of all, you'll be a better testimony, a finer representative for your Saviour, whose giving of Himself made it possible for us to say, "Thanks be unto God for His unspeakable gift" (2 Cor. 9:15).

PROCRAS-TINATION AND ITS CAUSES

Scripture, Acts 24:22-27
Felix trembled, and answered, "Go thy way for this time; when I have a convenient season, I will call for thee."
(Acts 24:25)

W hich of us has not at some time said, "I have to get at that project ... tomorrow"? The tendency to put things off is as human as the tendency to want other things right away. It is an expression of basic, fallen, human nature. Let's look at some of the causes of procrastination:

• *Misplaced priorities.* We often give attention to the trivial while missing the eternal. Governor Felix heard Paul's Gospel message, but in the back of his mind he also heard all that he might have to give up if he were to embrace Christianity—power, prestige, his very lifestyle.

• *Self-interest.* Solomon cautioned, "Say not unto thy neighbor, 'Go, and come again, and tomorrow I will give'; when thou hast it by thee" (Prov. 3:28). Though Felix often had Paul for "visits" after their initial encounter, his ulterior motive was that the apostle might buy his freedom and in turn pad the governor's pocket (Acts 24:26).

• *Mistaken idea of our right to the future.* We often put off important actions or decisions on the assumption that tomorrow will provide us the opportunity to get it done (that was Felix's line). Not so. "Boast not thyself of tomorrow," warned Solomon (Prov. 27:1). And James, the apostle of directness, said, "Your life is a vapor.... Ye ought to say, if the Lord will, we will live, and do this, or that" (James 4:14-15).

• *Mistaken assumptions.* The people of Noah's day assumed it would not rain. Some of Lot's family assumed there was time to get out of Sodom. Felix assumed that Paul would rather be physically free than a "prisoner for Christ."

Small thought here
Dear friend, don't let misplaced priorities, self-interest, presumption, and mistaken assumptions rob you of being an effective servant of our blessed Lord.

PROCRAS-TINATION AND ITS CURES

Scripture, Proverbs 3:5-6
He shall direct thy paths.
(Prov. 3:6)

Yesterday we looked at some *causes* of procrastination. Today I want to suggest some cures:

• *Recognize procrastination as a sin, and repent of it.* James said, "To him that knoweth to do good, and doeth it not, to him it is sin" (James 4:17). Pray specifically and in faith for deliverance from your tendency to put things off.

• *Spend enough time with your Lord to get a clear sense of His direction.* You will save yourself many wasted hours and steps if you spend more time waiting at "headquarters" until you get your marching orders for the day.

• *List the things that need to be done and prioritize the list.*

• *Start with the most important item on your list.* You'll find that it is also the most difficult. If you can't get started, say to yourself, "*If I were going to start on this, what* would I say or do?" Then follow through on those ideas, and presto, you've done it!

• *Set deadlines for yourself.* Make a challenge of bettering your own time for any given task. Ask yourself, "Which do I enjoy more: dawdling, or the solid satisfaction of accomplishment?"

• *Make a habit of conscious dependence on the Holy Spirit.* Pray your way through every task. "The Lord shall guide thee continually" (Isa. 58:11).

• *Make a lifetime habit of immediate obedience to what you know is God's will at any given moment.* Too often, what we label as procrastination is just plain disobedience.

Small thought here

Wait on God, dear friend, until you know His will. Place the most important element of His will at the top of your list and then get at it!

WE NEVER CALLED HIM "DAD"

Scripture, 1 Kings 2:1-4
*And he charged Solomon his son, saying . . .
"Keep the charge of the Lord thy God, to
walk in His ways."
(1 Kings 2:1, 3)*

Looking back, I can see the reason behind my father's vigorous objection to being called "Dad." For him, the term meant that he had become old and carried with it more than a trace of disrespect. He simply refused to grow old. Even when glaucoma was taking his eyesight, he would ride his bicycle daily, squinting along the curb with the last vestige of vision left in his one good eye. God must have sent an extra detachment of angels to protect him on those occasions!

A kindly brother in the Lord said to him one day, in congratulating him on his seventy-fifth birthday, "Brother Cook, isn't it wonderful to know the Lord in your sunset years?" My father, who always reserved the right to be impertinent while chalking it up to his convictions, answered: "Did you ever hear such rot? I'm not in my sunset years—I'm having the time of my life!"

"I don't know, Boy," he once told me, "but it doesn't sound right: Old Dad Jones . . . Old Dad Cook! That doesn't sound as though you thought very much of the person!" So we compromised: I called him *Pop*, my sister called him *Papa*, the relatives called him *Charley*, and the Sunday School kids in Howard Nelson's new church in Cleveland called him *Doc*. But we loved him . . . for many reasons which I'll be sharing with you.

Small thought here
Take some time today, and for the next three days, to think about your earthly father or mother. Ask our blessed Lord to bring to your heart and mind some of the contributions they have made to your life.

WHY
I LOVED
HIM

Scripture, 1 Timothy 4:11-16
Be . . . an example of the believer.
(1 Tim. 4:12)

There are many reasons why I loved my father. For one, he was real. Whether he was arguing with you or advising you (he never hesitated to tell you how you could live your life better) or wiping away a small boy's tears with the heel of a hand hardened by a half century of manual work, you knew he was thoroughly and transparently sincere. My father had a limited tolerance for superficial joking and jesting. He would often remind us that for "every idle word that men shall speak, they shall give account thereof in the day of judgment" (Matt. 12:36). Not a popular concept nowadays, but certainly biblical! Oh, he could laugh as heartily as the next person, but he wanted you to know that when he said a thing he meant it. When he promised something, whether it was a bicycle or a spanking, he kept his word. It was impossible for him to hide his feelings. When he was glad he showed it and when he was displeased you knew it—immediately. Such a personality can produce choppy domestic weather, but the squalls pass much sooner than when dealing with a chronic sulker.

Pop was real in his prayers. I sometimes grew weary at their length but there was never any question that he *meant* what he *prayed!* And I shall never forget the mornings when I would awake at 5:30 and see my father kneeling beside the gas stove that served both to prepare food and to heat our little rented room. "God, bless my boy today!" he would pray. "Keep him from sin and lead him in the way everlasting." You never forget prayers like that!

Small thought here
Let me ask you, dear friend: Are you *an example of the believer?* Do you mean what you *say* and mean what you *pray?*

HE KNEW HOW TO LIVE

Scripture, Colossians 3:12-17
And whatsoever ye do in word or deed, do all in the name of the Lord Jesus.
(Col. 3:17)

My father truly knew how to live. Perhaps this statement may seem strange when you realize that he never made much money, never was able to save any, never owned property, never had insurance, and except for five or six of his eighty-three years, he never owned a car (the rest of his life he rode a bicycle). He taught me that to enjoy life, its thrill and its pathos, you have to face it head-on with what you have. Today's fashionable discontent with all but the newest model never entered his mind. Whatever he had and however he felt at the moment he savored and enjoyed to the full.

Was he happy? He would whistle so shrilly that the sound threatened to pop one's eardrums; and the house would rock with his chin-music version of "The Irish Washerwoman." Was he blue? There were plenty of times when the loss of his life companion, who died shortly after I was born, came over him in waves of grief. He would settle into the old rocking chair, get out the hymnal and sing, "Oh, they tell me of a home far beyond the skies; oh, they tell me of a home far away!" And before long a smile would show through his tears. After church and Sunday dinner, Pop would get out his bike, put me on mine, and together we would spend the entire afternoon distributing Sunday School papers and magazines to unchurched homes. In so doing, he served his Lord, and got his boy delightfully and contentedly tired—in spite of no Sunday baseball!

Small thought here
My father enjoyed what he had, without the ulcer-breeding cry for "more." Of course, by today's standards it was a hard life and considered by some to be unnecessarily Spartan. Still, I recall with nostalgia the joy of living that was his.

HE HOOKED HIS LIFE TO ETERNITY

Scripture, 2 Corinthians 4:15-18
*We look not at the things which are seen
. . . for the things which are seen are
temporal: but the things which are not
seen are eternal.
(2 Cor. 4:18)*

For my father, everything had to pay out for souls, for God's glory, for eternity—*everything!* When I wanted a small box camera and was trying every legitimate means of persuasion (plus some polite blackmail) to get it, he remarked: "That'll be great, Boy! How are you going to use it to win souls?" Pop hooked his life to eternity. He would not be in conversation with a person more than five minutes before the talk would veer to eternal matters. How he did it, I used to marvel. Watching and listening, it was hard to realize that as a child he was so shy that he would run away from home rather than meet a stranger. And that he grew up with, "You'll never amount to anything!" ringing in his ears. Yet this father of mine—shy and unaffirmed as a boy—this amazing combination of Prussian positiveness, Germanic grumpiness, and Celtic charm, found a way to talk to everyone he met about the Saviour he loved.

When I graduated from high school, I wanted to go into auto mechanics. "Listen, Boy," he told me, "you'll be a better mechanic if you put a year of Bible under your belt. If God wants you to be a mechanic, you'll want to serve Him and win souls through that work. I'll stake you to a year at Moody Bible Institute, if you wish. Then you can go ahead with this career, OK?" I learned later that it cost him his lunch every day for a year to be able to pay for my room and board. He did it gladly, *to hook his boy's life to eternity.*

Small thought here
I want to be that kind of father—real with God and man, my life uncluttered by the chronic covetousness of our day—living every moment with the awareness that eternity is soon. And it's forever. Thanks, Pop, for teaching me that!

ALL
THAT
WE
NEED

Scripture, 2 Peter 1:1-8
*His divine power hath given unto us all
things that pertain unto life and godliness.
(2 Peter 1:3)*

When I was young, my father used to say to me, "My boy, I have to provide food, shelter, education, and loving care for you. That's part of my job. But," he went on, "that isn't all. We have to build a life—your life—you and I. And there's something you have to work at too, my boy!"

We all know there are some things you get "for free" and others you have to work for. Every one of us who is God's child begins with certain clearly defined dimensions in his life. This is the Apostle Peter's point in his second epistle when he says God has not only given us His grace (1:2), but also all things "that pertain unto life and godliness" (1:3) and "great and precious promises" (1:4) which are the key to Christian character and holiness. There isn't anything you will ever need to live the Christian life that has not already been given to you.

You may recall the story of the elderly couple taking their first ocean voyage. They had scrimped and saved to get enough for their steamship tickets. Then, they thought, "We must have food for the journey." Carefully they measured out cheese and bread and some dried meats—all they could afford. They hoped it would last until they reached their destination. Day after day they doled out the daily ration and ate it solemnly in their cabin. Just before the trip ended, someone discovered that these people had been eating alone in their cabin and inquired why. When the man and woman explained that they were trying to make the food last until the voyage's completion, they were told, "Why, all your meals were included in your steamship tickets! You could have been eating as much as you wished, every day."

Small thought here

All you need for a blessed, fruitful, satisfying Christian life is already yours. Claim it. Make it your own!

FOR STARTERS	**Scripture, 2 Peter 1:3-8** *Grace and peace be multiplied unto you through the knowledge of God, and of Jesus our Lord.* *(2 Peter 1:2)*

Before commenting on faith's "additives," we need to take inventory of some of the things we're going to be adding *to*—some of the gifts we have received from the Lord by faith, without working for them.

• *His grace is free.* "By grace are ye saved, through faith, and that not of yourselves, it is the gift of God, not of works lest any man should boast" (Eph. 2:8-9). God gives us saving grace, keeping grace, enabling grace, sufficient grace, grace to live and grace to die.

• *God's peace is free.* "Peace which passeth all understanding"—you can't define it, weigh it, or nail it down, because it is altogether divine. But you can experience its wonderful supporting strength! Peace is the quality of God, entering into your very nature (John 16:33).

• *God's joy is free.* Our blessed Lord Jesus said, "These things have I spoken unto you that My joy might remain in you, and that your joy might be full" (John 15:11). *Full* means "running over." Your cup may be small, but it can overflow a lot!

• *God's power is free.* What kind of power? The Apostle Paul wrote that the power that works in the believer is the *same power* that God "wrought in Christ, when He raised Him from the dead" (Eph. 1:20). Resurrection power is ours—*now*.

• *God's equipment for the Christian life is free.* "According as His divine power hath *given to us* all things that pertain unto life and godliness, through the knowledge of Him" (2 Peter 1:3).

Small thought here
Are you aware of how rich you really are? Now, urges Peter, build on *that*—add to *that!* We'll see how *diligence* ties in tomorrow.

MAKE THEM YOURS!

Scripture, 2 Peter 1:3-8
*All things ... through the knowledge of Him
that hath called us to glory and virtue.
(2 Peter 1:3)*

How do we appropriate the "all things" of which Peter spoke? By getting better acquainted with the Lord and applying His Word to our lives. The "all things" become real to us, first, "through the knowledge of Him." This means personal, intimate knowledge, as one has of a close friend. Spend time with your Lord and your character will be modified heavenward.

Second, appropriate the promises in God's Word. Let your soul feast on the thought that God forgives your sin. He makes you His child; He opens up heaven to you. He gives you "exceeding great and precious promises" (1:4), over 30,000 of them! He takes His very nature and gives that to you; He wants to live His life through you! I know from personal experience that God's Word in the mind and heart makes a difference in one's attitudes and decisions. While still a pastor, I embarked on a vigorous program of Bible memorization and meditation. Soon after I began, one of my deacons remarked, "Hey, Preacher, your preaching is different—what happened to you? Whatever it is, keep it up—I like it!"

So there you are. All these things given to you—free. But don't just stand there, looking. Appreciate! Appropriate! By faith—you and God working together—extend the borders of your Christian life. Peter goes on to tell how this is to be done—with diligence. *Diligence* means "thoroughness, completeness." Don't quit until the job is done.

Small thought here

Many a person, in the pressure of some trial or under the conviction of some great spiritual experience, has started a life of dedication to the Lord's will. But somewhere along the line, he or she has quit. It is time for us to renew our consecration, to consider finishing the job.

HE IS ABLE ON CHRISTMAS, AND ALL YEAR LONG!

Scripture, Hebrews 2:9-18
We see Jesus, who was made a little lower than the angels for the suffering of death, crowned with glory and honor.
(Heb. 2:9)

Believers know that the beauty and majesty of the Christmas story, by itself, would have little meaning were it not for its place in God's redemptive plan. His plan included not only the Virgin Birth and Bethlehem's manger, but also Calvary, the empty tomb, and the risen, glorified Lord! It is this connection which we wish to explore on this Christmas Day.

The very purpose of the Incarnation was for "the suffering of death." The Cross was not just a historical event; it was a legal transaction as well! Since that time, Satan has no legal right to the believer, and the feeblest child of God is encouraged to "resist the devil, and he will flee from you." Because Satan is a defeated foe, the believer is delivered from the awful fear of death. Certainly, physical death still occurs; but the sting, the curse, and the hopelessness have been removed *because Jesus came!* We now have a high priest who can be "touched with the feeling of our infirmities." Because He "suffered, being tempted," He knows how we feel when we are tempted, and "He is able to save them to the uttermot that come unto God by Him, seeing He ever liveth to make intercession for them."

Here, then, is the logic which undergirds our Christmas joys: Christ came to earth, miraculously born, sharing all our testings, so He could die for us. He died so we could be free from that which has always been the fingerprint of satanic damage: the fear of death. He came to die that He might deliver!

Small thought here

For the believer, "Merry Christmas!" means, "I'm free, and delivered from the fear of death! And I have a Saviour who knows all about me and is able to save and keep me!" Thank God that Jesus came! Thank God for Christmas!

ADD VIRTUE

Scripture, 2 Peter 1:3-8
Add to your faith virtue.
(2 Peter 1:5)

Life breaks up into little segments, like pieces broken off a loaf of bread. For each of those pieces of life, so to speak, you and I must form the habit of trusting the Lord Jesus Christ with the same abandonment we demonstrated when we came to Him for salvation. In today's text the Apostle Peter lists some of the things we are to add to our faith, the first of which is *virtue.*

When my daughters were very young, our family went to a restaurant to celebrate a special event. We looked at the various entries on the menu. Almost at once I saw what I wanted, and so did Mother and our older daughter. But our younger daughter, only about four at the time, was uncertain. To tease her a little, I took the big menu, put it under her face, and said, "OK, Dearie, what would *you* like?" Her eyes filled with tears and she looked up at me and said, "Papa, I just want what you want!" Well, at that point she could have had the whole world with a pink ribbon around it!

You know, God is waiting for the very same declaration from you and me: "Father, I just want what You want." That is *virtue*, and we obtain it by faith. Virtue is the quality of being spontaneously good, goodness that goes beyond the hope of reward. How do you achieve it? Simple. When the Lord Jesus Christ has control of your life, then His desires become yours. The psalmist exclaimed, "I delight to do Thy will, O my God. Yea, Thy law is within my heart" (Ps. 40:8).

Small thought here
There is a dynamic principle at work within the believer's heart. Paul identifies it: God works in you to *will* and *do* His good pleasure (Phil. 2:13). To will—that's the *want-to*. To do—that's the *power*. God does both for you when *His will* is your highest priority.

**ADD
KNOWLEDGE**

Scripture, 2 Peter 1:3-8
Add to your faith . . . knowledge.
(2 Peter 1:5)

Knowledge requires digging. I told our students at The King's College that a prayer meeting is no substitute for doing homework. God will never, in answer to prayer, help you remember something you did not first learn. Nor will He, in answer to prayer, bypass His Word and reveal directly to you the truths that you could find by reading or studying your Bible.

There is another kind of knowledge that comes by faith, as God blesses His Word and the Holy Spirit applies it to your life. That knowledge is an intimate acquaintance with the Lord Jesus Christ. "Acquaint now thyself with Him, and be at peace," we read in the Book of Job (22:21). Here is a mysterious yet wonderfully thrilling truth: the next time you pray, say, "Lord Jesus, just as I trusted You as my Saviour, so now I want to trust You to reveal Yourself to me while I read your Word and wait before You." I promise you, such prayers never go unanswered.

Years ago, while a guest in a lovely home, I was also the victim of an agonizingly busy schedule. I soon found that if I were to survive the pressures and have something fresh to share in the three to seven evangelistic meetings I had each day, I had to meet the Lord early in the morning, before the family awoke. I remember praying earnestly one morning, "O Lord, please hurry! There's not much time left before my hosts awaken!" Precisely at that moment of my urgency, the Lord graciously opened up the passage I had been studying and gave me a whole heartful of truths which I shared joyously throughout the day.

Small thought here
See the glorious combination: *Truth*—propositional knowledge—is yours if you will dig for it in the Word. *Triumph*—dynamic, personal knowledge—is yours by faith, if you will pray and believe for it.

ADD TEMPERANCE

Scripture, 2 Peter 1:5-8
Add to your faith . . . temperance.
(2 Peter 1:6)

We usually associate *temperance* with abstinence from alcoholic beverages or with some other form of self-control. While that is not totally inaccurate, it seems to me that a truer assessment of what temperance is all about lies in the concept of "inner strength." We've all heard the expression, "He lost his temper." Or, "Hold your temper!" It derives from the process whereby steel is *tempered*, or toughened, by heating and working it until it has the proper degree of hardness. This is the kind of inner strength and toughness that God produces in us by faith.

Paul prayed for his friends at Ephesus that they might be "strengthened with might by His Spirit in the inner man" (Eph. 3:16). Indeed, scriptural temperance, as I understand it, is not self-control, but rather God-control. It involves our bringing to Him every area of our lives that needs changing. Then we must start trusting Him to change each defeat into victory. And He will!

Another important dimension of *temperance* is its moderating aspect, illustrated in the maxim, "Justice should be *tempered* with mercy." Perhaps you've experienced this firsthand in a situation where you have let someone "off the hook" rather than exact your full "pound of flesh." How wonderful that God by His blessed Holy Spirit is building our inner strength as well as our capacity to temper justice with mercy in dealing with others.

Small thought here

God may not always change your circumstances in answer to prayer, but He will change you—in the circumstances—and make you a victor instead of a victim. That's true temperance!

ADD PATIENCE

Scripture, 2 Peter 1:5-8
Add to your faith . . . patience.
(2 Peter 1:6)

Some years ago we acquired a new puppy, a Doberman of all things! That breed has a bad name because it has been used as an attack dog, but our household's version was a very friendly and enthusiastic creature—"man's best friend"! Was he noisy? Yes. Dirt-bearing and flea-bitten at times? Yes. But he was eminently affectionate and strong. Rusty loved to jump up to greet you—and what a greeting you got! Thus the first thing he heard in the morning and at intervals throughout the day was, "Rusty, stay down!"

Interestingly enough, our expression "stay down" is very much akin to the word rendered *patience* here in 2 Peter. And patience—whether in animal or man—has to be *learned*. Many of us admittedly have a fairly short fuse. We need to learn the blessed, gentle art of waiting for God to act in His own time and way. He is *never* late, never makes mistakes, and His timing is exquisitely beautiful.

You may have heard the story of the man who was seen wheeling a baby carriage with a crying infant inside. As he moved along the sidewalk, he was saying, "Now be patient, Albert. Be quiet, Albert. Albert, don't fuss." A lady who was about to pass him said, "Sir, it's wonderful to hear you talk so soothingly to your baby." "Oh," the man replied, "*I'm* Albert." See what this dear fellow was doing: he was speaking to his own heart, as we often need to speak to ours. "Stay down! Be patient."

Small thought here

We are to be patient in prayer and intercession, patient when reversals come, when health is lost, when bereaved, when criticized by family and closest friends. Why? Because those testings bring us to a place of new awareness of Almighty God!

ADD KINDNESS

Scripture, 2 Peter 1:5-8
Add to your faith . . . brotherly kindness.
(2 Peter 1:7)

If you went to Sunday School as a child, or read Bible stories at home, you will remember the story of Joseph. Sold into slavery by his jealous brothers, he nevertheless—by God's providence—ended up as prime minister of Egypt, second in command of that very powerful ancient nation. You may also recall that toward the end of the story, Joseph revealed himself to his brothers, forgave them, and told them "it was not you that sent me hither, but God: and He hath made me a father to Pharaoh, and lord of all his house, and a ruler throughout all the land of Egypt" (Gen. 45:8).

Later, when their father Jacob died, the brothers feared that Joseph would remember what had happened in the past and would "requite us all the evil we did unto him" (50:15). But Joseph told them not to be afraid. He said that, though they had meant to do him in, so to speak, God had turned it into good—for all concerned. Then you recall that blessed demonstration of *brotherly kindness* when Joseph said, " 'Now therefore fear ye not: I will nourish you, and your little ones.' And he comforted them and spake *kindly* unto them" (50:21).

Kindness—like courtesy—is really love in work clothes. Paul told the believers in Rome to be "kindly affectioned" to one another (Rom. 12:10). To the saints at Ephesus he said, "Be ye kind one to another" (Eph. 4:32). And to the Colossians: "Put on . . . kindness" (Col. 3:12). How does God show us the riches of his grace, dear friend? In "His *kindness* toward us in Christ Jesus" (Eph. 2:7).

Small thought here
According to God's Word, every believer is a *habitation of God* —through the Spirit (Eph. 2:22). So God's kindness is in you too. Show His kindness to someone today!

| ADD LOVE | **Scripture, 2 Peter 1:5-8**
Add to your faith . . . love.
(2 Peter 1:7) |

One of the most powerful examples of God's love comes to us from the life of Corrie ten Boom. Sent to a Nazi concentration camp for hiding Jews in her home in Holland, Corrie found, as Isaiah promised, "a hiding place from the wind and . . . tempest" (Isa. 32:2).

Corrie survived that concentration camp and after World War II was used of God in a mighty way. On one occasion she was asked to come to Munich, Germany to minister to a group of believers. It was there she saw him, the former S.S. man who had stood guard at the shower room door in the processing center at Ravensbruck. Suddenly all of the pain and humiliation came flooding back—the roomful of leering, mocking men; the heaps of clothing; and her now-dead sister's pain-wracked face. As the church was emptying afterward, the man came up to Corrie, thanked her for her Gospel message, and thrust out his hand to shake hers. Angry, vengeful thoughts boiled within her. Then, realizing the sinfulness of her thoughts and that Jesus had died to redeem this wretched man, she thought: *Am I going to ask for more?* "Lord Jesus," she prayed, "forgive me and help me to forgive him." Corrie tried to smile. She struggled to raise her hand to take his, but she couldn't. She felt nothing—not the slightest spark of warmth or charity. So she prayed again: "Jesus, I cannot forgive him. Give me Your forgiveness." And as she took the hand of the former S.S. officer, the most incredible thing happened: from Corrie's shoulder, then down along her arm and through her hand a current seemed to pass from her to the man. And into her heart sprang an almost overwhelming love for this man who was once her enemy.

Small thought here
Corrie commented, "When God tells us to *love* our enemies, He gives, along with the command, the *love* itself." Hallelujah for that, dear friend, as we come to the close of another year.

Be thou an example of the believer in word, in conversation, in charity, in spirit, in faith, in purity.
(1 Tim. 4:12)

Be a Blessing
BY LEADERSHIP GIVING!

"This they did, not as we hoped, but first gave their own selves to the Lord and to us by the will of God" (2 Cor. 8:5). What a commendation the Apostle Paul gave the churches of Macedonia. Indeed, they were glowing examples to all the other New Testament churches for they did not allow their afflictions and poverty to slow down their work for God. Their readiness to give and to go beyond what might normally be expected of them is at once a challenge and an inspiration to all. You can similarly inspire others by your willingness to be a good steward of that which God has given you. It is the "extra" that makes the difference, whether serving, or preparing, or praying, or giving. And God honors and rewards with a satisfied heart what is truly done for Him.

Robert A. Cook